The Pantarch: A Biography of Stephen Pearl Andrews

Heads & Headlines: The Phrenological Fowlers

Books and Book People in Nineteenth-Century America

Antiquarian Bookselling in the United States: A History

BOOKS EDITED BY MADELEINE B. STERN

Women on the Move (4 volumes)

The Victoria Woodhull Reader

Behind a Mask: The Unknown Thrillers of Louisa May Alcott

Plots and Counterplots: More Unknown Thrillers of Louisa May Alcott

Publishers for Mass Entertainment in *Nineteenth-Century America*

A Phrenological Dictionary of Nineteenth-Century Americans

Critical Essays on Louisa May Alcott

A Modern Mephistopheles and Taming a Tartar by Louisa M. Alcott

Louisa May Alcott Unmasked: Collected Thrillers

Modern Magic

The Feminist Alcott: Stories of a Woman's Power

BOOKS CO-EDITED BY MADELEINE B. STERN

Selected Letters of Louisa May Alcott (with Joel Myerson and Daniel Shealy)

A Double Life: Newly Discovered Thrillers of Louisa May Alcott (with Myerson and Shealy)

The Journals of Louisa May Alcott (with Myerson and Shealy)

Louisa May Alcott: Selected Fiction (with Myerson and Shealy)

Freaks of Genius: Unknown Thrillers of Louisa May Alcott (with Shealy and Myerson)

From Jo March's Attic: Stories of Intrigue and Suspense (with Shealy)

Old Books, Rare Friends

*Two Literary Sleuths and
Their Shared Passion*

LEONA ROSTENBERG
AND MADELEINE STERN

Doubleday

NEW YORK   LONDON   TORONTO
SYDNEY   AUCKLAND

PUBLISHED BY DOUBLEDAY
a division of Bantam Doubleday Dell Publishing Group, Inc.
1540 Broadway, New York, New York 10036

DOUBLEDAY and the portrayal of an anchor with a dolphin are trademarks of
Doubleday, a division of Bantam Doubleday Dell Publishing Group, Inc.

Book design by Claire Vaccaro

Library of Congress Cataloging-in-Publication Data
Rostenberg, Leona.
Old books, rare friends : two literary sleuths and their shared passion /
Leona Rostenberg and Madeleine B. Stern.
p.   cm.
Includes index.
1. Rostenberg, Leona.   2. Stern, Madeleine B., 1912–   .
3. Antiquarian booksellers—United States—Biography.   4. Book
collectors—United States—Biography.   I. Stern, Madeleine B., 1912–   .
II. Title.   III. Title: Old Books, Rare Friends.
Z473.R77R65   1997
381'.45002'092—DC21   96-37176
CIP

ISBN 0-385-48514-X
Printed in the United States of America
June 1997

3   5   7   9   10   8   6   4

To Madeleine
with love and gratitude from Leona

To Leona
with gratitude and love from Madeleine

A friend may well be reckoned
the masterpiece of Nature.

RALPH WALDO EMERSON

CONTENTS

PROLOGUE

EARLY ONE MORNING IN SEPTEMBER 1995, THE TELE-
phone rang. We were still in the East Hampton cottage we had
rented for the summer, and we thought that by now the deluge of
calls would have diminished. Toward the end of August we had been
interviewed by Dinitia Smith for the *New York Times,* and her article,
"Of Faithful Friends and Alcott Experts," had set our phone "ring-
ing off the hook." Dinitia Smith had made a delightful pastiche of
our long friendship, our fifty-year partnership in the rare book business, and our writings, especially those concerned with the double
literary life of the author of *Little Women.*

"This is Doubleday calling. We've read the article about you in
the *Times,* and we were wondering whether you would give us a
book."

We were not sure we had caught the name Doubleday. "Who is
this?" we asked.

"This is Betsy Lerner, a senior editor at the publishing house
Doubleday."

A little surer of our ground, but still taken aback, we asked,
"What sort of book did you have in mind?"

A few possibilities were mentioned briefly. Then Betsy Lerner
suggested, "How about a joint autobiography? You do seem to have
a different story to tell."

Now our reaction was a mixture of astonishment, uncertainty, and disbelief. We would have to discuss the possibility and get back to her. And, yes, we were returning to the city in a few weeks. Perhaps we could get together then.

Between the September telephone call and the meeting with Betsy in October, we did talk about it. Not seriously at first—how could we be serious about a joint autobiography? Sitting together in the sun parlor, walking together on the beach, we toyed with the idea. Betsy had suggested we had a "different story to tell." It was true, when we looked at our friends—all of them married, most of them retired; their lives differed from ours. But what precisely had Betsy meant? How, specifically, were we different? In what ways did we have a "different story to tell"?

If we began at the beginning, there was difference there: in our background. Our parents were second- and third-generation German-Americans, comfortable, educated, admiring learning but taking it in stride. There was security in the home, financial and emotional, and the feeling of security settled into the bones and gave strength. Our parents took it for granted that we would move forward, and they helped the process along not only by precept but by example. They were the role models of our youth.

Then, too, in matters of religion, we were minorities of a minority. We were Jews, but descendants of Jews who had carved a radical path in Judaism, leaning less on Hebrew in our devotions than on English, eschewing Orthodox diet, knowing no Yiddish, taking the Union Prayer Book for our gospel. An Orthodox Jew could say to us Reform Jews, "Why, you're not even Jewish!" and a Jewish member of the Ethical Culture Society could regard us as conservative. Here too there was a difference.

We perpetuated the difference by living at home as long as we had a parent alive. Most of our friends (as well as our older brothers) moved out from under the parental roof as soon as they married or could afford their own flat. We *chose* to live at home because we were happy there. We enjoyed the company of our parents; we regarded them as companions, and in the course of our close relationship with our immediate families, we were nurtured and coddled. In a way it was almost a continuity of our childhood.

The educational process that our parents began for us continued. Graduate school came after college, partly a result of the national Depression. Formal education was followed by self-education, and self-education became a habit. We never stopped studying. Even today, after fifty years in the rare book business, we learn something from every book that passes through our hands.

The basic reason for much that has been different in our lives is of course the fact that neither of us married. There were men in our lives, but they remained on the fringe of our lives. Neither of us felt more than a mild interest in them, never enough involvement to contemplate a permanent relationship. As a result, we would have no children, but, as Mady's mother said, "People don't miss what they've never had," and perhaps this is true.

The *Times* article that generated the Doubleday call also generated some speculation about our sexual lives. Several readers inferred from it that our relationship was a Lesbian one. This was a misconception. The "deep, deep love" that existed and exists between us and that is mentioned in Dinitia Smith's last paragraph has no bearing upon sex.

Louisa Alcott wrote that she had taken her pen for a bridegroom. In a way, our children too were our books. Leona, dominated by the concept that the printer-publisher was an agent of civilization, took as her province seventeenth-century England and wrote several respected and distinguished books in defense of her thesis. Her original thesis, also substantiating the creative role of the printer-publisher, had been rejected as invalid when she presented it as her doctoral dissertation at Columbia University in the 1930s. In the 1970s her later books were accepted in lieu of that dissertation. The rejection, along with the subsequent reversal, would change the course we both traveled and prove one of life's most productive ironies.

Madeleine, meanwhile, continued to consume reams of paper. She started, as so many writers do, with a tedious autobiographical novel, and later plunged into feminist biography with lives of Margaret Fuller, Louisa May Alcott, Mrs. Frank Leslie, and an anthology entitled *We the Women*. Her reaction to the 1960s resulted in two offbeat volumes, one on a nineteenth-century American eccentric reformer, the other on a firm of phrenologist-publishers.

Before, during, and after all this, Leona made the startling discovery of Louisa Alcott's pseudonym and her pseudonymous sensational shockers, and Madeleine traced those shockers and assembled them in a succession of anthologies.

If books were indeed our children, we had large families.

Basically, the principal difference between us and most of the world is that for more than fifty years we have been partners in an unusual, sometimes esoteric business—that of rare books. It is a business in which knowledge is power, and the arts of detection often play a leading role. The electrifying alertness to what is unusual or important in an early printed book has been given the name *Finger-Spitzengefühl*. When *Finger-Spitzengefühl* is coupled with serendipity, the gates of paradise open for the dealer in old and rare. Leona learned of those fascinations during a long apprenticeship, and Madeleine learned of them from Leona. We have both been lured by the fascinations for half a century and we continue to be lured by them.

Through all that time our friendship has sustained us. Our partnership in business is also a partnership in life—the partnership of "Faithful Friends" who share "a deep, deep love."

Our Doubleday contract calls for a book in which detection and *Finger-Spitzengefühl* play a major role both in rare books and in the unmasking of Louisa Alcott's double literary life. It also calls for a "different story." We have thrilled to the chase in our hunts for rare books. With deerstalker and magnifying glass we have uncovered our finds. In the old and the rare we have made connections, connections between past and present, between our books and our selves. We shared the thrill of the chase and the joy of the find. But we shared something else too. We shared our differences. All that is here in the "joint autobiography" of two friends who led and are still leading their "different story."

BEGINNINGS

Leona 📖 T O   R E A C H back into the realms of childhood requires integrity and self-discipline. Time tends to gloss over all the events, the places, the loves, the hates, the fears. For me the passing years have embroidered childhood memories into a fabric of joy and love. But, of course, there is always so much more.

My earliest actual recollection is reaching the first shelf of my parents' bookcase at age two, and hearing my mother cry, "Leonchen is tall enough to reach the first bookshelf. She was looking at the books. She will be a writer one day and that I know." Thus began a family prophecy that I would live out, here and abroad, when few women became scholars of bibliographic history.

In the family pictures taken that same year, I am shown seated in a small armchair, laughing and gurgling as I hold a newspaper, my little silver eyeglasses adjusted, "reading", the news of 1910. My older brother, Adolph Jr., was also photographed, wearing a white sailor suit, his eyes alert, appraising the scene around him—the photographer in his studio bent over his camera, the camera covered by a large black cloth.

My very lovely mother, Louisa, was the first-born child of a successful New Orleans wholesale jeweler, Leon Dreyfus, and his wife, Bertha, both émigrés from Germany. The oldest of seven, she held sway over her siblings and was spoiled by her father, who, intrigued by her talent for dramatic elocution, showered her with gifts and called her his little Sarah Bernhardt. She attracted men by her charm and her beauty, but somehow did not hold them, and by the age of thirty she was desperate for a husband. Finally, in 1902, when she was thirty-two, she ensnared a German physician six years her junior, Adolph Rostenberg, not entirely suited to her temperament. Imbued with German male superiority, he regarded women as suitable agents of *Kinder und Küche* (the nursery and the kitchen). They were married Christmas Day of that year. Despite my aristocratic mother's social ambition, they settled in the Bronx, where my father had begun his practice of general medicine.

I recall our tall dark house on Washington Avenue. Next door was a stable whose distinctive odor I loved, although my mother never failed to pull out a handkerchief to smother her nose as we walked arm in arm to the big shopping center on Tremont Avenue. Compensating for the stable fumes was the scent of a garden to the left of the house. It bordered a small red brick building bearing the words NEW YORK PUBLIC LIBRARY. "Let's go to the liberry," I'd pester my mother almost daily. "Library," she'd correct. "Liberry," I replied.

Once there, we walked into a room ominously labeled "For Adults Only," where Miss Graves, the senior librarian, would greet my mother cordially. "I have saved a new book for you, Mrs. Doctor." Maybe it was Somerset Maugham's recent hit, *Of Human Bondage*. Maybe it was the latest Mary Roberts Rinehart. "Don't you want to go to the Children's Division, little Leona?" Miss Graves would always inquire. There, I was surrounded by rows of books bound in bright reds and blues, greens and yellows. One of the first I recall pouncing upon had large illustrations of the Presidents, entitled *Picture Book of Our Great Leaders.* "Can I take this?" I asked my mother. "Certainly, darling." Proudly I marched off with my selection, still sniffing the musty dusty odor of books, a smell that was somehow warm and comforting and exciting all at once and would remain with me forever.

In the basement of our house were the kitchen and the dining room. The first floor was devoted to my father's medical office—off limits to the children—the second to the living room and my parents' bedroom, where we were always welcome. It was to the third floor, known as the children's domain, where I'd take my book and sequester myself. There my brother, the strong, the valiant, the daring, the wild Adolph Jr., became the archvillain of my childhood—my brother, who not only dared me and double-dared me but triple-dared me to do every sort of childhood prank imaginable. He was a big fellow for his age (when I was four, he was seven and a half) and spent most of his time when not at school sliding down the bannisters or procuring worms from the backyard to frighten me. Mostly he triple-dared me to climb a snowy fence in my socks or stick my finger into boiling water or drink a formaldehyde concoction he'd made on the sly in my father's office. And yet occasionally we played together, tearing around the dining room, Adolph violently knocking over the chairs until one struck him in the head. At that point I remember crying out with some concern but mostly glee. "A has another hole in his head," I sang out until I noticed the blood that streamed from his forehead. Father came to the rescue and staunched it. Glaring at Adolph, he exploded, *"Du wilder Junge, du!"* (You wild boy, you!), and stamped out of the room.

And so we grew up in the house on Washington Avenue, where most of my pleasures took place indoors. My mother did not permit me to play with the neighborhood children. Mostly Italian, they were born of immigrant parents, and, according to mother, were given to smoking, wild fights, and playing cards in the street. To the feeling of German superiority she had inherited my mother added a touch of snobbery. Her prejudices were grounded in the belief that her ethnic heritage was better than that of others.

My father, a most musical gentleman, acquired a pianola in 1915. Many Sundays the family was summoned—my mother's sisters and brothers and their offspring—to a musical recital performed by my father. Envisioning himself as Paderewski's understudy, he dressed in a cutaway coat, striped trousers, a wing collar, and an ascot adorned with a pearl stickpin, and solemnly sat at the pianola "playing" the Moonlight Sonata or a Chopin waltz. The children, stiff in white starched dresses or suits, were not permitted a single beep. We were compelled to listen to Daddy adjusting the levers of the pianola, pressing on the pedals, emoting effusively. At the end, the adults applauded the performance and congratulated the performer. The children raced out of the room and released their pent-up energy in a pillow fight. Usually on Mondays, after Daddy had left the roll in the pianola, Adolph Jr. played it back, pressing his foot on the pedal and awaiting the clack, clack, clack of the finale, when the roll wound itself up. It was not unusual for my father to enter at just that moment, grab his firstborn by the ear, and plant a swift slap on his left cheek. Of course, he never hit his sweet Leonchen.

On other Sundays, all of us, joined by my mother's brother Max, his wife, Amy, and their daughter, Marion, two years my junior, climbed into Daddy's Ford to visit Mother's family in faraway Ridgewood, New Jersey. Our mothers commanded Marion and me to sit down simultaneously, smoothing our stiffly starched white skirts to avoid any possible creases. While our mothers and we were squeezed into the back seat, Adolph Jr. was placed on a small collapsible chair that rolled around constantly. The car crossed the great Hudson River on the ferry—probably one of the most exciting events of my childhood. Always there was an Italian singer on board who carried on his shoulder a little monkey, dressed in a short red velvet jacket and a cocked pageboy hat. While his master wandered around the many cars, the monkey held out a tambourine, into which pennies were tossed. Upon our reaching the dangerous Jersey shore, Daddy's Ford inevitably suffered a flat tire, calling forth a handpump to pump the tire, midst Daddy's fulminations against his wife's *verdammte* family and the entire State of New Jersey. When we'd finally reach Ridgewood, we were always received with love, good food, a field to walk, and gardens to play in.

Indoors, my grandmother, my parents, my aunts and uncles gathered to play whist. My mother, arrayed in a much admired new costume, always kept score. Her costume had been produced by my mother's dressmaker, Mary Walsh Conroy. There was a huge tribe of seamstresses who paid house visits in those days before mass-produced retail apparel. Mary Conroy was one of the personalities in my early background. The third Friday of every month was devoted to her visit. Miss Conroy was a large, heavyset woman with a white powdery face. Her bosom was ensconced in a tight-fitting pink cotton blouse; her full pleated skirt would not have recommended itself to the atelier of Coco Chanel. She arrived before lunch and remained for the rest of the day, executing Butterick patterns with elaborations by my mother. She also designed my dresses, which I utterly detested, preferring the gaudy ginghams hanging from racks in Hearn's or Adams Flanigan department stores.

"Tand till!" Miss Conroy commanded, a row of straight pins protruding like sentinels from her mouth. "Stand still," my mother interpreted, "while Conroy pins your hem." Deftly, Conroy extricated pin after pin from her mouth and inserted it in my skirt.

I learned what Catholic meant from Conroy when I asked my mother why we always had fish when Conroy came. "Miss Conroy is Catholic, darling," my mother explained, "and we will conform to the demands of her faith." "But we eat fish, and we're Jewish!"

Conroy dominated the lunch conversation, embroidering upon the exploits of her family, especially her brother James Michael, a policeman posted in the nearby Bathgate section. "Do you know that Jim caught two Eye-talian fellers stealing oranges from a ped-dler!'' And she added, with her particular brand of prejudice, ''We should stop the Eye-talian immigration.'' Frankly, I was more inter-ested in brother Jim's two daughters, the twins Jeanne Frances and Margaret Cecile. ''You wouldn't believe those two girls are twins. Margaret Cecile has the most beautiful long blond curls,'' Conroy remarked, eyeing my straight brown hair sympathetically. ''Jeanne Frances has gorgeous black hair and sings like an angel.'' During one visit I remember Miss Conroy coughing so hard at lunch she nearly choked, then pulling a fishbone out of her mouth with the same dexterity with which she extracted straight pins. Without missing a beat, she helped herself to a large portion of apple pie and com-mented, ''My sister-in-law Maureen uses Flako crust for her lemon meringue.'' At this point Daddy, slightly red in the face, excused himself. ''I think patients are waiting for me in the office,'' though no office bell had rung.

At his departure Adolph Jr. produced from a matchbox his small pet, Jonathan, a turtle, which he placed on the tablecloth. Miss Conroy gasped. Jonathan scarcely moved, retiring to his shell. He too was overwhelmed by my mother's couturière. At this point Mother interjected, ''Adolphschen, take that creature off the table and get ready for school, young man, and be sure to take your sister's hand.''

Once outside the house, Adolphschen—known to his school-friends as Rusty because of his flaming red hair—adjusted his skates, threw his books, tied in a red leather strap, in my direction— ''Here, shrimp, carry them!''—and sailed off. I trudged slowly behind. By the time I got to school, Rusty was engaged in a fistfight with his former friend, Shorty Williams.

Adolph Jr. never took my hand, never took me across the street. At the big crossing at Webster Avenue he raced ahead, look-ing for one of his many pals. And so it was that my mother's dream of brotherly protection for me never became a reality.

As we grew older, I became aware of my parents' consultations and their growing excitement about finally owning their own house. One day my mother said, "Darling, I am going to show you our new home. It is like a palace." And so we walked across Tremont Avenue from our rented house, up the hill to the Grand Concourse. One block west of the Concourse my mother showed me the new house. I had expected a palace like one of King Arthur's; I had expected crenelated walls and a high tower. I turned to her and remarked, "Oh, how you exaggerate."

It was in fact a lovely house of fourteen rooms, porches downstairs and upstairs, and I had a large room all my own, while across the corridor Adolph Jr. resided with his pets and his chemistry set. Amazingly enough, ours was one of only three houses on the street. Beyond were the fields, and when I went to school my mother cautioned me, "I do not want you to walk through the fields to school. Rather, walk on the Concourse." In those dim days the Bronx had not yet developed. It was a borough of private homes, gardens, and fields, a peaceful community. And yet even then my mother feared that in its fields might lurk a kidnapper or perhaps a rapist. Sensing her concern, I obeyed her.

By 1918 the peace was finally proclaimed by the shrill cries of newsboys with their "Extra! Extra!" Our housekeeper, Honora Eliot Macdonald, hailed the end of World War I with her victory hurrah: "Now let's kill the Kaiser!" Honora had a special distinction—she had six toes on her right foot. When I sought comfort from Honora after I had stubbed a toe, she confided in me, "Just think, honey, it would have been worse for me. I have six toes." I forgot my pain and asked, "Can I see them?" That evening when I visited her room, she displayed her extra digit. I looked closely, both fascinated and revolted. I did not ask to see it again.

As a child at P.S. 28 I had been imbued with an overwhelming love of country. At assembly we sang "My Country 'Tis of Thee" and "Hail Columbia," concluding with "The Star-Spangled Ban-

ner." Every day we pledged allegiance to the flag of the United
States and to the Republic for which it stands. The school walls were
adorned with portraits of our illustrious presidents—Washington,
Lincoln, and the incumbent, Warren Gamaliel Harding.

In 1921, when I was twelve, we spent the summer at Jackson,
New Hampshire, and one of the great events of my early youth took
place. A guest at the hotel, having advised my mother and aunt that
the President of the United States was visiting nearby Crawford
Notch, said he would be glad to drive the children over to meet
their glorious leader. My cousin Marion and I were selected for the
honor, and lo and behold, we saw, standing on a porch in Crawford
Notch, the leader of the United States, President Harding.

The President smiled at us benignly as we cocked our cameras in
his direction. As usual, I placed my hand in front of the lens,
prompting Mr. Harding to step down and address me: "Little girl,
that's not the way to take a picture. You must remove your hand
from the lens." I was in a state of ecstasy. The President of the
United States had addressed me personally. During this benevolent
scene the Fox Movietone News had filmed the great Mr. Harding
instructing a little girl. Now, feeling a close personal relationship
with the President, I trailed right after him when he strolled onto
the golf links. A member of the Secret Service promptly intervened.
"Little girl, you cannot follow the President onto the golf course."
"But I am a close friend of the President," I retorted at the ripe old
age of twelve. To no avail. Our close relationship had been cut
short.

Nonetheless, my patriotic fervor had been thoroughly roused
and I could not wait to report the event to my mother. "I saw the
President and I'm in the movies!" I cried. Immediately my mother,
almost as thrilled as I, telephoned the news to my father. As a result,
he spent three successive nights in a hot unair-conditioned movie,
hoping for a sight of his younger child amid the crowds. Finally he
was rewarded and saw the benevolent Mr. Harding instructing little

Leona in the photographic arts. It did not matter at all to him that Fox Movietone News had filmed little Leona with her back to the camera.

We spent the following summer abroad. My father had preceded us in order to take advance courses in dermatology offered at the University of Berlin medical school. My recollections of that trip are filled with churches, a few museums, and olfactory sensations. Being a Prohibition child, I was unaccustomed to the pervasive smell of beer and spirits with which all of Germany was redolent. When I returned home and was asked for my impressions of Europe, I replied, "It just smells different." People were interested in my reactions, since travel abroad for a middle-class family was uncommon. Actually we traveled first class aboard the Hamburg-American liner the *Resolute,* probably an extravagant plunge, though I can't see my darling aristocratic mother traveling any other way.

The following summer proved quite a different challenge. By then I was fourteen, extremely short, extremely shy, turning inward to my books and my literary endeavors. After reading "Evangeline" and "Miles Standish," I wrote a lengthy epic entitled "Peter van Dennsler," largely stolen from Mr. Henry Wadsworth Longfellow. Around the same time my parents gave me a birthday gift of Louisa May Alcott's Little Women series, each book bound in brown cloth. I devoured the novels one after the other, although I wrote no epic as a result. I had few friends outside the pages of my books. Disturbed by my excessive shyness, my mother took action and decided to send me to camp, where I would perforce mingle with my contemporaries. In my mind it would be a question of sink or swim.

The camp she selected, first and foremost, was one that fulfilled her social ambitions. I was the only camper from the Bronx, the only camper who did not attend private school, and the only camper whose clothes did not come from the paragon of children's fashions, De Pinna. I did not, at the time, know whether De Pinna was a statesman, a rare African animal, or a far-off country. I only knew that I had never heard of it, whatever it was, and was caught up short. Frankly, I was an anomaly in a camp of snobbish children, all of whom came from Manhattan and aped their mothers' every move. Nonetheless, my status as an oddity ensured a certain notoriety, and much to my surprise I found myself among the popular. They called me Peanut and elected me mascot of the Brown Team. Knowing very little about basketball, I stated with confidence that I played side center, but was readily forgiven when I could not follow the rules of the game. As the summer progressed I found I had many friends, and my shyness evaporated. The three years I would spend at Camp Kearsage on Lake Sebago in the State of Maine would somehow prepare me for the rough-and-tumble of Bronx high school life.

Madeleine 📖 FOR ME, LIFE BEGAN IN A seven-story apartment building on Lenox Avenue and 126th Street in Harlem, opposite Mrs. Hempel's boarding house. There on a hot summer day in 1912—probably on the kitchen table—I was born. My parents already had a son, now nearly ten years old. My mother had been cautioned against another childbirth and doubtless went through agonies when, at age forty, she learned she was pregnant again. Although I was certainly not planned, I was warmly welcomed—a little girl, and the first in all the family for a long time.

I never stopped feeling the welcome. In fact, I felt as if I was the fulcrum, the raison d'être, for the Harlem quartet. I felt far more important than I was, of course, but it gave a warmth to everything during my first decade. There was always a loving mother waiting for me when I came home, always a loving father to twirl me in his arms when he came back from his wholesale liquor business and met me on the street. As for my brother, Leonard, he was kind and sweet in an offhand way. He was remote—another generation really—and would become more remote as the years passed.

My father, Moses R. Stern, had been born to German Jewish émigré parents. They had emigrated, as my mother's parents had, during the early 1850s in the tide of German Jews who left their native land after the failure of the 1848 Revolution in Europe. They came for the freedom and economic security they felt they had lost. My father's parents settled in Hartford, Connecticut, as my mother's parents settled in Cincinnati, Ohio, both cities with sizable German Jewish populations.

My father's family remained in Hartford and my father remained a Yankee even after he became a New Yorker. He never lost his Yankee accent or his sense of humor. He was about ten years older than my mother—about fifty—and, to me, elderly in contrast to the parents of my friends. Yet he understood children and had a way with them. On Sunday mornings he took me sledding or to the lake in Central Park for ice skating, which he taught me, or to the Museum of Natural History. Later, he also took me to Sunday School, though he never, as far as I know, attended any temple service. He was a believer, especially in the hereafter, but never an observant Jew. He enjoyed me as I enjoyed him.

My father met my mother, Lillie Mack, in a bowling club in 1901, when bowling, like cycling, was a popular pastime for men and women, and they were married in 1902. My mother was a woman of extraordinary wisdom and understanding. She had graduated from Normal College—later renamed Hunter College—and as long as she lived she would be the auditor and perceptive critic of everything I wrote. She could also turn out the best apple pie in America with a minimum of effort. She was a twin, and her family, named Mack, moved to New York when she was six months old. The story was that my grandmother had decided she would rather be a lamppost in New York than the mayor of Cincinnati (a feeling I heartily concur with). Both families—my mother's and my father's—were comfortable though not wealthy, and had much in common.

After my parents' marriage they settled near my maternal

grandmother in Harlem, in an area I would frequently explore with my father. After dinner he would take me for what he called a constitutional, along the glittering highway that was 125th Street. There we would pass the well-lit shops, stop to watch a glassblower at work, glance at the great Alhambra Theatre, home of vaudeville performances; occasionally he bought me a bag of "plantations"— chewy chocolate-covered molasses candies—at Loft's. Harlem, not yet headed for its decline, had begun as the garden spot of Manhattan. Its array of brownstones, each with a well-kept garden, fronted quiet streets where lampposts were lit at dusk by lamplighters. Nearby shopkeepers knew their customers personally. The neighborhood seemed devoted to families, greenery, serenity. The only apartment house was the one where we lived, at 101 West 126th Street, on the corner of Lenox Avenue.

On the same street, at Number 133, my grandmother lived, a very old lady who suffered from a long-lasting and mysterious ailment and always wore black. Her illness had begun, I gathered, when her dearly loved husband—my grandfather—died, and it manifested itself in a refusal to eat and an inability to sleep. She lived with an unmarried son (my mother's twin) and an unmarried daughter, who must have been sore tried. From me she was always totally withdrawn. For the most part I paid her little attention and would scurry out to the backyard to ride the swing as high as I could. Once, with childish devilment, I hid in a closet and suddenly sprang out at her, but even then she demonstrated only the mildest consternation. She died when I was five, and on that day my mother said to me, "Just for today I'd like you to try to be quiet." My unfeeling response was "Do all the other kids in the street have to be quiet today?"

My Aunt Clara, wife of my mother's older brother Will, was another matter altogether. A stout, comfortable woman, she was a wonderful listener and she provided me with the most enthusiastic audience I have ever enjoyed. When I was a little girl my mother underwent an operation at Roosevelt Hospital, and during that time I stayed with my aunt and uncle, who lived in the neighborhood. For me it was an enchanted time. It included a celebration for my sixth birthday, so exciting and so filled with gifts that when the glorious day ended all I could say was "How will I ever do tomorrow without this day?"

One of the gifts, from my mother's cousin, was what I called my treasure chest. It was a brown box divided into a dozen compartments, in each of which was a selection of stationery supplies. There were paper clips and cards and keyrings; there were labels and rubberbands and pen nibs; there was everything a writer could dream of, and perhaps I fancied myself a writer even then. I kept that box for years, cherishing it.

One day during my "vacation" at Aunt Clara's, my father took me to see my mother in the hospital. She seemed very high up on her bed, so high that I thought she was elevated near the ceiling, and she looked down upon me with a loving smile but seemed very far away, and I was momentarily frightened. Then I was asked to recite a poem to entertain her, and, omitting the customary curtsey that preceded such performances, I stood near her bed and recited a comic ballad I had memorized entitled "Epaminondas." Years later I would learn that Epaminondas was an early Theban general, but there was nothing at all about any Theban general in my poem. My Epaminondas was a little boy who had all sorts of comic adventures. My mother was moved, not to laughter, but to a feeble smile. And my father grinned.

I loved my Aunt Clara and I also loved my independence. A year or so after my short stay with her, I decided that I would show my parents I could walk to her house on my own without escort. Aunt Clara lived at 119th Street and St. Nicholas Avenue, about half a mile southwest of us. And so one summer morning I took off. I walked briskly, filled with excitement. I knew I was breaking rules, but I also knew I had to prove to "them" that I could be on my own. I noticed very little en route—the idea was to get there as quickly as possible. Within ten minutes I appeared, unheralded and unannounced, in Aunt Clara's apartment. Her first words were "Does your mother know you're here?" When I said no, she phoned my mother immediately, but my mother had not yet noticed my absence and had not had time to worry. As for me, I had made my personal declaration of independence.

I was a tomboy from early on and played street games with the boys—tag and hide and seek, Red Rover and cops and robbers. One of the boys, Dickie Loeb, lived in the same apartment house. He was three years my senior but we became good friends. In fact, he initiated me into two of my most memorable early adventures.

As I look back now, I see that those adventures not only reflected my Harlem life but foreshadowed the life that would follow. On a bitterly cold winter's day Dickie suggested that we earn some money by shoveling snow. We rang the downstairs doorbell of a brownstone on our block and made a deal with the lady of the house, who was clad in a red jumper. We would shovel the snow off her areaway for thirty-five cents. She agreed. Dickie, about ten, and I, about seven, picked up our shovels and set to work. There were piles of snow settled on the paving stones, and it took us at least an hour to clear the area. When we were finished we rang the bell again to collect our fee. This time the lady who answered was wearing blue. She said she had never asked us to shovel the snow and she refused to pay anything. I was already making up a little story to explain what had happened. "I think she changed the way she looks and put on another dress just so she wouldn't have to pay us," I fantasized. Then we came to a decision: "Let's shovel it all back." It took us another hour, but right had been done, and that was important.

Dickie was instrumental too in the matter of my first paid job. A Mr. Joseph owned a small newspaper stand on the corner opposite our apartment; we could see it from our windows. One summer, probably the one after the snow-clearing episode, Dickie told me that Mr. Joseph needed an assistant and wanted one of us to "man" his stand. I must have been about eight then, and I was consumed with an unholy desire to beat Dickie and get the job. School—I attended P.S. 128—was over, and a long summer loomed ahead. I listened carefully to Mr. Joseph's stipulation. "Whoever gets here by 7 A.M. will get the job." Dickie's forte was never punctuality, and I easily got the job, having set my alarm a good hour early.

The relatives fumed. In fact they sent delegations to assure my mother she would be haled to court if she allowed me to take a paid job. She was as adamant as I. She understood my desire to command that corner post. More important, she knew that she would be able to determine exactly where her often wandering daughter was by merely glancing out her window. I got the job—and held it. Newsprint filled my nostrils and my soul. The variety of dailies and weeklies astonished me. There were racing papers and sporting papers and financial papers and story papers and foreign papers and of course plain newspapers. Most of them sold for two cents.

One halcyon day, while I was superintending the stand in my khaki bloomers, a man put down two cents for a daily paper. I handed it to him. Then he put down a dime. I asked him what it was for, and he answered, "That's for you." I did not understand. He had paid two cents for the paper he wanted, and he was giving me ten cents for handing it to him? How could that be right? It made no sense to me. "It's for you," he repeated with a smile, and he walked away. I was overwhelmed. This was what was called good fortune. This was what happened in fairy tales. I raced home later to tell my mother, and I think from that day on I became an optimist.

In between such ventures and adventures there were piano lessons—customary for girls from middle-class families, regardless of their inclination or talent. Every Monday Professor Frank paid us a visit and sat next to me at the upright Knabe in the living room.

Sometimes my parents listened to the performance. My first was a rendition of "To a Robin," my father occasionally humming along: "Robin, why do you sing, beautiful songs of the springtime? Tell me, where is your mate, singing both early and late?" Throughout, Professor Frank stoically controlled his disappointment at my complete lack of musical talent. He probably was intrigued—as I still am—by my costume. For some reason now lost to memory, I insisted upon wearing my Indian costume for my piano lessons. It consisted of long khaki pants, a tan beaded jacket, and a wide headband from which sprouted Indian feathers.

Long before I took my job I can remember the smell of newsprint when my father brought the paper home and I read the cartoon strip about Little Mary Mixup, the smell of library paste in school, the thrill of attending a performance at the Alhambra, a one-act in which two children had to walk through a pitchblack tunnel before they could emerge into the sunshine—darkness leading into light. But all the while the neighborhood was, as I often heard my parents say, deteriorating. A move was imminent. By then my father, who had been a manufacturer of vermouth with a huge establishment on West 57th Street ("Something to learn: Buy your vermouth from M. R. Stern"), had been forced by Prohibition into another business—bakers' supplies. The end of the First World War had ushered in an era of apparent prosperity. The 1920s were rolling along in their dazzling, optimistic, but ultimately destructive course. And Harlem was no longer attracting the German Jewish population with whom my family was most comfortable. We moved downtown and settled in an apartment on Ninety-ninth Street down the hill and close to Riverside Drive. There, my adolescent years would be spent. From there I would eventually walk each day to Barnard College, and after my brother's marriage and my father's death I would live on there with my mother until her death. The area was pleasant, prosperous, bourgeois, and the view of the lordly Hudson was always stirring. I would write several poems in its praise.

At nearby Joan of Arc Junior High School I formed a close friendship with Shirley Phillips, a friendship based in large measure upon our shared addiction to writing poetry. By then we were each writing a minimum of a poem a day, supplemented upon occasion by prose "rapsodies" [sic] to our English teacher. When, somehow, a copy of the Columbia University Bulletin of Information sailed into our ken, we scanned it and lit upon the entry for English s15, English Prosody. This was described as a three-point "course in verse writing." Particularly enticing was the promise that "poems of students will be discussed in class. The discussion will deal mainly with images as the foundation of poetry, and with versification." The course would be given in Columbia University's Hamilton Hall by Mr. H. N. Fairchild.

Although we knew little about versification, our lines were certainly filled with dazzling images, and there could be no greater bliss than to have our poems discussed in class. Shirley and I, now in our early teens, duly presented ourselves, that summer in the 1920s, to Mr. H. N. Fairchild. I would later learn that Mr. Fairchild possessed a delicate sense of humor, but he betrayed no sign of it when we applied for admission to English s15. We took the whole course and received his candid criticism of our endeavors. My poem to John Masefield he judged "not without merit," though my "metre breaks down." Next to my line "Your thoughts are pure as April rain," Mr. Fairchild wrote: "He used to work in a saloon." Not least among the little ironies of my life is the coincidence that I would re-encounter Mr. Fairchild in a few years' time. When he spied me in the corridor of Barnard College he would remember me. "You've arrived at last," he said. There he would become one of my mentors in the English Honors course.

Meanwhile, back at Joan of Arc Junior High School, I embarked one memorable summer upon my first trip abroad. When my mother's sister, my maiden Aunt Annie, and two of her friends decided upon a European tour and offered to take me along, my parents made the proposal. I could have the choice between this journey to distant lands or four summers in camp. Never suspecting that my life would be punctuated by annual book-buying trips abroad, I chose Europe and, in the company of the three single ladies, clutching my red leather-bound octavo entitled MY TRIP ABROAD, embarked on the S.S. *Stockholm* June 30, 1925.

That diary, still in my possession, hides, though not quite successfully, the homesickness I suffered from start to finish of the two-month trip. Still, as soon as we sailed, I entered the record with the usual exclamatory opening:

> *Well, we're off! The gangplank is lifted and caps and handkerchiefs wave in the breeze! Although, without, the climate is superb, my heart is not so light, as I think of the departure from my parents and brother. But I shall conquer this feeling! We have already dined, and now we have walked the deck, rather than to lie in the chairs.*

I celebrated my thirteenth birthday on board, and continued to pour into my journal long words in place of short ones, circumlocutions instead of direct statements, and my interpretation of the guide's explanations:

> *August 19, 1925. Paris. We drove to Trianon and walked about the peaceful forest and garden of Marie Auntoinette [sic], to which she would flee when weary of court life . . . At last we . . . turned to the Grand Trianon which contains many most interesting rooms, one of which is that prepared for Queen Victoria of England, who refused to sleep there, as it had previously been utilized by Duchess du Barrie [sic].*

My superlatives were scattered throughout my diary, along with my exclamations at the "WONDROUS" world that unfolded before me, especially at the "wondrous" North Cape:

Hammerfest: NORTHCAPE (aboard S.S. Irma July 28, 1925). We were in reality at the top of the world. High up above the remainder of that wondrous Planet called Earth, we stood, overwhelmed with awe. This renowned North Cape stands majestic and alone, in the waters of the Arctic, and a path extends to the topmost point from which one might proceed to the edge. A number of people ventured on this mysterious quest, in search of the "Midnight Sun," which we were advised would soon appear . . . The delicately colored clouds, bordered with brilliant gold, heralded the appearance of that ball of fire, around which the world revolves . . . On, along its neverending journey, the sun sped, until it was ready to rise to another continent and bring with it the return of dawn, and the departure of night.

After "the final words which I shall write in this little book," I returned home with my memories, my reports, and a mannish haircut from a Parisian salon—not yet popular back home. It made me the butt of considerable sarcasm at Joan of Arc Junior High School. Shirley was loyal, however, and we quickly resumed our way of life together. Always our adventures were interlaced with our readings in Sherlock Holmes and Horatio Alger, in *Wuthering Heights* and *Jane Eyre*. When it came to *Little Women*, it seemed always a matter not of reading but of rereading. Jo March was our alter ego—or we were hers. And then, too, our junior high school teachers were preparing us for senior high school. One way they accomplished this was by addressing us as "Miss." The trick was not to giggle when this occurred, to take it in stride—it was part of growing up. It was no child, but "Miss Stern" who was about to enter Hunter College High School.

YOU'RE SUDDENLY A "MISS"

Madeleine 📖 HUNTER College High School differed in three significant ways from most public high schools. It required an entrance examination and upheld high scholastic standards. It was an all-girls school with women teachers. Its principal, Louisa M. Webster, was a paragon of moral virtue.

Yet all this did not dismay me. Hunter College High School, nunnery though it appeared to be, was never a nunnery to me. As one of a small exuberant group of adolescent friends, I was happily unaware of the school's sequestered nature. One of our group was Helen Keppler, who had attended Joan of Arc Junior High School with me. When Helen suggested we go to see *Cyrano de Bergerac* on Broadway, my mother immediately expressed her approval: "If Helen Keppler wants to see *Cyrano,* she must be a very nice girl." She was less enthusiastic about the other members of our circle, regarding their Russian or Polish backgrounds as inferior to hers. Nothing about them bothered me. We attended classes, went to the theater, read poetry, gossiped and giggled, always together.

Mostly, we gossiped about our teachers. We giggled about our math teacher, whom we promptly dubbed Lizzie Poip—short for Perpendicular. In Latin we had a wonderful teacher who was in love with the classics. On her first trip abroad, she told us, she had journeyed to Rome, where she would never forget the thrilling, mellifluous cry of the conductor as the train pulled into the station—"ROMA." To me—to all of us—she turned Roma into Romance.

Our history teacher inspired Helen, who already had a dramatic flair, to some of her best acting. Miss Ver Planck, descendant of Dutch patroons, was an extremely well-cushioned woman who would enter our classroom, throw her books on the desk, and, before doing anything else, pull her costume into shape by tugging at her corsets. Helen did a great imitation of her. Before Miss Ver Planck's arrival she would march up to the front of the room, throw her books on the teacher's desk, and proceed to pull down imaginary corsets. One day, inevitably, Miss Ver Planck walked in during Helen's performance. Her last.

Our French teachers endeared themselves to us in different ways. One of them always appeared in riding boots and jodhpurs, sometimes partly hidden by a skirt. Another—Miss Dalton—raved on about the gratifying delights of *brioche et chocolat* in a French panegyric that inspired us all to rush to Constantine's and order *brioche et chocolat* after school. During school hours, to satisfy our adolescent appetites, we kept a communal jar of mayonnaise under one of the desks, each of us dipping a finger in as we felt the urge.

I'll never forget the incident during Miss Dalton's French class that threatened to change my future. While Miss Dalton was discussing the subjunctive mood, Helen took it into her head to toss a note to me in which she wrote that she and the great idol of the silent screen, John Gilbert, were having an affair. I immediately replied with a note to the effect that—what a coincidence!—I was going to give birth to Ernest's child. Ernest was then my imaginary lover, a gentle creature who combined the pure thoughts of John Masefield with the handsome features of Lord Byron. This time the note did not land on target. Miss Dalton saw it, interrupted her meanderings into the subjunctive, and demanded, in clear and unmistakable English, "GIVE ME THAT NOTE!"

On the way home from school I discussed my situation with my friends. It was without any doubt a difficult one. We attended a school where morality was enthroned. If our principal, the strait-laced Louisa M. Webster, saw a girl wearing rouge or lipstick, she simply walked up to her, took out a handkerchief, and wiped the girl's face clean. And now here was I—pregnant by Ernest. Miss Dalton would certainly decide that I had reached the depths of iniquity and I would be promptly expelled without court-martial. The only other possible decision she could reach was that I was insane. That decision, doubtless corroborated by a physical examination, would also result in expulsion. I had no choice really—I had to face the possibility that I would have to leave Hunter College High School and enroll in some business course at Gregg or Drakes or Eastman-Gaines. Maybe I should start applying right now!

The next day in French class Miss Dalton summoned me to the front of the room. My friends watched in consternation. I walked slowly to my doom. "Please conjugate the verb *aimer* at the blackboard," Miss Dalton directed me. I grasped the piece of chalk, resumed my studies at Hunter College High School, and took up my life again. Miss Dalton never said a word, and to this day I don't know if she read the note or simply ignored my adolescent humor.

Of all my high school instructors the one who influenced me most deeply and whom I adored was Hazel Sebring, my English teacher. Slight, short, olive-complexioned, with dark hair, she seemed to me the incarnation of poetry. Surely she lived most of the time with the Muse of Poetry. And just as surely I did too. At Joan of Arc Junior High, my English teacher Grace Macdonald had only just begun to enlighten me to the pleasures of poetry with her inspiring reading of Shelley's "Skylark." Miss Sebring continued, picking up where she had left off, reading poems aloud every day to the class. Her inspired readings were contagious.

The tangible results of that inspiration survive in a fifty-nine-page pamphlet, bound in stiff terra cotta wrappers, with the label POEMS on the front cover. The title-page reads *Poems Written by Students While Attending Hunter College High School.* The imprint is "New York, December, 1927," and the work was printed by the Cumberland Press. The poems are arranged alphabetically by author. My friend Helen Keppler is represented by two short poems, I by three. One of them is the octet on John Masefield, another is a love poem called "Late June," and the third is an invigorating paean to "This Autumn Day."

The pamphlet and the poems it contains were all produced by members of the Poetry Club, which I helped found and which Miss Sebring supervised. There is a picture of the club a year later in *The Argus,* the annual issued by students of Hunter College High School. Dated December 1928, *The Argus* includes not only poems and brief essays but pictures of the graduates, with mottoes describing them and an unsigned feature entitled "Pen, Pencil and Personalities." It is stated that "Madeleine Stern was influential in bringing the Poetry Club into being. Her poetry amply justifies the faith which the senior class showed in selecting her as the one most likely to become famous." I had won a number of medals at Joan of Arc Junior High School but none at all at Hunter; still, the confident assurance of future fame in *The Argus* was better than any medal, I thought.

In between writing poetry and studying Latin, French, algebra, history, and English, my friends and I talked incessantly and laughed mightily. Much of our homework was done on the Ninety-sixth Street crosstown bus, which carried us to and from school. I usually wrote out a Latin translation that the others copied, or communally we solved a problem in geometry. The bus driver on our route was a handsome Norse blond whom we dubbed Chico (from the movie *Seventh Heaven*) and promptly fell in love with. He was very tolerant of our antics, even when we spilled a whole bottle of ink on the floor of his crowded bus or blocked the exit while we loudly recounted some confidential tale.

The exuberance that characterized my school life was not quite duplicated at home. The pattern of my life had begun to change. My brother had married and left home. As a result, I now had two rooms to call my own, and I happily converted one of them into a study. Less happily, my father had suffered two strokes—one very minor, the other graver, affecting his walking. He sold out his business and spent his time at home reading all the books he had not read earlier—sets of Scott and Thackeray especially. My mother's older sister moved nearby and spent most of the day with us. She was what the nineteenth century would have dismissed as a "superfluous" woman—my maiden Aunt Annie, tall, thin, with carroty hair, who worried incessantly about me, carried my boots to school if it rained after I had left, and altogether lived a vicarious life. I rebelled constantly against her interference. Egoist Stern never thought of Aunt Annie's side of anything—only of how her limited life impinged upon my own.

The subtler problems resulting from such a home life never occurred to me. My mother held everything together with strength and wisdom, and I still believed that, despite my father's condition, my world revolved about "the one most likely to become famous."

Leona   NINETEEN TWENTY-TWO WAS AN important year for me. I graduated from P.S. 28 with a high award—a copy of *Lights to Literature,* inscribed to me by the principal—but was denied a formal presentation of the book at commencement because we were leaving the country to meet my father in Germany. He had now completed his courses in dermatology there, and we were to vacation *en famille.* Vacation meant shopping to my mother, and since the mark had fallen she was able to acquire Dresden china, beautiful hand-embroidered linen, and outfits for her offspring. Despite Junior's violent protestations, Daddy selected a morose green suit with a bilious matching overcoat for him. For me, my mother chose several poplin dresses adorned with tatting and embroidery, along with a large brown felt hat with an upturned brim. From my personal savings I bought a black fountain pen whose ink had to be pumped up and occasionally spilled over. Nevertheless, already fancying myself a writer, I was thrilled to own my first fountain pen.

When we returned home Junior immediately discarded his morose green suit, saying to my father, "Do you think I'm a Hun? I wouldn't be seen dead in school in this lousy outfit." For his birthday in late September he was given a gay plaid suit from Rogers Peet, an appropriate costume for a senior at Evander Childs High School.

As for me, I was about to become a freshman at the same high school. According to the New York City Board of Education, I could not attend the main building of that institution, although I lived exactly six blocks from it. All freshmen were assigned to the annex. The annex was in Wakefield. Even my father, whose practice had led him all over the Bronx, was unfamiliar with Wakefield. Its precise location would, as it turned out, remain forever unknown.

Attired in my blue poplin dress with matching socks and my brown felt hat, I set out for my first journey to Wakefield and my first day in high school. My costume was adorned with my new fountain pen, now suspended from a black ribbon around my neck. Following instructions from a family friend, I boarded the Webster Avenue streetcar, knowing that eventually I must transfer somewhere but not knowing precisely the spot. After an hour I asked the conductor. "You shoulda gotten out at 189th Street. You gotta go back there and take the crosstown." Nervously I awaited the return trolley. A lady eyed me sympathetically and asked me where I was going. "I want to get the 189th Street crosstown." "There is no such crosstown, honey." "But I must get to Wakefield," I answered. *She* had never heard of Wakefield and suggested that I return to Webster and Tremont and start all over again. Three hours had now passed. I was worn, hot, and utterly dejected. I took off my heavy brown felt hat and noticed that my blue poplin dress was spattered with black ink. My beautiful pen had leaked over my new dress. I arrived at long last at Tremont and Webster, walked up the hill, and finally was back home. "I missed my first day in school," I said, sobbing violently. Daddy immediately flew into a rage. "Those *Idioten!* To send a little girl to that *verdammte* place when she could walk easily to school! What *Dummheit!*"

The next day Daddy himself paid a visit to the main building of Evander Childs High School, six blocks from home. I never received a report of the comments he made there, but he was informed that if his daughter took German she could attend school in the main building. After his jubilant return he remarked to my mother, "Imagine! They suggested that Leonchen should take German. What other language should she take?"

Apprised of my admission to his building, Junior remarked, "Listen, kid, if you see me there, you don't know me." At a later date, long after I had recovered from my aborted trip to Wakefield, I spied my brother in conversation with his physics teacher. I went up and shyly said, "Hello, A." After a few seconds he condescendingly looked down at me, smiled at his teacher, and, as if excusing himself, said, in an abashed way, "The kid sister—what can I do?"

My so-called home room or official room during my freshman year was also home to the baseball team. These were the heroes of the school and they paid little attention to the small shy child Leona. A few of the baseball gods also attended my German class. There, when the teacher, Miss Ackerle, called upon me, I did not respond. When she called upon me a second time, the team pitcher nudged me: "She wants you!" I had not connected my new title—"Miss Rostenberg"—with "little Leona."

The disparity between elementary school and high school was enormous. Here I was, small, unaggressive, nurtured, a child in socks and short skirts, suddenly being addressed as Miss. My contemporaries seemed sophisticates, girls who used makeup and flirted with boys, women of the world. Many of these "sophisticates" lived in the recently built apartments along Creston Avenue. The neighborhood "fields" were beginning to vanish.

My first year in high school was lonely. I made no friends. I enjoyed few courses and utterly detested some. I loathed geometry, and my mother's consolation—"My little girl has a literary mind"—helped not at all when my math teacher, Miss Morley, announced, "The lowest grade goes to Miss Rostenberg." Amazingly enough, I had the temerity to report her public denunciation of me to the administrative assistant, who interceded on my behalf. The persistent Miss Morley insisted upon seeing my scholastic record, and when she noted that I had received A in English, A in German, and A in Latin, she immediately retreated.

It was not until my sophomore year that I met a former friend from elementary school, Lucy Bender. She had long curls, she was jaunty and loved pleasure—especially outside school. When she suggested we have a soda together, I eagerly complied. And I proceeded to play Follow the Leader for the next two years.

Lucy confided in me that she intended to become an actress and when she reached sixteen would leave school to go on the stage. Meanwhile, her behavior in class seemed designed to hasten her departure from school. Our botany course was attended by the majority of the baseball team and was presided over by one Miss Merchant, whose petticoats were much longer than her skirts. Passing around specimens of bean seeds and Indian nuts for the students to study, Miss Merchant saw Lucy open one of the jars, remove the contents, and begin to nibble at them. Near-sighted, Miss Merchant mistook me for Lucy. Immediately she wrote out a pink card: "Plays and keeps up a comotion almost daily." I was to take the card, along with a bean seed, to the principal's office. Indignant, I grasped the card, read it aloud, and rebuked Miss Merchant: "Miss Merchant, you have misspelled the word *commotion*. It should have two *m*'s." At this point Lucy rose and gallantly cried, "Let me go. I am the guilty one." Now we were really partners in crime.

Lucy Bender was not fully appreciated in my home. Her Russian background did not appeal to my snobbish mother. It was our much loved housekeeper, Babette Sternecker, who found Fräulein Lucy *"sehr amusant."*

Babette was an important personality in my domestic gallery, and to me she would become a mainstay for the next forty-five years. There had been nothing *"amusant"* about Babette's life. Born in the small Bavarian town of Straubing, she had been early orphaned and assumed the care of her sister and brother. Before World War I she had been engaged to a young harness maker, who was killed in the First Battle of the Somme. Her sister died of peritonitis shortly after. At the close of the war, having lost their small capital, Babette and her brother, lured by newspaper promises of a rich orange grove near Rio de Janeiro, immigrated to Brazil. The "rich orange grove" was a desolate waste filled with poisonous snakes. Shortly after, Babette journeyed to the Bronx, where she lived briefly with an uncle who advised her to find work immediately. She placed an ad in the *Staats-Zeitung,* New York's principal German-language newspaper.

My parents, in need of a cook-housekeeper, turned to the advertising pages of the *Staats-Zeitung.* Since my father was a German Herr Doktor, my mother advised him to interview Fräulein Sternecker. The result was inevitable. Babette made our home hers. When she stood in the kitchen she resembled a Madonna designed by Holbein or Weiditz for a German Book of Hours. At first of course she was lonely, but her loneliness was quickly dispelled when my brother brought home a stray puppy that had, like Babette, suffered from outrageous fortune. Soon Skeezie and Babette made each other whole. Babette respected the men of the house, A.

Junior, now a Columbia premed student, was Herr Adolph to her, the inspiration for her Hasenpfeffer and cherry strudel. I was always her Miss Leona. She loved me and she loved my dogs. And when Lucy came home with me after school, we could always feast on Babette's *kleines Gebäck*—her special hazelnut cookies.

As she had predicted, Lucy abandoned high school at age sixteen. She did not land on stage precisely, but she did attach herself to the delightful comedienne Bea Lillie, who allowed her to stand in the wings of the Palace Theatre and hold props for her. As for me, Lucy's departure left me quite desolate. Moreover, her antics and my own slavish devotion to them had played havoc with my scholastic career. There had been too many classes cut, too many Wednesday matinees, too many unprepared assignments. When I applied for entrance to Barnard College, I was turned down.

Madeleine   IN FEBRUARY 1929 I JOINED the freshman class at Barnard College. My immediate reaction was despair. As a February freshman I was out of step with my colleagues, who, having matriculated the previous September, were now knowledgeable veterans. In addition, I had been cut off from my high school friends, now mostly attending either New York University or Hunter College, and I felt their absence keenly. As my father observed, "You cried when you thought you might not be accepted at Barnard, and now you are crying because you are there." In time I adjusted, but it did take time. I philosophized with myself as I took the daily walk from Ninety-ninth Street near Riverside Drive up the broad streets of West End Avenue to Morningside Heights. The mile that led from comfortable, prosperous apartment houses to the purlieus of Columbia University on the one side and Barnard College on the other gave me a quiet, undisturbed background and just enough time for any necessary introspection.

During my first two years at Barnard I took the required courses except for freshman English, from which I was exempted. I continued writing verses, mostly sad ones. Contributing to my sadness was the fact that my old high school friends were not only at different colleges but had begun the process of pairing off.

Shirley, my junior high school companion, had fallen in love with an aesthetic young man named David, who balanced work in his father's clothing business with amateur acting. He starred in *The Valiant,* a play based upon Shakespeare's observation that "the valiant never taste of death but once." To me, David seemed all soul, though he certainly made his physical presence felt. At the same time my high school friend Helen was pairing off with David's friend Raymond—tall, handsome, graceful, and most enviable. I could not help feeling cut off, rather like the cheese that stands alone in the nursery rhyme. In a couple of years I would make use of that feeling and that nursery rhyme in my first published book.

But at that moment I expressed my state of mind and emotion in a convoluted letter to Helen. It is dated enigmatically "Monday—after sunset," and it confides to her: "I hardly know what it's all about—this thing called living. In some books I've been reading . . . I've gotten some new ideas. Norman Douglas, for example, in *South Wind* holds that life is really a very simple matter. The thing that makes it seem complex is the fact that we, considering ourselves quite significant, have established over us a deity. In my thinking, however, that is the one fact which seems an effort on the part of men to avoid complexity by ordaining the simple guidance of an overseeing companion—well, each in his own tongue."

Mine seems to have loosened a bit when I added the following revealing paragraph: "As for my emotional state, again I say, nothing happens. The seething has spent itself a little—but the need within me to be a gypsy lover, to love and be loved, all sufficiently still cries, for I am young yet."

In 1929, after completing one semester at Barnard, I spent my seventeenth summer at Richfield Springs, New York, a popular vacation spot. After my return home I wrote to Helen again, this time announcing that "I have grown enough to say I wish I had not grown. To make a short story shorter, in Richfield I met a man who seemed crazy about me. We took strolls at 1 o'clock in the morning, he kissed me in the park where it was dark save for the moon, he danced with me the 'Merry Widow Waltz,' and while we danced he sang to me, the exquisite words in French. I have not heard from him since I left the place—10 days ago . . . Needless to say, I have omitted many incidents which might aid in solving this riddle. He is a man, a 22-year-old boy. I could be mad about him. How I wish I could see him again! How happy I should be! . . . To love and be loved are, after all, what we are made for. It is better to be happy than to be interesting (Farewell adolescentia)."

My letter to Helen omitted one of the "incidents which might aid in solving this riddle." One evening, dancing to the "Merry Widow," I looked over his shoulder and saw nearby a radiantly beautiful young Spanish woman. I immediately called his attention to her and he soon began to pursue my "rival." My lover disappeared from my life. I had been too honest, too frank, too forthright, too outspoken. In my letter I tried to romanticize him into a mysterious shadow. Growing, I learned, could be painful.

The girl who wished she had not grown, and was facing her farewell to adolescentia with some misgiving, would soon be catapulted into a degree of maturity. Outside, the Great Depression had begun—lines of apple sellers appeared on the streets; soup kitchens opened for other lines of needy; banks began to fail; Hoover, seemingly untouched, was ensconced in the White House. Then, on September 24, 1930, at eleven in the evening, after I had just returned from a date, my father died suddenly of his third stroke.

My father's death was sudden but not unexpected. Handicapped by a major stroke, he had for several years lived a very quiet life at home. In 1930, when I was eighteen, he was seventy, and seemed very old to me. He took his condition with fortitude, but, in the way of young people, I was often embarrassed by it. On the night of September 24, I had been out with an attractive young man from the Virgin Islands who let me off at the house. I went upstairs. My parents were in bed but not asleep, and I began to tell them about the date with Albert. Then my mother and I saw my father go taut and heard a dreadful sound—the death rattle. It was over almost before it began. And I had lost my father.

It happened too suddenly to be fully realized at first. I mourned his loss, but I coped with it. My loss could in no way be measured against my mother's. I had lost the father who took a little girl sledding. She had lost her companion of thirty years. One of my mother's first acts after my father's death was to throw his letters away. She wanted no inquisitive eyes interpreting her love. My immediate and persistent reaction was gratitude that it was not my mother who had died. I knew I could not have borne her loss. I did bear my father's. It was only while setting the table for two instead of three, or looking hastily at the cushion on the living room sofa where he had habitually sat, that I missed him acutely, and one night I thought I saw him seated in my room. It seemed natural now that my mother and I should turn spontaneously to each other and become even closer.

At no time was it ever suggested that I leave college. In any event, work would have been impossible to find, and my parents had seen to it that funds were set aside for my education. One way of enunciating a farewell to my adolescence, and perhaps eventually of finding work, seemed to be intensive study, and by 1931 I had matured sufficiently to embark upon Barnard's Honors course in English literature.

That program was designed for me. It demanded no attendance at any classes, no tests, no term papers—only the supervision of an adviser from time to time. Not until graduation would I be required to prove my mettle. Meanwhile, I could sit in on any courses I wished, pursue my research and reading, consult my mentors when I desired to do so, think, produce, study—all on my own. And so I heard my old Professor Hoxie Fairchild lecture on *Hamlet,* and the drama specialist Minor White Latham discuss the conventions of the medieval stage. I listened as Charles Baldwin reincarnated Chaucer and as William Haller intoned John Milton. All of English literature spread out before me—a fertile field for me to wander. I spent hours at the Barnard and Columbia libraries and more hours at the New York Public Library. The Forty-second Street building was open in those days until 10 P.M., and I frequently sent slips in for books at 9:30, just to have a glance at them and reserve them till the next day. Barnard had given me a feast for my devouring, and I found myself ravenous, at last tasting the heady delights of intellectual independence, not a substitute for love, but another love altogether.

There was much at college then to lend variety to my life of scholarship. Always eager to earn money, I was thrilled when Professor Baldwin informed me that a titled lady whom he had met aboard ship desired a tutor in the art of prosody. She was the Countess Colloredo-Mansfield; she had married an Austrian diplomat, although she herself hailed from the Iselin family of Long Island. He thought I would enjoy the work. She offered three dollars an hour and wished an hour a week. For me this was manna from heaven. The art of prosody? Had I not savored that early on in the course Shirley and I had taken with Mr. H. N. Fairchild? Three dollars a week? That was a handsome income at a time when Dean Virginia Gildersleeve paid a student thirty-five cents an hour to walk her dogs.

I bused to the countess's domicile in Manhattan's East Seventies, arrayed as usual in a gingham dress and a beret. If she found my appearance amusing, she never let on. Instead, she showed me her poetry—some in English, some in German, much of it about mimosa—and we scanned it together, checking the rhymes, the rhythms, and the structure of octets and sonnets. During my senior year she moved to the tower of the Ritz Hotel. I was now nineteen and had a driver's license. I had also been able to purchase for a hundred dollars a much used early model Ford—a two-seater with a rumble seat. Still wearing some version of a gingham dress and beret, I drove up to the Ritz and was immediately accosted by the doorman. When he demanded whom I wished to see, I replied with some hauteur, "The Countess Colloredo-Mansfield." He eyed me up and down—gingham dress and beret—and asked, "Are you her maid?" "Indeed, not! I am her tutor!" I proudly ascended the tower to give my lesson in versification.

Meanwhile, my own verses found an outlet in the *Barnard College Quarterly,* from which they were reprinted in two anthologies, *Columbia Poetry 1931* and *Columbia Poetry 1932.* By the time I was studying for English Honors, however, most of my published writing was in prose and it was designed for the *Barnard Bulletin.*

The *Barnard Bulletin,* issued weekly, was in the capable hands of the so-called Brain Trust, Helen Block editor, Evelyn Raskin managing editor. I had a less responsible but to me far more attractive post on the paper. I was editor of a column captioned "Here and There About Town," subtitled "The Second Balcony." As a result, I was in the enviable position of having press passes to the theater once or twice every week. At a time when theaters proliferated all over the city—there must have been a dozen in those days to one today—playwrights were inspired to write for the stage, and theatergoers had a seemingly unending variety to choose from. The best seats in those Depression years were priced $3.30, but the second balcony afforded to the agile a clear if distant view for 55 cents. I had it best of all—it was all free to me. I went to the theater at least once during the week, and on Saturdays I frequently attended a matinee and an evening show.

Often I was escorted to the theater by a current "date." Albert, who hailed from the Virgin Islands, where his father had been consul from some European city, loved to tell me tales about native voodoo but was less interested in listening to my comments on literary matters. Another loved to wear a tux and made a great escort, especially for a Broadway opening. But none of my "dates" shared my passion for poetry and books. My relations with my male contemporaries were pleasant but casual. Strong rapport was missing, especially now when, at nineteen, I felt like a real pro, in fact more professional indeed than I would ever feel again.

For me in 1931 and 1932 the curtain rose upon melodramas, comedies, and tragedies, new plays and revivals: the dramas of Eugene O'Neill at the Theatre Guild; plays by August Strindberg and Luigi Pirandello and Somerset Maugham—plays to capture the imagination and loose the pen. Accordingly, in my critiques, signed M.B.S., I offered much free advice to playwrights past and present. After seeing Strindberg's *Father,* I suggested it "might be well . . . to cut off the last act and enlarge the first and second." From the depths of my vast experience I analyzed the characters in Pirandello's *Six Characters in Search of an Author,* finding one of them "pursued by the dual forces which torture elderly men." My most serious judgment was reserved for W. Somerset Maugham, who, I decided, had "not greatly developed since *The Letter*" and who "is not a playwright."

I covered more than the theater for "About Town," and, when I was not reading in the library or meeting my friends "on Jake" (the entrance to Barnard Hall, which had been donated by the philanthropist Jacob Schiff), I attended art shows, though my reports of them in the *Barnard Bulletin* were somewhat less judgmental than my theater reviews. In addition, there was always something exciting going on at Barnard—Rafael Sabatini might give a lecture on fiction; Joseph Auslander, a talk on American poetry. Amelia Earhart came to speak. Norman Thomas, the distinguished Socialist, advocated recognition of Russia and an end to war debts, and discussed the dangers of the next war.

I soon conceived the idea of presenting an art show right in the college, and invited none other than Ben Shahn, then on his way to worldwide recognition, to hang his paintings on Barnard walls and accompany the exhibition with a lecture. Shahn agreed, and I proceeded to prepare for the event. I thought of everything. I reserved a room, arranged for the hanging of the paintings, ordered a lectern and a loudspeaker, and planned through Housekeeping for tea, watercress and egg salad sandwiches, sponge cake, and cookies.

On the appointed day, my artist arrived at the appointed hour. But nobody else arrived. It appeared that I had not quite thought of everything. No notice of the event had appeared anywhere, not even in the "About Town" columns by M.B.S. I attempted to remedy my entrepreneurial lapse by running out and accosting every student who passed by with the enticement "Free tea!"

In May 1932 I graduated from Barnard with a Phi Beta Kappa key and with Honors in English. The latter had been granted after an extended written examination and an equally lengthy oral examination, in the course of which all my mentors questioned me about philology, literary genres, and British authors. I do not recall any specific questions or any of my answers. I do recall, however, that I wore my white beret throughout the interrogation.

Much had happened to me at college. I had made an effort to say farewell to adolescence, and I had matured to some extent. I had read widely and written profusely. I had savored the joys of independent scholarship. But it was altogether another occurrence during those years that would turn out to be the most important event of my life. When I was a freshman at Barnard I had met Leona Rostenberg.

Leona 📖 AFTER MY REJECTION FROM BAR-nard I had no anchorage. I wasted a year at Columbia Extension, arriving nowhere. By the spring of 1927 I realized that I would eventually need an academic degree, so I enrolled as a sophomore at Washington Square College, New York University. The subway trip to Astor Place was long and tedious, and the college, east of Washington Square, resembled a factory. There was no campus, no green, no quads, no distant spires, no geranium-lined walks. I attended courses in a building that resembled a storage vault.

Although the majority of students were men, there were a goodly number of women. A college degree was essential for any kind of career, especially in the humanities. Except for Lucy Bender, who had landed a job at Macy's, all my friends attended college. One or two were at NYU, and we shared courses along with gossip. Theirs was mostly about their boyfriends. As for me, I listened more than I talked. My own dating was confined to two or three sons of my parents' friends, with whom I had little in common. Dorothy Parker's lines ''Men seldom make passes/ At girls who wear glasses'' were frequently in my mind if not in theirs. And so it was to Elise's stories about her Arthur or Bernice's stories about her Harold that I listened while we walked beyond the NYU campus.

Beyond the college there was the handsome Washington Square Arch; there were the gracious red-brick Federalist houses just west of Fifth Avenue. And there was Greenwich Village, with its intriguing streets—Minetta Lane, Macdougal Street, Eighth Street with its score of antique shops, bookstores, intimate restaurants, cafés crowded with artists and writers, poets and aspiring geniuses.

Strolls in Greenwich Village, however, did not fully compensate for the hours spent in an office building. It was not until my junior year that I began to enjoy college life. I had made friends, but above all I had made a discovery: I had become impassioned with history.

In the fall of 1928, when I took a course in English history given by Joseph Parks, I began to realize the strong hold of past upon present. I was enchanted by his interpretation of the Tudor, Stuart, and Hanoverian dynasties. I read Lytton Strachey's life of Victoria and delved into Macaulay and Trevelyan. I later enrolled in a course on French history under the handsome André Alden Beaumont, whose appearance was as exciting as his lectures. He dazzled me with the colorful Age of Louis XIV, the Sun King, and he curdled my blood with his bloody descriptions of the Reign of Terror. At the time, events in the recently established Soviet Union were discussed not only in the newspapers but at practically every dinner table. A course offered by Alexander Baltzly treated the rise and fall of the Romanovs and explained to bemused students the Russian Five-Year Plan. Probably one of my most stimulating courses was entitled "The Renaissance." It introduced me to the beauty, the art, the literature, and the great names of the fifteenth and sixteenth centuries in Europe. It covered the revival of classical learning and its tremendous influence upon educated society. And, speaking of that influence, perhaps the most fascinating of all my courses in history was the one on Ancient Rome, given by the elegant and erudite John Kasper Kramer. I wandered through the Forum beholding the temples of Juno and the Vestal Virgins. I watched the gladiators in the Coliseum. And for the first time I understood the beginnings of Christianity, its development, and its subjugation by Rome.

I did not in my senior year have any premonition of my future career. But surely a forecast was signaled in a term paper I wrote for a survey course entitled "From Beowulf to Thomas Hardy." I researched the career, not of any literary giant, but of the first printer-publisher of the *Canterbury Tales,* William Caxton. At the time I was unaware of any significance about my choice of subject, but surely it indicated that my devotion to printing history had begun. On the front cover of my paper I copied Caxton's device: his initials W.C.

At commencement in 1930 I marched through the Hall of Fame with other aspiring B.A.'s. I now had knowledge of the Bourbon dynasty, the Romanovs, the twelve Caesars, and the Hapsburg succession. But how would this avail in the enveloping world of the Depression? How would my knowledge of the past help me confront the future?

Actually, without my realizing it, my future had been shaped during my senior year at Washington Square College. At that time I had met a Barnard freshman named Madeleine Stern. We eyed each other superciliously at first. Madeleine was a mere freshman at Barnard, and I was not Ivy League. Our meeting lacked warmth and portended little.

It took place in the Hebrew Technical School for Girls, a building on Fifteenth Street and Second Avenue, on a Saturday morning in September 1929. At that time the prestigious Temple Emanu-El sponsored a Sabbath School there for neighborhood children. It was run by one Henrietta Solomon, a former teacher in Emanu-El's Sunday School. Miss Solomon, a single woman of large physical proportions, ruled her domain with an informal, casual touch. For much of the morning she was ensconced at the telephone, arranging most of her social engagements while she superintended the school. She was not overly concerned with disciplinary matters, and altogether the Sabbath mornings had a light, carefree air.

We each had individual connections with Miss Henrietta Solomon, and it was those connections that, in the end, connected us. My connection with Miss Solomon began on shipboard during the summer of 1928, when my mother and I traveled abroad. The second day out at sea a tall woman wearing pince-nez hailed us. "Why, Louisa Dreyfus!" My mother replied, "Henrietta Solomon!" They embraced. "Henrietta, this is my daughter, Leona." For the next few days we tea-ed together. At one point Miss Solomon turned to me and asked whether I would like to teach at her Sabbath School. I was then entering my junior year at Washington Square College. I had had no formal education in traditional Jewish history. I had never attended Sunday School. But, unabashed, I replied, "I would love to." She answered, "You know we pay $2.50 a morning."

In September I prepared for my first paid employment by re-reading the Ten Commandments.

Upon my arrival at the school, Miss Solomon stated, "Leona, you will teach the young children. My niece has the older group." Since my formal education in Jewish history was nonexistent, my instruction would be based on the history courses delivered by Messrs. Parks and Beaumont. I told the children as much about King Arthur and the Black Prince as about the ancient Kings of Israel. They loved it. When the time for their Hebrew instruction arrived, I withdrew. Sitting in the back of the room, I prepared an overdue college assignment. When one of my most serious eight-year-olds approached, asking for my interpretation of a Hebrew word, I masked my ignorance and replied, "Do you think it would be honorable for me to help you?" My ability was questioned and my job was threatened many times, most notably when I staged a Christmas celebration in the Hebrew Technical School for Girls, having invited my old friend Lucy, who was as ever game, to impersonate Santa Claus's daughter.

The new year progressed uneventfully until, in September, we all welcomed a new teacher assigned to the older children of the Sabbath School. Miss Solomon heralded her arrival with the pointed statement: "We are getting a new teacher who knows all about Jewish history."

The "new teacher" had had a religious education at that very Temple Emanu-El where Miss Solomon taught. Indeed, she had been Miss Solomon's student and had been awarded a leather-bound copy of *The Book of Psalms,* inscribed by Miss Solomon to "dear little Madeleine Stern." When, in 1929, Miss Solomon realized that her school was attracting more neighborhood children than she had anticipated, she contacted Madeleine and offered her the going rate: $2.50 a morning. Mady had not yet been spoiled by the $3 an hour she would earn from the Countess Colloredo-Mansfield; $2.50 a morning still seemed rich reward.

It was in September 1929 when we were finally introduced to each other in the building at Fifteenth Street and Second Avenue. It was not a promising encounter. Neither was drawn to the other. A Barnard freshman? Not to be taken seriously. An NYU senior? Hardly impressive!

While I rehashed my lessons in Arthurian legend before my class of eight-year-olds, Madeleine referred to her voluminous index cards and proceeded from Genesis to Exodus for the benefit of her eleven-year-olds. At one point, when she was trying to interweave the theory of evolution with the development of the Jewish nation, and chalked in bold letters on the blackboard the word *evolution,* one bright boy raised his hand to ask, "Miss Stern, shouldn't there be an R in front of *evolution?*"

Despite our lack of any strong interest in each other, we were perforce thrown together. When the pupils were studying with their Hebrew teacher, we often met and adjourned to the ice cream parlor across the street. Our conversations, however, were certainly not memorable. Far more memorable was a comment made by the Barnard freshman in the presence of the NYU senior to a friend on the telephone: "Leona is lots of fun, but she is *no intellectual.*" From time to time during the long years that followed, that remark would be retrieved, aired, and chuckled over.

Meanwhile, the Sabbath School continued. In the spring, when the Hebrew festival of Purim was celebrated, Madeleine was given an extracurricular assignment by Miss Solomon. Miss Solomon's niece had presumably coached the children in a Purim play. The niece was unable to supervise a dress rehearsal, and the play was scheduled for performance that very day. Would Madeleine take over?

In her brash and indomitable style, the Barnard freshman did. She quickly discovered that not a single member of the cast knew his or her lines. All were totally unprepared for a performance before the expected parents. The play must go on nonetheless. When the curtain rose, chubby little Queen Esther was seen on stage looking bewildered. Madeleine was in the wings with the villain, Haman.

Haman heard his cue to walk on stage, but was rooted to the ground and refused to move. At this the freshman gave him a push and enunciated loudly and clearly: "Get out there, you damn fool! Move!" Those would be the only audible words heard during the entire performance. When Haman was catapulted on stage, his white cotton beard on his nose, he landed under a small table. Esther bent down to address him, and there he remained throughout the play. I was seated in row one with Miss Solomon. "Can I help in any way?" I timidly asked. I can still hear Miss Solomon's enraged reply: "You stay right here; it's bad enough as it is!"

Neither of us found it surprising when the Sabbath School closed at the end of the year. As a matter of fact, when I asked one of my pupils, "Eddie, will you be coming back next year?" his reply was, "Nah, I don't learn nuttin' here." The Barnard freshman and the NYU senior would never know for sure whether it was they or the Great Depression that ended the experiment on Fifteenth Street. But the friendship that began that year would prove to be more lasting—more lasting, perhaps, than even we were able to imagine.

Leona 📖 THE GREAT
Depression hit the NYU commencement class of 1930. Perhaps
we marched through the Hall of
Fame with some hope and aspira-
tion, but then we tried to find
work. I had even lost my $2.50 a
week job at Sabbath School. Despite my knowledge of the past, I
was unprepared for the present. I had taken no courses in education
and therefore could not even apply for a teaching post, the traditional position for women. When I was a child I had been asked the
inevitable question: "What are you going to be, little Leona, when
you grow up?" My reply had been unhesitating: "Me—a reporter!"
Now, if I could report on the divorce proceedings of Henry VIII or
the frivolity of Marie Antoinette, maybe I could also report on more
timely occurrences—the ineptitude of Herbert Hoover, the stagna-
tion of the country, particularly the predicament of my generation. I
would try.

A friend of my brother had a friend whose cousin had a job on
the Sunday *Daily News*. I had to avail myself of such a connection.
When I sought his advice, I was bluntly informed that there was

absolutely nothing available on any newspaper in New York City. However, maybe in Westchester . . . And so I found myself in Dobbs Ferry. Just how I got there remains a mystery. The would-be Nellie Bly finally confronted the editor of the local newspaper. And he confronted me—all of my four feet ten, my rumpled hair, my horn-rimmed glasses, my eager eyes.

"A job, kid? Why, we're lettin' people go. Why don't you try Tarrytown?"

"Is that very far from here?" My budget was getting very low.

"Just over the hill, kid. You can walk it."

"Just over the hill" took me three hours. My shoes were as worn as my spirit. Nonetheless, youth is resilient and by the time I reached the *Tarrytown Tatler* I managed to exude some hope and optimism. Neither was returned. A large, genial, middle-aged gentleman repeated familiar words: "A job, sis? Why, we're lettin' people go." He added with some compassion: "You're from New York. Why don't you open one of those apple stands? You can sell apples for five cents apiece!"

My Westchester mission had failed. I would try a different direction, toward the east. I boarded the IRT for the Battery, transferred to the ferry, and sailed across the bay to Staten Island. A bus took me to the office of the *Staten Island Advance*. The editor eyed me critically. "Where are you from, miss?" Afraid to tell him that I lived in the remote Bronx, I boldly answered, "Manhattan." He paused a while before commenting: "You can't commute here every day from Manhattan, kid. Besides, even if you lived across the street, I couldn't offer you a job. No jobs—no money—no nothin'!"

On the way back to the mainland we passed the Statue of Liberty, but her torch had dimmed.

A few weeks later, an old Berlin friend of my father visited us for dinner. Dr. Nicolai Cahen had been born in Russia and emigrated to the German capital, where he became a successful physi-

cian on the Kurfürstendamm. Drafted into the German army during
World War I, he was shortly suspected of being a Russian spy.
Accordingly, he was exchanged for a German prisoner of war and
sent to his native Russia. There, he was almost immediately suspected of being a German spy. Without further ado, the Russians
sent him to a typhus camp in Siberia. Obviously now—a decade
later—Dr. Cahen had a great story to tell, which he did at length at
the dining room table.

It appeared that he had also turned his great story into a manuscript. The manuscript, however, was in German, and Dr. Cahen
was looking for a translator. I pricked up my ears. Here, finally, was
something I could do. Thanks not only to my father but to my dear
Babette, I daily aired the German I had studied at Evander, and as a
result I was fairly fluent. Besides, had I not taken a course in Russian
history under Alexander Baltzly at NYU? Dr. Cahen's story titillated
me. I immediately asked, "How about me?"

Dr. Cahen was delighted, the family applauded, and terms were
discussed. I was to receive $100 upon publication of the opus, enti-
tled *From the Spree to the Amur*. Dr. Cahen had a contact—though not
yet a contract—with the publisher Boni, Liveright. He planned to
return to Germany but would leave the manuscript with me, and I
would present the publisher with my translation.

Dr. Cahen's travelogue was truly astounding. It included of
course his deportation to Siberia and his stay in the typhus camp
near Stretensk, a Cossack village in Asiatic Russia. There were colorful descriptions of Amur in East Siberia near the Manchurian
border. The work had an exotic quality that I sought to convey in
my translation. There was much excitement in the doctor's account
of the Bolshevik Revolution of 1917, when the Red Army fought the
White Army in the east. More and more, *From the Spree to the Amur*
began to resemble a wild movie script, and I plodded on, spending
four or five months with the deportee from Germany and the es-
capee from Siberia.

When the task was completed I reported to Dr. Cahen's contact at Boni, Liveright, and was told to bring the manuscript down. I did so, and spent the weeks that followed ranging in mood from high anticipation to miserable despair. All doubt was resolved with a peremptory phone call from the Boni office: "Miss Rostenberg, we suggest you come down and pick up the manuscript. We are so inundated with manuscripts about the Red Russians and the White Russians that we simply cannot add the Cahen book to our list."

At the time, my crestfallen spirit was lifted by my friendship with another German émigré, Carl Flanter. Carl was good-looking and charming, and for me in my early twenties it was a gratifying experience to be seen walking down the street or down a movie aisle or into a restaurant like Lindy's next to this handsome specimen of masculinity. I tried to convince myself that I was in love with him. But beyond the externals, there was little substance. His academic background was almost nonexistent, and his main ambition was to make a success in the glove business. Try as I did to find his conversation fascinating, I had to admit to myself that it was boring. Even my family, who would have liked to see me married, remained unenthusiastic about Carl and his future. Our relationship petered out—as had my reportorial career and my translation of *From the Spree to the Amur.*

The only affirmative thing I did, it seemed to me, was cast my first vote for the President of the United States. In November 1932 I voted for Franklin Delano Roosevelt. He would not take office till the following March. Then perhaps we would see some change for the better. Meanwhile, what was there for me to do? Incapable of finding work, many of my contemporaries, male and female, were going to graduate school. I decided to join their ranks and work for a Ph.D. in history at Columbia. In the fall of 1932 I registered at Morningside Heights, selecting courses for a major in medieval history and a minor in modern European history. My courses were rounded out with lectures on American colonial history, Alan Nevins on historiography, and the brilliant Carleton Joseph Huntley Hayes on nationalism. I have never forgotten that red-letter day, January 30, 1933, when Professor Hayes, speaking before his large hushed student audience, solemnly said: "Ladies and gentlemen, today President Hindenburg has named Adolf Hitler Chancellor of Germany. The world will never be the same again."

Carleton Hayes discussed the future. Alan Nevins discussed the past. In his course on historiography he instructed his students in the use and value of source material. I was assigned a study of the origins of the Great Fire of London in September 1666. To reconstruct that devastating event, I consulted the diaries of John Evelyn and Samuel Pepys, both eyewitnesses. The two accounts conflicted. While Pepys declared that the fire began in loose timber adjoining the house of John Martyn, printer to the Royal Society, Evelyn stated that it began in St. Paul's Cathedral. I had to weigh the veracity of both accounts. For this I needed a third eyewitness, and even then the accuracy of his account could not be taken for granted. At all events, there was no third eyewitness who had left a diary account of the Great London Fire, so I was left hanging in the end. The precise locale of the kindling of that fire was never determined. But I had been led to the mighty question "What is truth?" I had learned the value of skepticism. And I was on my way to the glories as well as the hazards of scholarly detection.

Although I found the wan smile of Austin P. Evans somewhat specious, he succeeded in transporting me into the medieval world of feudalism: its great manorial landowners, its serfs, the tillage of the soil, the knights in armor, the ladies, the courts of love, chivalry, the jousts, the prelates, the threat of the Turk, the crusades, the position of the Jew. Professor Evans conveyed it all.

I was to realize that the lowly position of the medieval Jew persisted on Morningside Heights one day in early 1933, when Professor Evans summoned me to his office. In the course of a consultation about my projects, he looked out of his tall window in Fayerweather Hall and said to me: "Miss Rostenberg, do not set your sights too high. You have two grave disadvantages. You are a woman and a Jew." Was this another roadblock in my future? Was I wasting more time at Columbia? I rallied sufficiently to reply, "There is nothing I can do about either, Professor Evans." And I left the office.

Professor Lynn Thorndike preferred to be called "Mr." He sidled into the lecture room wearing his customary dark green suit and discoursed upon the wonders of twelfth-century astrology, witchcraft, the occult, and mysticism. Like Professor Evans, he gazed out the window rather than at his audience, and mumbled his observations. During his seminar on medieval intellectual history he assigned to me a topic that I thoroughly detested: the influence of the medieval Arabic astrologers on Western culture. I was to translate the Latin prefaces of writings by Albumasar, Alkindi, Albohazen Hali, and their associates. Since I did not know the difference between the Big Bear and the Little Dipper, I found the subject of astrology superfluous. The distaste that accompanied my translations was alleviated slightly by the advice of two brilliant seminar students with whom I formed a warm friendship, Ben Nelson and Blaise Hospodar. The former was Thorndike's darling; the latter a Hungarian and fine Latin scholar. Both tried to share with me their belief that somehow connections existed between Arabic astrology and modern civilization, and, thanks to them, I completed my work for the seminar. "Mr." T. was delighted with the results.

Sometime in 1933 I had spied a familiar face on campus. The Barnard freshman who had been my old Sabbath School colleague was now doing graduate work at Columbia. Madeleine Stern had re-entered my life. We immediately arranged to have lunch to bring each other up to date. It was then the floodgates were opened. Where before we had looked down upon each other with some disdain, we felt more like equals in the academic world that surrounded us. We met regularly from that time on, shared our pleasures at soda fountains and in double features, and especially in the theater. A lifelong friendship had begun in earnest.

Madeleine's friends soon became mine, and as Shirley was married to Alvin, and Helen was deeply in love with Raymond, we both felt that we were being left alone. Mady would pursue this theme in the novel she worked on from time to time. The result of all this was of course that we were thrown together more and more. It was with Madeleine now that I discussed my problems, from the infrequency of a Saturday night date to my mother's habitual and annoying query after I did have a Saturday night date: "Did you ask him to call again?," from the difficulties of Arabic astrology to the peculiarities of Lynn Thorndike. And by 1936, when I was facing the prospect of my oral examination for my Ph.D. degree, it was Mady with whom I shared my concerns.

I had been immersed in reading for my orals for more than a year. Even during the WPA concerts I attended with Mady—Haydn and Mozart for fifty cents—I was reviewing in my mind the annals of Charlemagne, Henry III of England, the House of Medici, and all the way on to the Industrial Revolution. By the time a date had been set, my head felt completely compartmentalized—so much so that I would allow no one to touch it lest I lose track of a fact.

Indeed, I was expected to spout innumerable facts on April 20, 1936, the day of my orals. I was seated next to the chairman of the board, the astral Mr. Thorndike. Around the table sat the "greats" of the Columbia history faculty: David S. Muzzey; Charles D. Hazen, authority on the French Revolution; the internationally known Carleton J. H. Hayes; Eugene Byrne, medievalist sitting in for the absent Austin Evans. The questioning was brisk and included one or two queries about Thorndike's Arabic astrologers. With Hayes I discussed the Congress of Vienna and with Hazen the Thermidorean Reaction of the French Revolution. The orals even included an extraneous question based upon Dante's *Divine Comedy* leveled at me by David Muzzey. After I had replied, my head suddenly felt lighter. By noon the interrogation was over and I joined two friends for lunch. As we walked through the campus, we encountered Professor Muzzey, who stopped short, took my hand, and said, "Young lady, you covered yourself with honor." Now my heart felt as light as my head. I saw no barriers ahead of me.

For some time I had been thinking about the subject of my doctoral dissertation. Having handled many incunabula—fifteenth-century books—in connection with the Arabic astrologers, I had become deeply interested in early printing. The influence of the press in spreading knowledge and shaping opinion during the Renaissance and later Reformation seemed to me an innovative subject for a doctoral dissertation. What had been the role of the printer-publisher? How large a readership had there been? Had the printer's prefaces given any indication of his point of view and purpose?

In a state of high excitement I bounded up the six flights of Fayerweather to Mr. Thorndike's office. He rose and congratulated me on my orals.

"I am very pleased, and now I wish you to continue with research on the Arabic astrologers for your dissertation." I was momentarily stunned. How could I dare to remind Mr. Thorndike that I had but little interest in his Arabic astrologers but was consumed with interest in my printing-publishing project? In 1936 no one dared oppose Lynn Thorndike. Nonetheless, I bubbled on with my alternate plan, discussing the possibility of researching early printer-publishers as molders of reform and scholarship. Thorndike remained silent while I persisted. I had even given thought to the locale for my research. I would go to Strasbourg for two reasons. That city had been a center of humanism and the Reformation; its libraries were world famous. Second, although Strasbourg was officially a French city, its culture was German. Now, with the threat of Nazism, I would be safe and secure in a French city. In addition, my expertise was in the German language, and Strasbourg—ever a political football—was German in background.

At this point Mr. Thorndike interrupted my enthusiastic flow: "Your printers were mere hacks—utterly uneducated. They had little if any influence. I see no validity in such a subject."

"I think I can establish my point of view, Professor Thorndike," I said quietly. "I'd like to give it a chance."

Young and brash, I determined to go ahead with my Strasbourg printers. I tried to forget about Thorndike's lack of enthusiasm for my subject. Preliminary research confirmed my point of view that printer-publishers did indeed influence their readers. Reading a preface to an inflammatory sermon by Martin Luther, I found statements by the publisher pointing to his personal involvement in the Reform movement. I realized that the publisher not only agreed with the Reformer's tenets but wished to disseminate them. In a humanistic text by Erasmus I found a preface endorsing the author's ideology by the university-trained publisher Schürer, who boldly added a Latin injunction: "Buy! Read! Enjoy." I knew I would find more such prefaces. I was sure I could convince Mr. Thorndike once I prepared my dissertation. For all this I had to go abroad and settle for several months in Strasbourg. Over the years I had accumulated the vast sum of $700—about $7000 today—sufficient for the voyage abroad and maintenance in a Strasbourg pension. As I laid my plans, I began to weaken. I would be separated from my parents and from Mady. I would be living alone in a distant city. But I had to go ahead. I had to complete what I had begun. On August 5, 1936, I sailed aboard the *Aquitania*—first stop, Le Havre.

Madeleine

Madeleine 📖 WHILE LEONA PURSUED HER doctorate, I settled on a master's. Like so many 1932 college graduates who had no jobs but did have some savings, I enrolled in graduate school. At Columbia I continued the kind of program I had begun at Barnard, taking courses in English literature from medieval to Victorian times. The *Cambridge History of English Literature* was my constant companion, and it became infused with my cigarette smoke as I plodded through the pages. Almost all my women friends were smokers, some using cigarettes to affect a social ease and grace; others, more dependent upon them, becoming chain smokers. I myself was convinced that without a cigarette in my mouth I could neither study nor exercise any creativity. All unconscious of future revelations about nicotine, my mother would say to me, "Why not—as long as it's not dangerous." And so I smoked my way through the *Cambridge History of English Literature.*

My specialty at the time was the literature of the Middle Ages, and I selected as the subject of my master's essay the life and career of Mary Magdalene as interpreted in medieval poetry and prose. My great-grandmother had been named Magdalena and I had been named Madeleine after her. Perhaps that was one reason for my interest. Another was that I was intrigued by this disciple of Jesus in whom I had detected a split personality, so I pursued her literary appearances. I pursued her in Columbia's Low Library and in the New York Public Library, and I pursued her so intensively that I found myself following her portrayals by later writers well into the nineteenth century. My master's thesis was turning into a hefty tome. At seminars with my old friend Professor Baldwin, when a small group of students chanted medieval hymns and discussed Dante's *Divine Comedy,* I discussed the conflict between sinner and saint in the Magdalene of English literature. In the fullness of time, by the early spring of 1933, my thesis—my tome—was finished.

I proceeded at that point to do what most other writers of master's essays did: I brought mine to the secretary of the English Department for retyping. This was standard practice at the time. One evening I received a telephone call inquiring: "Miss Stern, do you have a copy of your master's thesis?"

"No," I replied. I had no copy. The original was the one and only, and that was safely deposited in the English Department office. Then I heard from the other end of the line: "I'm afraid that two thirds of your paper has disappeared from this office. We have the first third—that's been retyped.''

My mother and I dashed to Columbia immediately. We spent part of the evening going through Columbia rubbish bins. Two thirds of Mary Magdalene had simply disappeared. Her role in literature between the sixteenth and nineteenth centuries had evaporated. So, perhaps, had my master's degree. It was not until considerable weighty consultation had taken place that the Columbia powers-that-be decided to accept the first third of Mary Magdalene in lieu of the whole and grant me a master's.

The Magdalene experience had two important effects. It encouraged me to pursue research well beyond any limits I might have originally set. After all, if my thesis had not been so long, I would not have received a degree. At the same time, the incident discouraged me from going on with graduate work. I was tired of listening to lectures. But I was agog to pursue independent research. I was also eager to earn some money even in Depression times. I had already taken the extensive examinations, written and oral, offered to candidates for teaching positions in New York City high schools. It would be months before the results were announced. Meanwhile, I would have at least one free semester—six months in which to write what I pleased, think as I pleased, do as I pleased. As it developed, the year 1933 had brought me more than freedom. It had brought me the reunion with my fellow teacher in Sabbath School with whom I would begin to share much of my life.

Now I shared with her, in exchange for her thoughts about Arabic astrologers and intellectual history, my cogitations about what would become my first published article. Entitled ''Hungry Ghosts,'' from a line by Conrad Aiken—''We are the hungry ghosts of the selves we knew''—and subtitled ''Flux of Identity in Contemporary Literature,'' the study centered on a subject and a field I had never academically pursued. Now I was pursued by the dualism of human nature, and as I had followed Mary Magdalene through the ages, I searched for the core of identity in Strindberg and Dostoevsky, in Proust, Eugene O'Neill, and T. S. Eliot. I ended the article, which appeared in 1935 in the *Sewanee Review,* with the remark, "The writer thinks it about time she took the infinity of her selves for an airing."

With Leona I aired my infinity of selves and discussed plans for a follow-up article in the *Sewanee Review* that would concern flux of time in literature. With Leona I discussed the entry into my life of a young man named Alter Fischof, who had read something I published and wanted to meet me. My mother, thinking he might be a killer, objected, and I was forced to meet with him initially chaperoned by two tall friends. The second time Alter and I met he noted, "I see you came without your cohorts." Actually, he was no killer. He was, strangely enough, a rabbi, though without a congregation, and a very brilliant man. Although he took pains to introduce me to his mother, our relationship did not last. I seemed to enjoy talking about it all to Leona far more than experiencing it.

At no time did I ever feel any parental pressure to marry. I am sure that my mother would have liked to see me married—but married to the "right" person, who would be a companion in an understanding and permanent relationship. Marriage for the sake of marriage meant nothing to her, any more than any of the "shows" of life did. I too would have relished such a marriage. But none of the men I dated really shared my personal passions for writing and for books, and hence never had a true share of me. Leona did. In this respect our friendship was both uncommon and intense, though always in a platonic way. Helen's husband, Raymond, appreciated this and eventually said, "Mady and Leona are the most perfect couple in our circle." For the most part, Leona and I were too busy confiding in each other and enjoying our confidences to analyze our friendship.

In 1934 I became a teacher-in-training in English at Theodore Roosevelt High School. I was expected to act as a kind of secretary to the head of department, to teach a little, and to observe much. Besides, Theodore Roosevelt High School was in the Bronx, not too far from Leona's home. On Friday nights I usually bused to her house from school and we digested the week that had passed with the wonderful dinners prepared by Babette. My salary as teacher-in-training was $22.50 a week. Although I was earnest about the work and eager to please my superiors, I did not find the act of teaching fulfilling in any way. I went through the motions, but I did not rejoice in them. The pay was tempting, though, and, living at home as I did, I could put money aside.

But I knew that teaching left something to be desired. I had a tendency to simplify too much even for below-average students. One such class had been assigned Old Testament stories, and in order to explain as lucidly as possible the dual responsibility of the Judge of Ancient Israel—active leader of the host in war and sedentary justice passing sentence on crime—I clarified a bit too graphically: "The Judge of Ancient Israel," I informed my pupils, "had two duties to perform. One of these he performed standing up, and the other sitting down." The class's literal interpretation of my metaphor triggered much unintended hilarity.

By the summer of 1934 I felt I had put aside enough money to go abroad. Leona could not come with me; by then she was too deeply involved in preparation for her Ph.D. My mother agreed to accompany me, and on July 4 we boarded the S.S. *Washington,* for what would be my literary trip to France and England. Throughout, I recorded my reactions in letters to Leona and my other friends as well as to a five-year-diary, practically all of which was consumed with indexed details of the two-month journey. From Chartres to St. Germain-en-Laye, from Dinard to Dinan, from the Bibliothèque Nationale to the Musée Rodin, I wandered and wrote and wrote and wandered. I stopped long enough at the Paris quais to make my first purchases of rare books, noting that the books were

> *kept in grey tin boxes unlocked to show the public. Some American & foreign books in paper covers & some 16–18th century French & Latin. I bought a 17th-century Ovid for 40 francs and an Erasmus L'Éloge de Folie with*

Holbein drawings 17th-century, for 140 francs . . . [and a Baudelaire translation of Poe for 3 francs]. Different owner of every few stalls—some women in heavy black petticoats who are eager to unlock the precious wares and a few men with carroty mustaches who knew something about books.

Years later, when Leona and I were partners in the rare book business, we would sell that seventeenth-century Ovid and the Baudelaire translation of Poe, as well as the French Erasmus with Holbein illustrations. Indeed, the *Praise of Folly* would be the focus of a book we would one day co-author under the title *Quest Book—Guest Book: A Biblio-Folly*. The Quest Book of the title would be Erasmus's masterpiece.

In England the literature I had studied came alive for me. At the Bodleian I saw the guitar Shelley had given to Jane. In Salisbury I saw Florence Nightingale's bed, owned by her dear friend Arthur Hugh Clough. My mother and I sat in a tent in Regent's Park during a drenching rain to see John Drinkwater play Prospero in *The Tempest*. Wherever there were bookstores I was lured, from a second-hand shop in Bath to D. M. Beach's in Salisbury to Foyle's in London.

Prospero had drowned his book in *The Tempest*. I was getting more and more eager to open mine. I was quite sure that, though I would have to teach, teaching was not my "book." It would have to be the background to what I really wanted to do—write. When we returned home from "My Literary Trip Abroad," I went back to teaching and to researching unpaid articles for scholarly periodicals.

I went back too to Leona, but now our friendship was given another dimension. Her brother Adolph—A. Jr.—had begun to play a role in my life. Chaucer, having put him on the road to Canterbury, would have called him a very "sudden" man. Now, reincarnated in the twentieth century, a young physician, he was still a very "sudden" man, brilliant but condescending, a man who went after what he wanted with single-minded determination. No, the twentieth century would not have called him "sudden"; it would have called him "macho." Yet he was often fascinating to be with, and our association had ups as well as downs. His medical practice never deterred him from his innumerable hobbies; stamp collecting gave way to tropical fish, botany to mathematics. For a time I was probably one of his hobbies. Curiously, he never called me Mady, just Stern; and I never called him Rusty, just A. In the end we realized that there was basically little love between us. He wanted to be married and selected me for the post of wife. I went on to another nonsuitor.

Bill was far less "sudden" and "macho" than A. A lawyer in the immigration office, he was also an amateur violinist, and I frequently played the role of audience for the quartets he assembled. He had an interesting and original mind, but he was certainly not ready for marriage or for any permanent relationship. In addition, he had a vulgar streak that he manifested upon occasion. I recall a performance of *Tristan* that he classified unhesitatingly as "shit." At the time, he succeeded in shocking me.

I am not sure just how Leona reacted to all my confidences. All I remember is that the imparting of those confidences gave me considerably more pleasure than the experience that triggered them. And this told me quite definitely that I should not marry her brother A or his successor Bill, and perhaps I should not marry anyone.

This feeling did not make it any easier for me to watch on the sidelines the pairing off of friends. Shirley had married and had a baby. Helen would marry Raymond as soon as they had put a little money aside. Besides discussing all this with Leona, I did what came most naturally to me: I put my observations into prose.

I had begun my novel in college, but now it took on more precise focus. I called it *We Are Taken,* from Edna St. Vincent Millay's *Buck in the Snow:*

> *This is my testament: that we are taken;*
> *Our colours are as clouds before the wind;*
> *Yet for a moment stood the foe forsaken,*
> *Eyeing love's favour to our helmet pinned;*

Death is our master,—but his seat is shaken;
He rides victorious,—but his ranks are thinned.

It was not death that was master in my *We Are Taken,* but rather love and the conventions in which my lovers sought security. I based my novel upon the progressions of the nursery rhyme "The Farmer in the Dell": "Heighho the Derry-oh, the Farmer in the Dell"; "The Farmer Takes a Wife"; "The Wife Takes the Child"; "The Child Takes the Nurse." Inevitably, as in the rhyme, the Farmer runs away, the Wife runs away, the Child runs away. But the Cheese stands alone. And as the Cheese that stood alone, I dominated my novel, observing the taking and the running away, and, in the end, being left. It was a simple enough conceit for a first novel, but it took off from a pretentious prelude and did not quite succeed in making its point.

I dedicated *We Are Taken* to my mother, who had listened with what seemed like appreciation to my readings from it. In 1935 the novel was published by a small firm, the Galleon Press, with offices in New York's Flatiron Building, at 175 Fifth Avenue. My mother had seen in a New York newspaper the press's announcement that it was looking for manuscripts, especially novels. A few prior attempts at placing *We Are Taken* had been unsuccessful, so when my mother suggested I try Galleon, I did. Its two heads, Gerta Aison and Kenneth Houston, were both enthusiastic about my submission. They were also enthusiastic about their press, which they described as "publishers of fine editions and books of distinction." My elation at seeing my creation between boards was tempered by some reservation. Perhaps I should have waited longer and tried more distinguished houses with wider distribution. But at twenty-three I could easily wave such a thought aside when I rode downtown to the Flatiron Building on top of a double-decker, hugging the thought that I was on my way to "my publisher." Actually, though the publication gave me a great feeling of satisfaction, accomplishment, and sophistication, there was not much "of distinction" in *We Are Taken*. My friends, of course, read it with undisguised curiosity; to them it had the appeal of a *roman à clef*. A review in the September 15, 1935, *New York Times* was not too sanguine. The novel, the critic conceded, has "lusty lungs, sensitiveness, a desire to probe and an unabashedness at its own nakedness . . . But it bites off more than it can well chew." A provincial paper, the *Blackwell Daily Journal*, of Wewoka, Oklahoma, thought more highly of *We Are Taken*, which it described as a "unique book . . . a succession of narratives concerning the problems of young girls. Their hopes and disappointments, their loves and hatreds, their racial and religious differences—all are depicted with a sympathetic understanding." As for the heroine, she was, in the reviewer's estimation, "unusual," with "an ultra-modern mind . . . forever seeking for solutions to troublesome mysteries . . . an intriguing personality who evolves at length into worthwhile womanhood."

The *Blackwell Daily Journal* was not only kind but optimistic. At the time I did not feel that I had in any way evolved into "worthwhile womanhood." I felt just like the Cheese, still standing alone. Thanks to the publication of my novel, I now had an ambition to see in print anything and everything I might write. The only problem was that I wasn't sure just what it was I wanted to write. Before long I would be truly and literally bereft. The confidante to whom I had unburdened heart and mind would soon be off on her own search and her own adventure. Leona would be living her own life among old books and new people in a city three thousand miles away. And I, having come this far, seemed at a standstill.

STRASBOURG
ON THE RHINE

Leona 📖 THERE IS A wide gulf between travel abroad in 1936 and today. Travel to France aboard the S.S. *Aquitania* took six days. Life aboard ship was pleasant enough; most of the passengers were English or American; their language and customs were mine; and so the ship was almost an extension of America. But watching couples do their mileage around the deck was often painful for me. Envious of their closeness, I longed for Madeleine's companionship. In addition, as a woman sailing overseas alone sixty years ago, I lacked the hail-fellow-well-met freedom of later decades.

Aboard the *Aquitania* I did meet a young woman with whom I developed a casual friendship. She was bound for Vienna to see her father, and we arranged to spend the first night in Paris together, each departing the next day for her respective destination. When the boat reached Le Havre, my shipboard acquaintance discovered she could make immediate connections to Vienna, so I found myself suddenly and completely alone in Paris.

I registered at the Terminus, a small station hotel near the Gare de l'Est, checked my trunk through for the next day's trip to Strasbourg, and took the Métro to the Louvre. With little enthusiasm I gazed at the *Winged Victory,* Leonardo's *Mona Lisa,* and the other masterpieces in the Grande Salle. I walked through the Tuileries Gardens, kicking the pebbles, yearning for the familiar. I walked on the rue de Rivoli, on to the Champs Élysées, seeing little, and close to the Arc de Triomphe stopped at a café for brioche and coffee. The endless day finally ended back at the Terminus, where I immediately wrote letters to my parents and Mady.

The following morning, my courage and animation renewed, I took the train for Strasbourg. Here I was met by an acquaintance of my brother, Freddy Gall, whose welcome was dutiful but unenthusiastic. "Jesus, you have a trunk! That'll detain me no end." "You don't have to wait," I replied. He waited, accompanied me with trunk to the Pension Elisa, 3 rue Goethe. "See ya!" he cried as he hopped out of the cab and departed.

I was escorted by a Madame Betzner, *propriétaire,* to the fourth floor. The room assigned me—number 19—resembled a discarded operating room. The bed was white, the washstand white, the armoire white. Madame Betzner took me to the window to gaze across the street at the signs U. CLOT ÉPICERIE and A. DRIZEHN TABAC. I did not see the signs but rather the large porch surrounding the house in the Bronx, my dog Chimpie jumping into a chair, Babette in the kitchen, my mother playing bridge with my aunts, my father giving me a bear hug, meeting Mady, walking arm in arm, laughing and giggling, going to a double feature, and later devouring a fudge sundae. Madame Betzner roused me from my revery and told me that supper was at seven.

At seven I entered the dining room, although I believed I could not eat. There, I was seated alone at a small table. The large center table was occupied by retired French military and their spouses. I saw no one under fifty. I ate my meal much in the manner of a Trappist monk and retired to my room. On the table was a letter. It was from Madeleine. She wrote: ". . . I've been feeling a great respect for you—your courage—and your determination to follow the path you've set for yourself . . . You're doing something so fine and important for yourself." At the moment I had neither courage nor determination. I began to wonder why I had come.

My reasons for coming to Strasbourg were made evident only the following morning, when I took myself and my umbrella to the university library and went to the office of the director, Monsieur le Docteur Ernst Wickersheimer, who rose politely when I introduced myself and said, "Ah, Madame, I am just writing to Professeur Thorndike. We are both interested in early science." I felt this was a bad omen. Monsieur le Directeur continued, "He has written to me about your project and I will take you directly to Monsieur le Curateur des Livres Anciens." I followed him down the hall to an office marked F. RITTER. When we entered, Monsieur Ritter, a rather tall man with a receding hairline, stood up, shaking strands of tobacco from his duster, and extended his hand. Monsieur le Directeur made a few introductory remarks and departed.

I discussed my project with Monsieur Ritter who became extremely excited as I talked. *"C'est magnifique,"* he declared. "I shall be happy to assist you in the selection of books. It is an important project. As you know, our library has one of the greatest collections of incunabula and early sixteenth-century books. I will now take you to our reference room." Here on the shelves were weighty volumes listing the library's holdings in two main divisions, one marked *Avant la Guerre* and the other *Après la Guerre.* I was not certain whether the reference was to the Peasants' War or the Great War. Monsieur Ritter, balancing himself, pulled down a hefty tome labeled ER— ET. *"Voilà—le Grand Érasme."* He pulled out a call slip on which he indicated the call number, author, and title. "Big deal," I thought. "We do this daily at the New York Public Library." He then introduced me to the chief of the reference room, Herr Fischer, who sported a toothbrush mustache, a stiff cravat, and a white duster. He eyed me suspiciously, bowing stiffly. Monsieur Ritter at this point whispered to me, "You must tip him." I looked at Ritter questioningly. "Tip him? Every time he brings me a book?" "Not *every* time" was the reply, "but frequently."

Soon my days began to fall into a routine. I worked in the library, searching for prefaces by early printers of texts by "le grand Érasme" and other humanists. In the afternoon I occasionally visited the library of the Protestant Seminary St. Guillaume, where the young seminarians regarded me as the great granddaughter of Frau Luther. Here were paraded volumes relating to the German Reformation, and their prefaces indicated the reform point of view of their printers.

On a rainy morning during a consultation with François Ritter, there was a knock on the door. A tiny man, more like a pencil shaving with white hair and a white goatee, stood there. Monsieur Ritter jumped up. *"Ach, mein freund, Herr Heitz."* He turned to me, saying, "This is Monsieur Paul Heitz, the famous authority on the early woodcut." Monsieur Heitz greeted me: *"Sie sind nach Strasbourg gekommen mich zu besuchen!"* (You came to Strasbourg to visit me!). I smiled. *"Natürlich."*

Paul Heitz was indeed a celebrated scholar and a very kind old man. He took me around the city and showed me where, during the War of 1870, he had hidden. He took me to his office, where he displayed his great collection of woodcuts, sixteenth-century New Year's cards, and a Roman fountain pen. He plied me with worm-eaten peaches brought from his garden and a quince *"pour Madame votre mère."*

A few weeks later Monsieur Heitz invited me to dine at his home. I was warmly received not only by Frau Heitz but by the bewigged family ancestors, who looked down from the walls. Père Heitz enthusiastically gurgled his soup while Madame, a short, rotund lady, attempted to put me at my ease by suggesting conversational topics of homey familiarity.

"Tell me, Fraülein, how is everything now in Nicaragua?" Nicaragua, I repeated to myself. What is it? Confusing it with an avant-garde author and the leader of a local assembly district, I finally recalled its existence.

"Everything is just great in Nicaragua. Nothing to worry about," I assured her.

As Madame, now satisfied, concentrated on her turbot, Père Heitz took up the *"art de parler."* He delivered a lengthy peroration on fascism and the pro-German sentiment of many Alsatians.

"My dear child, there is some German in every Alsatian. And if there is a war—and there will be a war—many in this city will welcome their German neighbors. There are many *collaborateurs,"* he concluded, waving his knife at me. "You have gangsters in your great country; we have *collaborateurs."*

Happily, upon my return to the pension, I found a letter from Madeleine about that "great country" of ours: "Everybody is election-conscious here, and talk is very political," she wrote. I knew it would be her first presidential election, and we were both ardently hoping for a second Roosevelt term. Mady was teaching now, and she reported that a notice had appeared on the English bulletin board: "Political Topics. Please avoid all controversial matter. Use the same précis material for the entire class. Do not let them choose their own material." In America, it seemed, the antagonism between the extreme right and the extreme left was intensifying. Mady herself mentioned that she and Bill had gone to a "rally in Madison Square Garden for the support of the Spanish leftists . . . Spain holds the center of attention." And she added, "New York is upset by the prophecy, recorded in the *Times,* as well as *New Masses,* of a massacre of the Jews in September. The papers will really print anything."

Despite the nostalgia evoked by letters from home, the days passed and I began to relax in my Strasbourg existence. I became familiar with the city, its present and its past. I explored the magnificent cathedral, with its dazzling stained glass and its great nave and pulpit, from which my Reformers had thundered their messages centuries earlier. I wandered through Petite France, its narrow crooked streets and gabled houses with dormer windows. I walked past Zum Hasen 1579, glanced at a sturdy paneled doorway, dated 1618, and overheard remarks of the natives, gesticulating, calling out loudly—always in German. For all the Teutonic overtones, I was becoming intoxicated with Strasbourg, once called Argentoratum, the Silver City.

Now, when I visited Ritter's office, I noticed that he stood as close as possible to me, and at times his hands strayed. When I moved away, he moved after me. He finally said, "Liebchen, I have fallen in love with you. I cannot work anymore. I think of you night and day." I looked at him as if he were mad and patted his hand. That night I wrote to Madeleine:

> Hold your seat, darling friend, wait till you hear. Ritter—the head librarian—has fallen in love with me. He is at least 50 years old, Mady, and a grandfather. What the hell I'm going to do I don't know. He's a nice enough guy but he smells of beer and garlic. I like him as the curator of books. Me— I'm the Strasbourg siren.

Mady responded quickly to my confidences, asking detailed questions about what she called my inamorato and demanding immediate replies. She addressed me as "Miss Amorosa" and was not at all surprised that "the librarian professeur is enamored of you" and concluded that he "must have a lot to him if he has shown such excellent taste." As for herself, despite outings with Bill and one or two D'Oyly Carte performances of Gilbert and Sullivan, her letter—all her letters—reflected a noticeable loneliness, describing her weekly visits to the Metropolitan Museum where she studied the catalogue as she viewed the masterpieces of Rembrandt and El Greco, Velázquez and Goya. "I get a very adolescent kick out of recognizing the painter of a work I've never seen, and find I take to this particular form of aesthetics far more rapidly than with music.''

She listened to music nonetheless over radio or her Decca phonograph, but she listened alone. She read Freud's autobiography and Arnold Bennett's journal, but did not mention discussing the books with anyone but me. She was writing again—a play based upon her teaching observations—but only her mother ''listened to it, and thought it 'natural.' '' Already Mady was thinking in terms of the next summer and perhaps a return to Europe: ''Made a list of the paintings I want to see at the National Gallery & the Louvre.'' Her aloneness filtered through her letters. And so did her love: ''I am sure we shall be friends for always . . . We shall grow—but not apart.''

As for me, I was hardly a ''Miss Amorosa.'' As I continued my work, with Ritter watching me in the library and Herr Fischer observing the two of us, I found myself in love not with François Ritter—dear old Ritter—but with the books selected from his shelves. I felt their great age, the wonderful printing, the beautiful paper, the wide margins, the aroma, the woodcuts, the early six-teenth century rising from their midst. I was in love with the bind-ings, many stamped pigskin with rolls depicting the heads of the Caesars, angels, or putti, others showing the likeness of Luther, Melanchthon, or other great reformers.

In the pension I had grown friendly with a bewhiskered gen-tleman who occupied a fourth-floor room near mine. Georg Walther was intelligent, had a good sense of humor, no money, and sat in my room eating my cookies and grapes. He occasionally asked me for a loan, which I did not give him. From time to time we went out together and one evening we visited the large sprawling café on the Place Kléber, the Taverne Kléber. A huge beefy waiter took our order: a cup of coffee and a glass of wine. After twenty minutes the waiter appeared and literally threw our orders across the table. As Georg began to protest, a great hulk of a man in a filthy apron loomed over me, screaming, *"Heraus!* You are no good woman. You are a *verdammte* Jew!'' The surrounding tables took up the refrain in a violent chorus: *"Stinkende Jüdin!''* I could scarcely rise from my chair.

Once outside, I leaned against the lamppost, my entire body shaken. Georg tried to comfort me. "There is much anti-Semitism. We are close to Germany." I stayed in my room all the next day, Sunday. I was afraid to go out. The Silver City was much tarnished. When I reported the incident to Ritter, he looked somewhat surprised. "But, Liebchen, how could you have gone there with that Georg? Didn't you know the Kléber is Nazi social headquarters in Strasbourg?"

I decided I had to get away. I left for Paris, where I had a distant relative who treated me as his little Yankee cousin. Albert had a charming apartment in the Parc Monceau district, where he cooked omelets in a frying pan that bore the remains of many preceding lunches. "But, Albert, don't you ever wash your utensils?" "It gives a better flavor, ducky." With Albert I visited the top of the Eiffel Tower, French cafés, and the Opéra Comique. Alone, I scoured the bookstalls and hesitated over the purchase of a history of French printing by Audin. Ritter had suggested that I visit the eminent bookseller Leo Baer, and I did so. He showed me his collection of early printed books and I consulted him about the purchase of the Audin, which I was still considering. He strongly encouraged me, and the four-volume set became mine. A bookseller's reference library had begun. I returned to Strasbourg with renewed enthusiasm to complete my work.

Ritter greeted me with open arms. He came to my room and cried, "How I love you. You are my Bettina." I eluded his passionate embrace by looking steadfastly out the window at u. CLOT ÉPICERIE and A. DRIZEHN TABAC. François Ritter's growing sadness contrasted with my increasing exuberance. We both knew that soon I would be going home.

A recent letter from Mady had announced, "I am planning a European trip next summer. Please . . . let it be for both of us. Next month I'm going to make inquiries. First to Russia, probably in a collective unit . . . Then, biking in England." I had little desire to visit Russia in a collective or individual unit, nor was I keen on cycling in England. But I would, of course, love to show Mady all my old haunts in Strasbourg and in Paris, and I replied that I would be thrilled to go abroad with her, but at the same time I warned her that Europe was changing rapidly. "I have observed so much," I wrote to her, "including the approaching end of old Europe as Strasbourg is old world. Fascism is spreading throughout Europe. Here I am in Strasbourg—supposedly a French city—and everything about it is German. There are swastikas right across the Rhine and there have been episodes which I have not mentioned. Everything seems to be teetering and ending. Nonetheless," I added, "this stay stamps my future. Some aspect of printing will be my overall interest. I know my life work now and I hope I can pursue it. See you at the pier, ducky!"

GLENGARRY AND ALPENSTOCK

Madeleine 📖 BETWEEN the French Line's pier, where the *Lafayette* disembarked in November 1936, and the pier of the Anchor Line, where the S.S. *California* set forth in July 1937, months of work and months of companionship intervened. I taught, not too contentedly, worked on an article about propagandist literature, and confided my difficulties and satisfactions to Leona. Leona reviewed the notes she had taken in Strasbourg, tried to substantiate her premise that the printer did exert an influence on the books he circulated, and shaped and reshaped her thesis. Her confidences were punctuated now and then with her doubts—doubts not about her point of view but about Mr. Thorndike's. But with the prospect of our first trip abroad together coming nearer and nearer, doubts were dismissed, difficulties forgotten, and together we rejoiced, sometimes uncontrollably, at what lay ahead. We were in our twenties, America was looking up, and the world was our oyster.

We prepared for the carefree journey. Carefree but bookish. We obtained a copy of a *Guide to European Hotels,* 1937 issue, and studied it with the utmost diligence, noting names and prices only a bit more seriously than we noted accommodations. After all, who cared about accommodations? We cared about euphonious names, romantic locations, and low prices, and on those grounds we made our selections. We then proceeded—not to write for reservations—but simply to check the hotels in the book and tell our parents to direct their letters to the hostelries indicated. That was the preparation— the background—for our first trip abroad together, "our hearts were young and gay trip" of 1937, and indeed that was the reason for some of the adventures that lay ahead.

Our arrival in Scotland set the tone for most of the journey: it was not only carefree; it was hilarious. The *California* anchored in Glasgow at five of a misty morning. We immediately decided that it would be a waste of time to go directly to Edinburgh. Why not get all those lochs and trossachs en route? And so we joined a bus tour through the land of Sir Walter Scott. As we rumbled through the lochs—Loch Vennacher, Loch Katrine, Loch Lomond—we became sleepier and sleepier, dozing through much of the Rob Roy country, the glens redolent of the Lady of the Lake and Bonny Prince Charles.

At Loch Katrine we had to change buses, and a bit of melodrama was added to our trip. A porter climbed down with the luggage and asked Leona, "Miss, is this the 'andle of your grip?" Leona screamed as she saw her new valise with a gaping hole through which most of her undergarments were seeping. "Don't worry, lady, I'll tie it up."

The crippled grip was flung onto the top of bus number 2, which carried us to Stirling. There we and all our impedimenta from America had to board a local bus for Edinburgh. It was rush hour in Stirling, so the two intrepid travelers from New York had to stand all the way to St. Andrews Square. Before we arrived, I thought it might be wise to consult the bus driver about the Beechwood Hotel, which we had selected from the *Hotel Guide*. To my amazement, he had no knowledge of that hostelry. But being an optimist, I assured Leona that the Beechwood was probably so elegant that a bus driver would never have heard of it. And so our uninformed bus driver dumped his passengers and their luggage at Edinburgh's St. Andrews Square.

Each of us promptly and successfully summoned a cab. As we entered the first, the rejected driver yelled at us, "I hope you both git killed today." With this parting shot, we drove off and airily announced, "The Beechwood Hotel."

"Never heard of it" was the cabbie's response. We were beginning to lose faith in the *European Hotel Guide,* not that it made too much difference, since we had not booked any reservations. Exhausted and somewhat desperate, we implored the driver to find us accommodations.

"You know the King and Queen have just been here and there's scarce a vacancy in all of Edinburgh."

"Oh, take us anyplace," we begged him.

We were finally deposited at the Bruntsfield Private, one of a series of residences with rooms for tourists, where the paucity of soap was compensated for by the quantity of oatmeal for breakfast. The next morning the rains fell, but we began our explorations of Edinburgh: Castle Hill, the Royal Mile and the Tolbooth, Holyrood and the desolate sodden Cannongate Churchyard. The cemetery flaunted a large placard of its "specialties," including the grave of the celebrated musicologist Dr. Charles Burney, which I was inexplicably inspired to visit. The curator led us over the wet gravel paths to a monument. " 'Tis Dr. Baron," he announced. "But I wanted Dr. Burney," I insisted. "Oh, what's the difference?" Leona, ever practical. "This will do."

We traveled by motor coach to the pseudo-Gothic "castle" in Abbotsford-on-Tweed, where, as the guide reverently proclaimed, "Sir Walter Scott penned his beautiful works." I mused in my diary: "Scott must have had fun wandering about the country, drawing up his horse to breathe inspiration from the Horsebend—a marvelous stretch of hill country plaided with farm—collecting relics of Mary of Scots and Rob Roy—& then proceeding to write about them & receiving more relics from admirers such as George IV.''

Inspired by the glories of Scotland, we each purchased a glengarry, the Highland headgear for men, and wore it for the rest of the trip. So accoutered, we sought the whereabouts of the ''elegant'' Beechwood, the hotel of our original choice. After a morning's journey we found it; it was a pub on the outskirts of the city. Sure enough, our mail was waiting for us. So too was the dawning realization that the *European Hotel Guide* had betrayed us, and that we had better make a few reservations down the road.

Actually, at our next port of call we did not need to book rooms in advance. At Keswick we found our Skiddaw Hotel immediately and were given a room in the attic overlooking the hills around Derwentwater. The English Lake Country brought the Romantic poets alive for both of us but especially for me. In the garden of Wordsworth's Dove Cottage in Grasmere we snapped pictures of each other in our glengarries, and then walked up Langdale Hill, filled with the scents of sweet grass, honeysuckle, and roses.

Leona was aware that a descendant of one of her Strasbourg printers had emigrated to the English Lake District. He had Anglicized his name from Schott to Scott and been rewarded for good deeds with a baronetcy. He was now Sir Samuel Haslam Scott. She wrote to him, informing him that she was at the Skiddaw and asking for an interview. He replied on a postal card addressed to Leona at the hotel and adorned with his name, his title, and his armorial crest. She read his message, regretting his inability to meet with her because of an arranged garden party, but, despite her disappointment, she preened her feathers at hearing from a milord. She immediately replaced the postal card on the letter rack where she had found it so that others would be apprised of her place in the social world. The proprietrix at the Skiddaw was not impressed, and after a couple of days she remarked to Leona, "I am certain that everyone has by now read your card and I suggest you remove it."

The highlight of our Keswick stay, however, was not Sir Samuel's communication but, rather, Buttermere Round. As we wrote home:

> *Today will possibly be one of the dearest in our remembrance of this trip. We drove to Buttermere Round in a coach & four driven by 4 brown bays & a driver whose tophat was grey. We saw the Lake Country more closely than you can imagine. The speckled stones on the hills were really sheep; the little white dots, vicarages & homes; the variegation in greens & yellows, really farm land in strips. We circled round the hills & saw their scars of brown earth, the old stagecoach roads cut round them—& the sun on everything. The smell of burning charcoal, heather, rose blossoms, manure—& low-lying hills around Buttermere Lake & Derwentwater. We held tightly to our seats as the tallyho crunched down the steep Honnister Pass & we looked triumphant as people paused to snap us. Once in a while the driver let us hold the reins. Naturally the English could not do without their tea, and so the mugs were passed aloft as we neared Buttermere Lake. It was truly unforgettable.*

Wales, on the other hand, was quite forgettable. Why we went there we never really knew. It is true that Carnarvon Castle, with its crenelated walls and towers, the seat of the investiture of the Prince of Wales, was bedecked with royal emblems and pennants in honor of the King and Queen, who had just left. We immediately seated ourselves on the throne they had vacated, though in our ever-present glengarries we looked not exactly regal. Nor did the town, despite the flags and bunting for Coronation Year. At its cinema, *Tarzan Escapes* followed *The Gorgeous Hussy,* and Carnarvon seemed to us like an ill-smelling woman dressed in her Sunday best.

To reach a place called Llandrindod Wells we took a long, roundabout train trip that included at least five changes. By the time we arrived at Ye Wells, we had absolutely no answer to the question why we had come. Llandrindod Wells was a spa where saline or chalybeate waters were dispensed for internal and external use in connection with liver complaints. Ye Wells was patronized almost exclusively by what seemed to us the British middle class in its senile stages. Canes were much in evidence. The dining room presented a mass of white heads and elaborate evening dresses. Fish and rice pudding were savored with languid enthusiasm. As for us, we appeared at dinner in our everyday suits with drooping skirts, cameras still slung about our necks. One evening as we departed the *salle à manger* we heard a brief conversation behind us:

DOWAGER NO. 1: What do you suppose they are?

DOWAGER NO. 2: Why, Americans of course—what *could* they be?

Between our lack of diplomatic éclat and the worsening weather, we decided to abandon the land of chalybeate waters and head for London. Meanwhile, however, we had been very cautious and had actually booked reservations in advance. In what seemed like an inspired moment, I remembered a very nice hotel, the Belgravia, near Euston Station, where I had stayed as a child on my first trip abroad. Accordingly, I wrote a letter to the Belgravia's proprietrix, and, to our amazement, a reply was almost immediately received. It was addressed to "Dear Miss Stern," it recalled fond memories of "dear Miss Stern," and it looked forward with eagerness to "dear Miss Stern's" return with her "dear friend" Miss Rostenberg. The Belgravia response seemed a trifle peculiar to us on two grounds: it was surprisingly exuberant for such a communication, and it lacked any formal letterhead. However, who were we to question the ways of London hôteliers. We felt very reassured, having secured reservations in advance.

When we entered a taxi at Euston at 9 P.M., I confidently imparted, "The Belgravia," and the cabbie drove us off. He did not, however, stop at any nearby hostelry. Instead, he drove on and on and on, until I called to him, "The Belgravia I meant was right near the station. Where are you taking us?" "Oh," he replied, "that Belgravia burned down about five years ago. But there's another one with the same name, and I'm taking you there."

At long last we confronted what looked like a private residence in an advanced stage of dilapidation—a shabby, scruffy rooming house. Simultaneously we began to have qualms, and requested the cabbie to leave our luggage on the street while we went inside. A frowsy red-haired woman greeted "dear Miss Stern" and "dear Miss Rostenberg" and led the way up five flights of steep stairs. En route we glanced about us, heard a few peculiar sounds, saw a few men scurrying about, and passed a number of closed doors. Although we had specialized in medieval history and English literature, we had a fairly good idea of the nature of this particular Belgravia. By the time we saw the moth-eaten divan and the Murphy bed in the room we had so carefully booked ahead, we were certain of it. "Dear Miss Stern" and "dear Miss Rostenberg" would not enroll for advanced courses at the Belgravia. "We think there's been some mistake," we muttered. We were no longer "dears" as we fled downstairs and slammed the door behind us. We retrieved our luggage and, finally, with the aid of a bobby, located another cab and sought refuge in London's American asylum, the Strand Palace. Once in our immaculate room, we embraced each other and laughed aloud. "We could have made some money instead of spending it, for a change."

We had each seen London before, but now for the first time we were discovering it together. And because we were together, the city was transformed. We wandered its mews and lanes and courtyards; we breathed its mingled scent of fish and roses; we rejoiced in its surprises; London became for the two of us a feast for devouring.

Together we explored its art treasures—the Soane Museum, where, we were told, the Queen Mother Mary often sat for hours. We sat there, too, transported by Hogarth to the eighteenth century and corruptions that were still familiar in our time. We bused to Chiswick to see the Hogarth House and to Holborn to see the Dickens House. At the Tate we inspected the Blakes and more Hogarths, and we walked forever—through Whitehall and Trafalgar Square and Charing Cross to the Strand, to Regent Street and Oxford Circus. We walked along Victoria Embankment under a full moon and saw Big Ben shining in its light. Together we fell in love with a city so various and now so new to us.

Being American tourists, we chose for our first all-day excursion a visit to Stratford. The memorabilia of the Bard's home, consisting mostly of land deeds, litigation suits, and indentures, did not interest us particularly, but the timbered Elizabethan dwellings carried the flavor of Shakespeare to us, and we were entranced by a performance of *The Winter's Tale* at the Memorial Theatre. We topped the day with high tea at the Judith Shakespeare Inn, and on the bus back to London we dreamed happily of the seven stages of man and of woman.

One of our happiest days in London was a day that now in retrospect pointed the way our lives would go. We spent the morning at Foyle's and the afternoon at the British Museum. At the former we bought, ''with 3 shillings & delight,'' as we wrote home, a copy of Conway's *Flemish Artists* for reference when we crossed the Channel. At the latter we were transported not only into the past but, had we realized it, into our own future. Leona wrote to her parents:

I weakened before the manuscript Psalters and Books of Hours—Flemish, French, Plantagenet—incunable editions of Petrarch, Boccaccio, Caxtons, the Gutenberg Bible—the traveling library of Sir Julius Caesar. Then in the Print Room we called for the Leonardo cartoons and sketches and actually touched the paper he had worked on. Before we left we saw the Elgin Marbles and the life pulsing beneath the sculptured drapery. The beauty of the East pediment frieze of the Parthenon came to life before us. We were overcome, bewildered, suffering from mental indigestion and fallen arches, but high tea at Fuller's restored us.

Our journal entries for July 26 record our reactions to "one of those great perfect days to be talked about in years hence"—our first trip together to Oxford: "We rambled about the quads inhaling Amores Academici, snooping about Oriel, Magdalen, Merton, Brasenose, their gardens and cloisters. However, the greatest thrill for us was the Bodleian Library. It is so rich in age & history that it all seemed incredible & we couldn't realize that we were standing before Magna Carta, the Anglo-Saxon Chronicle, the Chanson de Roland, the First Folio of Shakespeare." We left the Bodleian hand in hand, mindful of all we had studied and were still studying. I wrote at the end of my journal entry: "L is the best person with whom to go on an exploration of this kind. She treads the old pavements in the same way that she handles incunabula—breathing in with respectful appreciation the musk of centuries past."

A day at Liberty's and Harrod's brought us back to earth. We exchanged a couple of pounds for gloves and hankies, scarves and what we learned to call scent, to give as gifts. (When we asked for toilet water, we were directed to the ladies' room.) Before our departure from London, the Snewings, whom I had met when I was abroad with my mother, invited us to Simpson's. Over the succulent roast beef and Yorkshire pudding, Mrs. Snewing regaled us with acerbic comments about the woman who had ensnared the Duke of Windsor and caused the recent abdication. "We just don't talk about them if we can avoid it," she said. "If she hadn't been a prostitute it would have been very nice."

At Wembley Stadium, where the Snewings invited us to view a water sports contest between Germany and England, we saw other, more ominous signs of the times. As we reported in our diaries, it was "a bit nauseating to see the swastikas flying above us. The Germans took the races and water polo contest very seriously, played carefully and fiercely for their Führer, and much to our disgust won practically everything. The English were more light-hearted & seemed to realize they were playing games . . . As the Fräuleins dashed leagues ahead, we could not help thinking of England, that 'royal throne of kings,' that 'sceptred isle,'—you are so small, so brave, so chivalrous—but you will be helpless . . . a small island that has been proud for a long time. We wonder how much longer.''

We left the small island for the continent with high anticipation, the journey entailing the train to Dover, a three-and-a-half-hour wind-swept sail aboard the *Côte d'Argent* to Ostend, and then another train trip to Bruges. There, we fell in love with this city of Bruges, this city of canals where swans floated and every time our boat passed beneath a bridge we had to duck. After the hurly-burly of London we were enchanted by the red-tiled rooftops, the shrines in niches, the cobblestone walks. At the Hôpital de Saint Jean we saw the Memlings and Van Eycks, and at the Panier d'Or in the Grand' Place we ate our *omelettes fines herbes* facing the Belfry of Bruges, which chimed a tune every quarter hour. There too we heard a carillon concert, and Leona wrote in her diary: "It's almost impossible to write of the beauty of this night with the towers of the belfry cutting the sky & supported by two tremendous shadows looming upwards—lights flooding the Square & the chimes carilloning forth and there we sat. Something rare that will never happen again—two people who are dear friends before the Belfry of Bruges.''

The past took over from the present in Bruges. On the Langestraat we found ourselves in the midst of a medieval procession honoring either Saint Anne or Satan—we were not sure at first—but then voices were clearly raised in the prayer *"Anna, ora pro nobis.''*

The nearer, more ghastly past came alive for us at the cemeteries of World War I—Passchendaele and Tyne Cot—where British mothers and sisters and friends came to visit their dead. After Hill

A *conventional honeymoon. Lillie Mack Stern and Moses R. Stern at Niagara Falls, June 1902.*

"M*y very lovely mother" Louisa Dreyfus Rostenberg, 1914.*

My elegantly attired father
Adolph Rostenberg, 1914.

Madeleine contemplating the news,
ca. 1915.

Leona chuckling at world events, ca. 1910.

M*adeleine in a goat cart. Harlem, 1918.*

Leona with her brother Adolph Jr.,
Peck's Bad Boy, 1914.

Madeleine with her big brother
Leonard Mack Stern, ca. 1919.

Leona, Bachelor of Arts, NYU,
1930—farewell to the "factory."

The contemplative scholar: Madeleine, Hunter College High School graduate, December 1928.

Madeleine with the captain of the S.S. Stockholm during the "wondrous" trip abroad, 1925.

Leona in Strasbourg-am-Rhein, August 1936.

"Scots wha hae" Leona and Madeleine with Glengarries, London, 1937.

"Nonpareil of booksellers" E. P. Goldschmidt of London.

Our "five-doored pagoda," Ogunquit, Maine, 1938.

Leona in dory no. 3 with Chimpie and Glengarry, 1938.

Madeleine with her chicks "Meg, Jo, Beth, Amy," 1944.

LEONA ROSTENBERG

takes pleasure in announcing

that she will engage in the sale of Rare Books

at

152 East 179th Street
New York 53, N. Y.

Tremont 8-2789

"A brave new firm," 1944.

60, where we were shown a trench—a so-called luxury trench—used in World War I, and where the British lost fifty-eight thousand men defending Ypres, Leona meditated in her journal: "I thought I had realized some horror of the war in the educational propaganda at home, but this, the real thing, and a 'luxury trench' . . . made me realize I knew naught of war. Down in the earth, black, foul-smelling, damp . . . then water knee-high—soldiers slept & had their wounds tended—after these quarters they were expected to go over the top or up Hill 60. It's incredible & it's hell." At Ghistelles the sight of a Krupp cannon—the Big Gun—inspired her to specu-late: "One wonders what would have happened if the Germans had won, or what might happen or will happen should fascism link & play with Krupp cannonry."

For one dollar in 1937 one could take a rail trip through all of Belgium. We availed ourselves of this gift and spent a day at Ghent. There, we hailed a carriage whose enthusiastic but not entirely accu-rate driver described the sights. Everything, he assured us, was *"très ancien."* The Maison des Bateliers was *"onzième siècle";* the Château des Comtes de Flandres *"dixième—très, très ancien";* the Maison de Van Artevelde even *"plus ancien—neuvième siècle";* and the oldest of all—over there—was built in the *"huitième siècle."*

Brussels was ultra-modern by contrast. We varied our sight-seeing there with repeated visits to the Musée des Beaux Arts. We concentrated on the Breughels, Elder, Younger, and Third—so vivid and realistic that, as Leona put it in a letter home, "his people are alive, coarse, their spittle is seen, their belches heard." At the end of the day we relaxed in the Café des Boulevards, dining *al fresco* on luscious fillet, a dame blanche with café drippé, topped by a gold-tipped cigarette and an anise pastille. Truly this was Europe, the sophisticated continent of Europe. Truly this was the life.

We saw yet another Flemish version of life in Antwerp, when we visited the Plantin Museum. In that building the printing office of Christophe Plantin, who left France and settled in Antwerp in 1548, was restored and his records preserved. Had we known that one day we two would be buying and studying and selling the books he printed, we might possibly have been even more exhilarated by the museum than we were. But as it was, I was sufficiently thrilled to write in my journal:

This morning a feast of Plantin imprints at his sign of the Golden Compasses near the Rue Nationale. The house is almost intact as it was in 1575. There are 36 rooms most of which are filled with vellum-bound books; the walls are of oak, the ceilings beamed, grisaille & stained glass windows. The presses, metal impression plates and wood blocks are on exhibition & it doesn't need much of an imagination to hear the machinery humming, to see the proof-readers examining copy, the servants on the rough stone kitchen floor, a man lighting the fires between rows of Delft tile, & Mme Plantin sitting for her portrait by Rubens. The house is built on the quadrangle style with an open court of greens.

Somehow, after the Plantin Museum in Antwerp, it seemed appropriate for us to move on to Strasbourg, where Leona had studied the work of other sixteenth-century printers. Now she would show her tarnished Silver City to her friend, and her excitement upon her return was such that she nearly collapsed when she said "rue Goethe" to the cab driver. From then on her *déjà vu* came to life for me.

"I saw L's room at the Pension Elisa and ate the marvelous food she had here last year. I saw the letterbox where she mailed her letters & the benches where she wrote them. We wandered down the Quai des Pêcheurs to the Place Corbeau and her excitement became mine. I know how she feels, and how strange it seems to her to be here again, unlocking the pension door, walking up the old steps and thru the same streets."

At the library I met Ritter, who seemed "stunned with happiness. He lovingly fetched books for his inamorata and angled for opportunities to be alone with her." He showed us around the library where Leona had worked, and guided us through its stacks and domed reading room onto the roof, from which we could see the spire of the cathedral. Later Papa Heitz took us for a vegetarian lunch at the Pythagore and showed us his printing relics, his woodblocks, rare books, and incunabula leaves.

Everywhere I retraced Leona's footsteps with her through this German city that is supposedly French, to the Petit Rhine, where swastikas wave, to the city archives and the Taverne Kléber, still Nazi social headquarters. Now I could better understand those months when Leona had worked on her own in a remote and foreign city. It was obvious that Ritter still loved her, though she felt toward him much as she had before. It was clear too that, despite his love, she had been very lonely working in Strasbourg, scratching away at her desk, doing things alone—always really alone. But she was alone no longer. We were together, sharing the past, creating a future.

We shared so much, from family background to what has euphemistically been called single blessedness. Although we had dated several men, neither of us had ever really been committed to any one of them. We shared our sense of humor and our love of adventure. Above all, we shared a growing passion for books and the printed word. We lived together in the life of the mind. There we stood on common ground. We loved each other, asexually, platonically, to be sure. The fact that we were two women instead of man and woman did not seem to have much bearing upon our relationship as far as we were concerned. Already we were beginning to identify with each other, to end each other's sentences, to divine each other's thoughts.

From Strasbourg and its ghosts we moved on together to Switzerland and its adventures. In Interlaken we added alpenstocks to our glengarries and, so attired, confronted the glories of the Alps. Each day we set forth from the Pension Iris to try this road or that cowpath, to cross a footbridge or scale a wooden fence. We sailed on both lakes—the Brienzersee and the Thunersee. At Brienz we visited the atelier of the woodcarver Huggler-Wyss, and later, on our walk to Heimwehfluh, we actually saw his woodcarvings walk before us. Our rucksacks stuffed with box lunches, we set forth on the day's adventures—a trip to Mürren where cowbells tinkled and *Grüssgotts* welcomed us, where models for our woodcarvings stroked their beards and carried packs on their backs. Along dirt paths, past frozen waterfalls we walked, clumping our alpenstocks.

After an excursion we strolled along the Hoheweg and dropped in at Bücherer, king of watches, where I bought a gold watch for my beloved mother. First, of course, we examined every watch in that emporium of timepieces, and finally selected a beauty. Unfortunately, however, when we examined it back at the Pension, the hands had not moved since the time of purchase. We raced back to the Hoheweg, where we were regaled with profuse apologies. The management had forgotten to insert the movement.

We consoled ourselves for the Bücherer oversight with marzipan pastry at the Café Schuh. In the evening we ambled to the Kursaal for flag-swinging or an alphorn recital. I wrote rhapsodically in my journal: "Pastry and sun and green grass and L beside me sitting in the Alps. Truly Das Oberland, Das Oberland, Das Oberland ist schön."

We added tokens to our alpenstocks as we visited towns farther aloft—for each village a small medal to nail onto our sticks. We sat waiting in misty rain on the porch of the elegant Hotel Victoria Jungfrau, hoping the sun would appear so that we could take the trip up the Jungfrau. We spent a strange and slightly hilarious day journeying by bus to Lucerne via the Rhone Glacier. Our stolid, imperious, and very German blond driver took seven hours for the outward trip, but at Lucerne, impelled to be in Interlaken in time for supper, he announced that he would make the return in only two hours. As I recorded in my journal:

Everything passed smoothly at first & we were thrilled by the Aare-Schlucht whose river gushes white over the grey boulders of the gorge, by Grimsel Pass over vertiginous cliffs, by the Rhone Glacier where a native blew "God Save the

King" on his alphorn. We left the chamois and the St. Bernards when we arrived in Lucerne, but when we left Lucerne the fun began. Our driver, to make up for lost time, took it into his head to race through mountain passes, over precipitous cliffs and curves, at 80 miles an hour. We screamed for him to slow down. "Passengers do not set the pace," he warned, and then reduced his speed to an impossible crawl. The remaining passengers included a woman from Wisconsin and a timid Dutch couple.

Boldly suggesting we all abandon the bus and charter a private car to take us back, I promptly discovered I had no money with me and could not participate in such a venture. Then Mrs. Wisconsin became ill, the Dutch couple demonstrated intense fear of the Germanic driver, and somehow we all made our way back to Interlaken. The day was a peculiar combination of lieblich scenery, majestic mountains, carefree spirits, and a strangely insinuating threat. We recovered from it, however, and were both, as Leona wrote in her journal, "happy as only we can be together in the Alps."

Yet, as "our hearts were young and gay" trip neared its end, Leona's journal revealed that her happiness was intermittent. We had only one more port to call before returning home, and that realization, coupled with concern about Mr. Thorndike's lack of enthusiasm for her subject, dashed her spirits from time to time. As she wrote, "A long winter stretches ahead and my night's rest is sometimes destroyed by mean shadows portending the return to reality." But our next—our last—port of call was Paris, and shadows of the long winter were not yet upon us.

"In Paris at least we won't have any hotel problems," Leona asserted confidently. Certainly we foresaw none. In Strasbourg we had written ahead to a small hostelry on the Place St. Augustin, where Leona had stayed the year before. "It's nothing grand," she had said, "but it's pleasant." And so we wrote to the manager Monsieur Laplace, and Leona emphasized that we would pay no more than fifty francs a night, the same as she had paid last year. Monsieur Laplace wrote as ingratiating a confirmation as the proprietrix of the Belgravia had sent us. He would be delighted to see her again with her friend, at the same rate as last year. We realized later—too late—that the franc had inflated since Leona's stay at the Malesherbes.

When we arrived, however, I was not as elated by the Hôtel Malesherbes as I had hoped to be. First of all, I realized that the *ascenseur* seemed to be very limited in its operations, ascending readily enough but seldom descending. Second, the hall lights were known as *minuits,* lighting up for only a few seconds before a timer extinguished them. Third, our *chambre à coucher* left much to be desired. Upon close inspection, I decided that the drapes hid a quantity of dust, and, after we had both done our laundry, we proceeded to consult a Paris hotel guide. There we discovered that, thanks to our ignorance of currency fluctuations, we were paying as much for the meager accommodations of the Malesherbes as the excellent Left Bank Hôtel Lutétia charged for a double room with bath. Such a situation could not be tolerated, and, despite our dripping laundry, we decided to arrange for an immediate departure from Monsieur Laplace and the Malesherbes. We would concoct a plausible story to account for the sudden change of plan.

With crocodile tears we approached the proprietor, informing him that my nonexistent only sister was dying in Antwerp. Like all Frenchmen, Monsieur Laplace took a reverent interest in necrological matters and expressed profound sympathy. However, when we added that we must rush to her bedside immediately, he and his sympathy were transformed. Now Monsieur Laplace became a fury incarnate. His face reddened, he jumped up and down, he paced back and forth, he scratched the seat of his pants, and simultaneously screamed at us and made out several bills. Despite my grief, I examined them carefully and informed Monsieur Laplace that he had charged us for three nights instead of one. We compromised on two nights and proceeded to repack. As we gathered up our wet laundry, Leona kept murmuring, *"Ah, ma soeur, ma soeur."* The chambermaid, hovering over us, was puzzled and, pointing to me, said, "I thought it was *her* soeur." "Oh, what's the difference?" Leona replied in perfect French.

From the Lutétia on the Boulevard Raspail in the heart of the Left Bank we rejoiced to explore Paris together. We reveled in everything, from the *clous* in the gutters to the *pissoirs,* from the Citroën buses to the mustachioed boulevardiers. Together we gloried in the vistas of Paris, seen from the narrow lanes and cobblestones of the Left Bank or from the broad and elegant expanses of the Avenue de l'Opéra or the Champs Élysées. Together we roamed the Louvre, stood before the *Winged Victory* in her windblown pride and beauty, strolled past the worshippers of *Mona Lisa,* on down the corridor des Italiens to our particular treasures. We wandered through the shops together, seeking suede and leather gloves at the Galeries Lafayette, where we were squirted with gallons of free, very strong perfume, and at the Grand Maison de Blanc we were surrounded by mountains of embroidered hankies and colorful scarves. We rested our weary legs in the Tuileries Gardens, and tea-ed happily at Rumpelmeyer's—not on tea, but on *cresson* sandwiches, *tarte de noix,* and *chocolat chaud.* In the evenings we dined on *châteaubriand, haricots verts,* and *pommes frites,* and spent a few hours at the Cinéac. There we watched, not the News of the Day, but a dog seated near us who, with rapt attention, followed a cartoon about a misunderstood puppy and a naughty cat. Everything was possible in the City of Light. For us together everything was pure joy.

Paris was *en fête* in 1937, hosting the International Exposition. Among the thousands of visitors we were struck by the Russian Pavilion, with its tractors and autos, its minerals and statistics, its air of "Look what we have done." In close proximity was the German Pavilion, where swastikas flew and Hitler's face was for sale on postcards. Of all the pavilions the one that interested us most at the time was the Spanish. There, Franco's name was not mentioned, for the pavilion was under the auspices of the Loyalists, and due honor was paid to the 1937 Armée Populaire. In one small corner of Paris we saw a microcosm of Europe and a portent of things to come.

Our political ruminations were interrupted by a professional visit. Perhaps it was her reaction to the flying swastikas that accelerated Leona's heartbeat. At all events, it bothered her sufficiently to make her consult a physician. Dr. Theodore Merrill, recommended by the hotel, hailed from Massachusetts. Perhaps his star asset was the fact that he spoke English. After a brief examination he diagnosed a "tricuspid valvular leak" and suggested that Leona take it easy for the rest of her stay. While he indited a lengthy epistle to Leona's father regarding her condition, we looked around the office. As Leona wrote in her journal: "His office reminded me of an antiquated junk room. The only thing that really appeared to pertain to his profession was a set of eye tests half hidden by an Empire tapestry. His collection of trash was topped off by a branch of the Washington elm."

We did not allow Dr. Merrill's diagnosis to interfere too drastically with our last days in Paris. We spent a great part of them scouting the bookstalls on the quais. Our journals record our reactions: "When the tin boxes were opened [I found] Lawrence's Lady Chatterley and his Defense, another copy of Baudelaire's translation of Poe—1857—Rousseau." Leona "got a nice little collection on printing—printers' marks, wood engraving, and the Bibliothèque Nationale Catalogue on the French Revolution."

If only we had known then that within less than a decade we would be partners in a rare book business that was selling Rousseau and Baudelaire and using Leona's "nice little collection on printing" for reference. But in September of 1937, when we embarked on the *Statendam* for home after our first trip to Europe together, the future seemed less clear and certainly less hopeful than ever. Rumblings of dissension and premonitions of global war mingled with our own uncertainties. Dissatisfied with teaching, eager to write but floundering for genre and for subject, I felt unanchored, unfulfilled. Leona was especially disheartened. She wrote in her journal: "So much nearer home; so much more miserable. I know the enormity of this admission but going back implies so much & I am so completely happy just going on endlessly with Mady . . . I can't stand the thought of its being over. I can't." The day before the *Statendam* docked in Hoboken, she recorded, "When I realize HOME tomorrow and all that goes with it, it seems impossible. I don't want to go back. To what? Futile hopes and anxiety about my dissertation— trying to hold my head up against a lack of accomplishment. After we have explored Europe together, how can I face my future alone?"

EBB TIDE

Leona 📖 REALITY HIT even harder and sooner than we had anticipated. Our mothers met us at the pier, more solemn than joyous. Mady had to give up the few remaining days of her vacation to help with a course in reading skills for the Board of Education. Far more serious was the news that my father was gravely ill. In addition, we were now separated after the glorious time together, and, as I wrote in my journal in late October: "Our beautiful trip is over more than a month. How hard to accept—how difficult to believe we won't don our glengarries, take alpenstocks in hand, and tramp the Hoheweg. It seems a bit trite almost to speak of these things when it's all been so dreadful— what with Daddy nearly gone—the hours of horrible uncertainty— never knowing, constantly dreading & all of us loving him so."

Within the next few weeks, my father made a marked recovery, and soon after was able to resume his practice. I was free once again to work on my dissertation, judging the results sometimes with satisfaction, sometimes doubt. I confided my doubts to Madeleine alone, who in turn was searching for a subject for her pen. After spending a day teaching grammar or reading *Silas Marner* to uninterested students, she longed for a more creative focus for her life.

In 1936 Van Wyck Brooks had published *The Flowering of New England*. Now, a year later, we devoured it, and after I read the chapter entitled "Alcott, Margaret Fuller, and Brook Farm," I suggested to Madeleine that she write a full-length biography of Fuller. The suggestion would take root, and Brooks's "electrical apparition," the "queen of Cambridge," would dominate Mady's life during the next few years.

Meanwhile I concentrated on work for my degree. My ongoing fears about the validity and presentation of a thesis that would establish the printer's influence upon his times arose partly from a lack of self-confidence and partly from Mr. Thorndike's ever-present insinuations. He still wished that I had selected a subject from his beloved Arabic astrologers, and, more important, he was not accustomed to opposition of any kind. Nonetheless I persisted, but not without the attendant fear that I would have to suffer the consequences of my independence.

Coupled with these anxieties was my distress at not earning money and relying on my parents for an allowance. And all this was exacerbated by the presence in our home of Dr. Fritz Levy, a young refugee from Nazi Germany, the son of my father's closest friend, whom my parents had invited to live with the family. He arrived in 1938, a politely annoying and somewhat patronizing physician, who, everyone was aware, was in search not only of a livelihood on these shores but of a wife. I was quite certain that Fritz had been imported not solely for humanitarian reasons, and I did not relish the situation into which I had been thrust. Fritz's interest in me was patently manufactured and I soon sensed its lack of sincerity. My parents, I felt, had placed me in an embarrassing and untenable position, and at one point I threatened to leave home. The matter was finally resolved when Fritz married another refugee and set up for himself. Meanwhile, I vented my feelings in my diary, where I wrote in November 1938: "I can scarcely write of what I fear—there's Czechoslovakia—and Hitler marching & marching—English perfidy and skulking France. On the other side of the sea all the world is mobilizing & soon bombs will be hissing & shrieking over Strasbourg. I can't stand it. It's also a question of my earning money to be independent of it all—including the miserable situation with Fritz."

Despite my immersion in research and passionate pursuit of printing in 1509, my fear of Thorndike's eventual rejection continued to haunt me. I had been influenced by Van Wyck Brooks, the acclaimed literary historian whose style was reflected in the first part of my dissertation. When I finally summoned up the courage to present that portion to Mr. Thorndike, however, his reaction was not entirely disdainful. "It seems to have some merit," he admitted, adding, "The style cannot attain acceptance. It is too popular. You must use more academic prose."

The dissertation was apparently still viable. We would enjoy a family get-together for Thanksgiving, the birth of friends' babies, even Lucy's marriage and sojourn in Mexico. We would relish Paul Muni in the role of Émile Zola and young Yehudi Menuhin playing Brahms's Violin Concerto with the New York Philharmonic.

As for Madeleine, she had already begun preliminary research on American Transcendentalism and on Margaret Fuller, feminist, author of *Woman in the Nineteenth Century,* citizen of the world who had taken the world as her province and accepted it. A summer in Maine would, we agreed, offer both of us the leisure and the opportunity to plunge deeper into our projects. The summer of 1938 was spent, as later summers would also be spent, in a rented cottage located one mile north of Ogunquit.

We found that cottage much as we had selected our hotels in Europe the year before—with the same touch of carefree hilarity. A young man in the English Department of Long Island City High School, where Mady had been transferred, happened to mention that he had had a great weekend near Ogunquit. Eager to summer in that area, Mady had asked where it was. The teacher had forgotten the name of the road, even the name of the town, and had no idea as to who owned the house, but he did recall that it was "the next to the last house on the dead end road a mile north of Ogunquit." With her usual optimistic persistence, Mady addressed an inquiry to:

THE OWNER

NEXT TO THE LAST HOUSE

DEAD END ROAD

ONE MILE NORTH OF OGUNQUIT, MAINE

That owner, Mr. Powers, then vacationing in Florida, actually received the letter, forwarded by a cooperative United States Post Office. And Mr. Powers would be delighted to rent his house, named Riverbank, for the season at two hundred dollars.

Our parents insisted that we inspect Riverbank in advance, and since Mady was teaching, I volunteered for the mission. It was the month of May, and Maine's wild strawberries were ripening and the grove of Scotch pines in which the little house was set exuded a wonderful aroma. A tidal stream nearby led to the ocean, and a dory was included with the rental. Enthralled, I sat with the owner on a little broken bench outside Riverbank, dilating on the beauty of the spot. Mr. Powers was pleased but did suggest, "Miss Rostenberg, wouldn't you like to look at the inside of the house?" The lease was signed after a whirlwind inspection, and I returned home to face the full-scale interrogation of Mady's mother, a superb housekeeper with a very sharp mind:

"What about hot water?"

"What about the stove?"

"What about refrigeration?"

"What about laundry?"

"What about a telephone?"

"What about marketing?"

"What about neighbors?"

And the final challenge: "What about garbage disposal?" To all this I shrugged my shoulders. "It's all so beautiful. Who cares?"

We cared a little more when we reached Riverbank. All three of us—Mady, my darling wirehair Chimpie, and I—were driven to the cottage by my parents' houseman, Warren, who, once we were unloaded, immediately drove back home. "I wouldn't stay a night in this dump" was his parting shot.

His description was fairly accurate. Riverbank looked less like a house than a five-doored pagoda on Tobacco Road. The rooms were stuffed with broken-down furniture; the kitchen boasted an iron sink and a wood-burning stove. There was no bathroom. Instead, there was a cold-water shower outside and, on the porch, a flush toilet with a swing door. But it was true that we did have a grove of Scotch pines, a tidal river, and an ocean.

It rained for the next three weeks. The roof leaked, the two "pioneers" subsisted on a spartan diet, and the garbage piled up. We had neither a car nor a telephone. Our only means of transport was the little dory. We did have ample time for our work, and I revised sections of my dissertation while Mady vibrated between writing melancholy verse and reading secondary sources on Margaret Fuller. We soon discovered that burning garbage, especially orange peels, was all but impossible and, once the sun re-emerged, we let it be known in the village that we needed domestic help.

As a result, at eight o'clock one night, Chimpie's shrill bark responded to a knock on one of our five doors. Mary Buono was about to enter our lives. She was a huge woman with a bandana on her head and a child in each hand. "Youse the gals that need help?" she asked. And the culinary interview began. Mady queried ingratiatingly, "Tell me, Mrs. Buono, do you know how to prepare Campbell's tomato soup?" There was a loud guffaw. "Even my Lilly— and she's only five years old—can make Campbell's soup." Mady posed a more sophisticated question. "Tell me, Mary, do you know how to prepare breaded veal chops?" to which the response was, "Jeez, lady, I'm a cook. You're so funny, you should write a joke book." For three dollars a week Mary Buono became an indispensable part of our Maine summers, and for an extra two dollars a month she even removed the garbage.

In her catechism, one of Mrs. Stern's questions had been "What about marketing?" This we accomplished by river navigation aboard our little dory. With Chimpie at the helm, we rowed to the village at high tide. There, we lingered at the butcher's and the grocer's and the baker's, always ending with a prolonged fudge sundae at the confectioner's. Finally, armed with our purchases, we trundled back to the river, only to find a mud flat in which our little dory was tightly embedded. Our only alternative was a long hot trek along U.S. 1, carrying our bundles and desperately holding on to Chimpie's leash. Chimpie was a very perverse terrier who invariably chose to walk backward at the same time as he chewed on his leash.

Before we chewed the victuals we had purchased, we tested them. Confirmed hypochondriacs, we sniffed most of our food before we cautiously tasted it. But now that Mary Buono was our "cook," all such problems would be behind us.

"Mary, what do you think of the cream?"

"It's beginning to turn, girls. I wouldn't use it. But I'll take it home and make a sour cream pie."

"This meat tastes funny, Mary. What do you think?"

"It's too fresh, girls—should have hung longer. You better not eat it."

"These cornflakes look green, Mary."

"Mold, girls. Don't eat no mold."

After two weeks had passed, Mary arrived, not with her children, but with their cart, later departing with most of our larder piled neatly on it. We often had an egg for dinner while the over-fresh steak and the turning cream disappeared from view. What strangely reappeared in view, however, were our chicken bones. They arrived in the form of a contribution from Chimpie. He had discovered Mary's garbage dump—right in back of the house.

Our Maine days were fragmented between bouts of work and

plunges into the icy ocean waters. They were punctuated too by the arrival of friends and family, some of whom did not tarry too long on Tobacco Road. We frequently invited them to the *spécialité de la maison*—a steak cookout prepared not by Mary but by us. Lacking a sophisticated modern barbecue, we simply dug a hole in the ground, filled it with coals, and then poured a can of kerosene before we lit a match. Over this conflagration we placed a grill, and over the grill our beautiful steak. The result was known as steak à la petrol. Most of our guests departed early the next morning.

During our first Maine summer in Riverbank, when my parents visited, we borrowed Warren and the car to drive to Concord, Massachusetts. Mady, now more and more intrigued by Margaret Fuller, had begun to seek the roots of American Transcendentalism, to trace Fuller's relationship with Emerson, and to follow the dramatis personae of *The Flowering of New England*. Before her *Life of Margaret Fuller* was finished, there would be several other visits to Concord, but this was the first and perhaps the most seminal, for in its course we wandered not only through Emerson's house, but through the Orchard House, the home of Louisa May Alcott. During the years that followed, Alcott would preoccupy both of us far more than Margaret Fuller.

Meanwhile, summer over and back home, I strove to tie up the loose ends of my dissertation as Mady was taking up the challenge of her Fuller biography. I was encouraged by a visit with the eminent Victor Hugo Paltsits, President of the Bibliographical Society of America and Keeper of Manuscripts at the New York Public Library. I had consulted with him from time to time, but he had never been more enthusiastic than now, when he emphasized his belief that I was on the right track—that it was time to assert the role of the early printer; that the size of editions and the prices of books all implied something of significance; that the practical side of publishing in the early 1500s had had a definite bearing upon the dissemination of learning and reform. If only Mr. Thorndike would agree.

In December, I presented my completed dissertation to Lynn Thorndike. And a few weeks later, during Mady's Christmas vacation, we left for Fuller researches in Cambridge, Massachusetts.

Through our rose-colored glasses, Cambridge seemed to combine the charm of Oxford with the grace of Concord. We pursued Margaret Fuller there. From our attic room in the Brattle Inn on Tory Row, we walked to Harvard's Widener Library, where we read the written records that reanimated her clothes and her diet, her friends, the concerts and cotillions she attended, the books she read, the life of her mind, her effect upon her world. From the Craigie Mansion to Mount Auburn Cemetery, where we drove over snow-covered roads in a hearse, we traced Margaret in the attempt to restore her and her world to life. We traced her in West Roxbury and Brook Farm; we traced, or tried to trace, her in Boston. But in Boston, West Street, where she had given her famous Conversations, was now the home of Thompson's Spa, and other Margaret associations on Bedford Street and State Street had become the locations of Jordan Marsh and a bank building.

We searched out, too, all of Margaret's living relatives we could unearth. The results were not always fruitful. Mrs. Roger Warner of Chestnut Street on Beacon Hill regretted her inability to find the manuscripts we knew she had. Margaret's nephew Freddie, who lived with his daughter Mabel in East Milton, was now age eighty-eight, "slightly rusty and detached." Mady's excited questions evoked but few answers except from Mabel, who finally exploded, "Why should anyone want to dig up that old stuff!"

We celebrated my thirtieth birthday on December 28 with a visit to the theater—the incomparable Bea Lillie in Noel Coward's *Set to Music*. Mady gave me two most appropriate gifts, more appropriate indeed than she realized—a pen and a Caxton Club reprint of Estienne's great work on *The Frankfurt Book Fair*. That very copy would be listed in a Rostenberg catalogue—our very first—to be issued in 1946.

Our notebooks filled, we returned home after what Mady called the "efflorescence of New England." I expressed it a little differently in my journal: "Now home to await the awful news—what I ever am going to do, not only about accepting the verdict but with life is a conundrum."

By mid-January of 1939 the verdict had been rendered, the conundrum posed. In a short note Mr. Thorndike stated that he could not accept my dissertation. As he had originally believed, the subject had no validity. The printers were mere hacks and had no point of view. If I wished, I might discuss the matter with him in his office.

Despite my premonitions, the verdict—in black and white—numbed me. Had my six years at Columbia been for naught? Nonetheless, I also felt aggressively on the defensive and eager to justify myself. I knew there was little point in questioning Lynn Thorndike, but I needed to question him, and so I took him up on his invitation. He simply reiterated his opinion, mildly suggesting that I do another dissertation on the Arabic astrologers. I walked down the six flights of stairs in Fayerweather Hall, my eyes blinded with tears.

Yet I could not dismiss my years of work. I would appeal if appeal were possible. Had not six Columbia professors judged my ability at my orals? How could one man have the power to decide the fate of my dissertation? The Dean of the Faculty of Political Science was then Dr. George B. Pegram, and I resolved to present my case to him. I might have given this a second thought had I known that Dr. Pegram was a physicist, former Acting Dean of the Faculty of the School of Mines, and author of *Electrolysis of Thorium Solution*. Dr. Pegram was quite pleasant, listened attentively, and, smiling, said in his Scottish burr, "Oh, write another dissertation."

Time works its little miracles, and in time my degree would be awarded. But more than thirty years would pass, and even if I had known about it then, it would have been cold comfort. As it was, I now had a life to reconstruct.

Having found no support at Columbia, I once again visited Dr. Paltsits at the New York Public Library. He was quite shocked at Thorndike's decision, saying, "I took a course in paleography at Morningside Heights some thirty years ago. They were a tough bunch even then. Unfortunately, I have no influence at Columbia. I wish I had, because I believe in your thesis." He shuffled some papers, looked thoughtful, and then said with a smile, "By the way, young lady, do you like to travel? There's going to be a meeting of the Bibliographical Society of America in Washington this December. I would like you to present part of your dissertation there."

I was overcome, but not too overcome to be silent. "I would love to."

"And, by the way," he continued, "there's an Austrian chap—one of those refugees from Vienna—who's planning to open a rare book business here in the fall. He needs someone who knows early printed books and the English language, and that sounds like you. Would you be interested? His name is Herbert Reichner."

DUAL
APPRENTICESHIP

Leona 📖 At 34 East Sixty-second Street I had expected to find a window luminous in its display of gleaming calf bindings, beautiful woodcuts, and handsome title pages. Instead, I confronted a scabrous brownstone, its steps leading up to a small sign: H. REICHNER ANTIQUARIAN BOOKS. I was greeted by a short pudgy man with black lank hair and thick lips. He introduced himself, opened the door of his second-floor apartment, and ushered me into a large front room filled with books and periodicals, catalogues, cartons and crates. Against the walls stood heavy mahogany bookcases partially filled. Two battered oak desks, two typewriters, and a stepladder surmounted by a can of Leather Vita completed the scene.

Mr. Reichner offered me a chair, and in an attempt at nonchalance I pulled out a cigarette. *"Nein, nein,* Miss. Do not smoke with the books." I had made a bum beginning. As he attempted to interview me in his halting English, I interrupted with "I do speak German." He relaxed and introduced me to his wife and child. They had all fled Vienna at the time of the Nazi invasion of Austria.

There, he had issued a journal for collectors, the *Philobiblon,* and had formed connections with leading antiquarian dealers in London and on the continent. Through them, and on his recent trip to France, he had obtained many fine early printed books on consignment.

"Did you get to Strasbourg?" I asked.

He looked at me sharply. *"Ach,* Strasbourg—*ja*—Dr. Paltsits told me you studied there. I am well acquainted with Herr Heitz and Herr Ritter. I am surprised that American women are interested in such things."

I dared not take umbrage at his remark. I desperately wanted the job. As it happened, he desperately needed an assistant. "I shall want you to help me with cataloguing; my descriptions must be in good English. Also, you must make some order here," he added, his thick stubby arm swinging out violently toward the disorder in the room. "Naturally, I cannot pay you very much. It is very expensive to live in New York. Besides, I shall require you only from nine in the morning until two in the afternoon—six days a week of course."

The next two weeks, I spent the hours from 9 A.M. to 2 P.M. (no lunch intermission) in helping Reichner arrange the room, lug books around, and shelve them carefully. This last was of supreme importance. Herbert Reichner was a man of pathologic neatness. His desk never bore any trace of disorder. His mail was stacked in two neat piles. He filled his fat European fountain pen daily in a precise ritual, never letting a drop of ink fall. This, a stack of multicolored pencils, and a heavy ruler were aligned in battle array on his desk. Those multicolored pencils were used to underline his recommendations to his customers. Heavy double underlinings stressed a book's condition; heavy triple underlinings emphasized a book's importance.

Herbert Reichner did indeed have many books of importance. His first catalogue, much of which I helped prepare, included books I had never seen before as well as titles that would one day appear in my own catalogues. In Reichner's front parlor, while he fumed about a misfiled order or ranted about a collector's ignorance, I studied and fondled the treasures of his Catalogue One: an incunable edition (1497) of an illustrated work on famous women beginning with Eve; a rare French edition of the *Ship of Fools;* Castiglione's *Courtier* in the first edition of 1528, published by the Aldine Press of Venice. With mounting excitement I turned the leaves of Fournier's *Manuel Typographique,* the great landmark in typography, and of Hepplewhite's monumental *Cabinet-Maker.* Holbein's *Dance of Death* in the rare first edition of 1538, Repton's *Landscape Gardening,* Adam Smith's *Wealth of Nations*—all passed through my eager and trembling hands.

My horizons were expanding with every book I handled, and as I became familiar with his stock I gradually learned to dismiss the uncontrolled ravings of my frenetic employer. It was not always easy. During a snowstorm he would greet me with the statement: "What happened? You are late—it is nine-seven A.M." After I typed a card for cataloguing purposes, he would cross it out and pencil in the word REDO, underscored in two wavy lines with his purple pencil. Author, title, and imprint had not been aligned evenly enough. When shipments were delayed because of the stringencies of the European war, the Customs Service was added to the United States Postal System for his excoriation. And soon I was delegated to serve as his representative at the Customs House.

Completely ignorant of the technicalities involved in "clearing through Customs," I presented a Notice of Arrival to a small harassed man behind the counter of the large circular room of the old Customs Building at Bowling Green.

"Fill it in, lady."

"Fill in what?"

"The forms," he wearily replied. "Here's the forms—fill 'em in: the ship, the date of arrival, the numbers, the charges, don'tcha know."

I meekly returned some inked-in spaces.

"Hey, lady, what about the convoision? Don'tcha know the convoision rates?"

At the wicket in the back the forms were usually returned to me marked "Unacceptable." The "convoision" from dollars into francs or sterling—pounds, shillings, and pence—was always incorrect. Forlornly, I handed my sheaf of rejected papers to the little man up front, who eyed me with some small sympathy.

"Hey, why don't your boss get a Customs broker? A cheapskate, huh? Gimme the papers, lady, or you and me'll be here all day."

The new stock that finally arrived after my visits to Customs was combined with Reichner's other holdings, and many of the items appeared in his first catalogue. At my manual typewriter I banged out three thousand address labels.

"When you paste the labels, Fräulein, be extremely careful. Be sure to center them on the envelope. There is not enough glue on the labels made here by these *Idioten*. You must mix the glue with your fingers and spread it on evenly. *Schön, ja?*"

While I stuck to desk and typewriter as well as to the envelopes, Herr Reichner corrected proof. His admonitions, underlined in red, were now addressed to the typesetters—the American typesetters "who are the most stupid ignorant *Idioten. Schweinhunde!* They have no feel, no understanding, for books." It was true that my own understanding of books was increasing even though he did not hesitate to address me as "Fräulein Dummkopf."

"He is probably insane," I told Madeleine as we had a late Saturday lunch at Schrafft's on Fifty-ninth Street and Madison. Over an egg salad sandwich on toasted cheese bread, I confided my feelings to her. "That man is really mad. I don't know how much longer I can take it." Yet I heeded the advice of my friend and my parents to ignore his tantrums and to learn, and the years I would spend with Herbert Reichner—"My Five Years in Siberia"—were shaping my future.

The first year with my erratic employer was particularly difficult. The spoiled darling of overindulgent parents, now at her first
job, had never been subject to the moods of such an individual.
When I was not coping with Herbert's mercurial nature, or studying
a particularly interesting volume, I was reacting to the progress of
the war. My diary recorded the climate of my times:

"Saw a marvelous art exhibit at the Met. Delightful especially
the Peales and portraits of 18th & 19th century Bostonians. All the
complacency of another age in contrast to the present. The bombs
fall in Europe and once again the lights go out. How insane it all is.
Russia now allies with Germany. The Russians are coming to the
defense of the poor, oppressed White Russians in Poland—ha, ha
ha. Reichner is as mad as ever."

Inside Mr. Reichner's office, the war seldom seemed to intrude.
There, once Catalogue One had been circulated, his customers—
many of them most distinguished—began to arrive. Having familiar-
ized myself with the great collectors of the past, I now met the great
collectors of the present: Lessing Rosenwald, whose holdings in
woodcut books and incunabula would go eventually to the Library of
Congress; William A. Jackson, the fair-haired boy of Harvard, already an eminent librarian; Zoltan Haraszti, Keeper of Rare Books at
the Boston Public Library, whose Hungarian accent charmed the
ladies of Beacon Hill; Rachel Hunt, the doyenne of botanical collectors, who insisted upon climbing the tall ladder to look at the
topmost shelf.

My day did not end at 2 P.M. I had fallen in love with old books
and I had begun to research on my own the subjects that illuminated
the scope of early printing. Gradually my articles appeared: "The
Printers of Strassburg and Humanism" (the subject of my Washington talk); "The Libraries of Three Nuremberg Patricians"; the career of the Basle printer-publisher Johann Oporin; "Andreas Rue,
Stationer of St. Paul's."

One of my articles, published in the *Library Quarterly,* attracted the attention of a Reichner prize customer, the distinguished collector Lucius Wilmerding. Mr. Wilmerding kindly invited me to view his library in his mansion at 1 2 East Eighty-ninth Street. "And certainly you may bring your friend," he wrote. Of our afternoon Madeleine recorded in her diary: "Visited the home of Lucius Wilmerding . . . 2 Alices in Wonderland. His home is a little gem set in a great city. The library is a large octagonal room lined with books, some having belonged to Elizabeth." She did not add that when the butler entered with a five-foot tea service she nonchalantly lit a cigarette, announcing airily, "Leona loves to pour."

Lucius Wilmerding was not only a first-rate collector but a most observant host. "Dump it in," he advised jovially. So I poured while Mr. Wilmerding discussed his books, other collectors, dealers, and my article, which reposed resplendently on his desk close to a signed photograph of King George VI and Queen Elizabeth. I felt regal by association.

I ascended less regal heights when I emptied Herbert Reichner's wastepaper baskets. Every time he threw a foreign catalogue away, I retrieved it, thus accumulating records of European dealers' stocks. Through their catalogues a new world of antiquarian greats unfolded for me: Maggs, Quaritch, E. P. Goldschmidt, Davis & Orioli, Weil—all of London; Olschki of Florence; Martini of Milan; Berès of Paris. I speculated about them. What were they like? Were they all mad too? Would I ever meet them?

Although I may not have been conscious of it, I was preparing and being prepared for the life of an antiquarian bookseller—a life implicit in the apprenticeship I was serving.

Madeleine 📖 SOME OF THE ARTICLES LEONA was researching during her Reichner days had nothing to do with sixteenth-century humanist-printers. Rather, they were centered on the career of Margaret Fuller, whose biography now consumed me. Leona's articles were outcomes of our joint visits to Boston, Cambridge, and Concord, and one of the most fascinating was "Margaret Fuller's Roman Diary." The diary was a tangible relic of the struggle for Italian independence and Margaret's last years in Rome. It had survived the shipwreck in which Margaret was drowned, in 1850, and Leona had edited it from the water-stained manuscript she had found at Harvard.

In my biography my purpose was to restore the writer of that diary to life so that I could honestly assert: "Here Margaret Fuller walks again, her blue chenille cord knotted in her hair, her carbuncle ring glittering on her finger, speaks again the words she actually spoke, thinks again the thoughts that once were hers." I was ambitious to restore both her persona and her background. My hours after teaching at Long Island City High School were spent, therefore, in reading and rereading the sources of Margaret Fuller's life. Eventually I wrote a series of articles that would, I hoped, become chapters of a full-length biography. In all of them I tried to reproduce Margaret's times and to reanimate her personality. My biographical technique derived from Van Wyck Brooks's methods.

Almost inevitably, he approved of the results. And since my *Life of Margaret Fuller* would be my first biography, I kept the recorded reactions of my readers—of readers like Mr. Brooks, to whom I submitted my articles; of readers for publishing houses; and eventually, after publication, of professional critics and reviewers. Their letters to me and their newspaper critiques, kept all these years in scrapbooks, trace the history of my first biography and point the way to my second.

Between June 1940 and Autumn 1941 my articles were carried by scholarly quarterlies, trial runs, so to speak, of what would become chapters on Margaret's early girlhood, her stay in Providence, her work on the *Dial,* her proletarian summer in the West. But finding a publisher for the biography would prove difficult. In

1940, while I was still *in medias res,* Viking came out with Mason Wade's *Margaret Fuller: Whetstone of Genius.* There was the pressing question of whether the market could sustain two biographies of a woman with dynamic but limited appeal. It was true that my point of view, unlike Wade's, was feminist. My own brand of feminism was probably in my genes. It came from within, it went way back in my life, and it was based on a strong egalitarian concept. Why should my brother—or any other man—be able to do thus and so if I could not? The egalitarian view continued, unconsciously or subconsciously, until, by the end of the 1930s, I could identify very naturally with the woman who had said of other women: "Let them be sea-captains, if you will." Neither Leona nor I was part of a feminist movement; a militant feminist movement did not yet exist. But my point of view was strongly feminist, firmly supportive of women's right to do whatever men did if they wished—to be soldiers or sailors, miners or sea-captains, if you will. It was early in the biographical genre for the infiltration of such an attitude, and it would take nearly half a century for such pioneer efforts to be valued.

In addition to the feminist approach to my Margaret Fuller, my technique was a revolutionary one, attempting to reproduce conversation and thought in a work of nonfiction. It was a technique that appealed to one critic at least, the distinguished author of the popular *Flowering of New England,* who, on September 27, 1940, wrote to me, renewing my determination along with my hopes:

> *I am delighted with your second chapter on Margaret Fuller, and I think you have worked out a most interesting form. I do not think publishers should be put off because of Mason Wade's book, for your treatment constitutes a mode of approach that makes the subject for me entirely novel. This accumulation of exact detail makes your book by far the best on the subject, assuming that you can carry it through to the end with the same skill, truthfulness and feeling for proportion. So far it is indeed a remarkable achievement. Only you must not*

slip even once. If there had been twenty biographies of Margaret Fuller, this would make the subject entirely fresh, and I hope you will persist and get it published.

What you are doing is a work of art . . . I have lived more Margaret Fuller *in these two chapters than in all the six or seven biographies of her. I do indeed congratulate you . . . and I should have no objection if you cared to show this to a publisher.*

I did indeed care to show "this" to a publisher, specifically to Mr. Brooks's publisher, E. P. Dutton and Company. John Macrae, firm president, responded:

November 19, 1940

I have been giving a considerable amount of thought to your manuscript, The Life of Margaret Fuller. *Frankly, I have enjoyed reading what you have had to say about Margaret Fuller. It seems to me that it is essential that you should complete* The Life of Margaret Fuller *. . . it is my strong feeling that you can complete the necessary work without having to go to Italy. I appreciate why you cannot properly go to Italy under the present conditions.*

I believe it would be wise for you to come down here to my office to have a conference with me . . .

There is no lack of books about Margaret Fuller. On the other hand, I feel that you have done something for Margaret Fuller which her previous biographers have failed to do.

The first conference took place on November 26, 1940, at 3:30 P.M. It was followed by other conferences, by presentations of partial manuscripts, and, at long last, by a working draft of the entire manuscript. Elliott Beach Macrae, Dutton's secretary and treasurer, reported to me on May 29: "I think we can safely say that we shall make an offer of publication providing our terms are acceptable."

As a result of the euphoria inspired by this statement, my mother, Leona, and I drove out to the White Turkey Inn in Danbury, Connecticut—by that time I had bought a little car—and our luxurious meal began with the inn's celebrated cheddar cheese soup. Of course we toasted Margaret Fuller and the book, Van Wyck Brooks, and E. P. Dutton, in wine provided by Leona. It was the kind of joyous occasion that can never quite be duplicated.

By this time, Van Wyck Brooks had read the entire manuscript and written an endorsement that would eventually be emblazoned on the jacket of my *Life of Margaret Fuller:*

> *I think this is a fine book, and I feel it should be published. It confirms all my feelings in reading some of the chapters in magazines. It is true that three other lives of Margaret Fuller have appeared, within the last fifteen years, and that Margaret Fuller is a limited subject. But this book is, of its kind, so very good that I feel one should ignore these facts.*
>
> *What makes the book so good is the mass of concrete detail, which has been handled in a masterly fashion. The author is saturated in her subject and in the context of the subject, and, as one who knows this context more or less, I can vouch for its general authenticity.*
>
> *The book is sound, and moreover it is immensely readable. It is a novelized biography but thoroughly grounded in fact, and it quite throws into the shade the lives I have mentioned. I think it is a capital book. There is still a large public for such authentic pictures of our way of life.*

Meanwhile, there were further visits to the Dutton offices on Fourth Avenue, often with Leona, and, during yet another summer in Maine, I continued polishing and revising. Now in the more habitable cottage called Sunnybank, not far from out first cottage, I completed the final version and wrote my foreword, beginning: "Every reader knows that with each generation comes the need for reinterpreting the past to the present. Today the purpose of biography seems to be to search out the parallels that exist between our day and earlier times."

Copies of my biography were emerging from the bindery by

December 7, 1941. Were there any parallels between our Day of Infamy and the days of infamy Margaret had observed in the Rome that during her last years had been "her country"? Now, a century later, our country was facing powers more baleful than any she had ever witnessed. Would the story of her life be at all meaningful to a nation taking up arms in its most horrendous war?

The question is answered by excerpts from the reviews. My first biography was undoubtedly a *succès d'éstime,* but it was also a financial failure. Most reviewers heaped praises on my head, but reviewers did not buy books. Those who did were concerned, not with the author of *Woman in the Nineteenth Century,* but with Pearl Harbor. I tried to concentrate on reviews rather than on sales, and for the twenty-nine-year-old author of a first biography I found heady praise indeed. On page 1 of the *New York Herald Tribune Books,* George Whicher called the biography "a consummate example of the art," re-creating "scenes and conversations . . . on the basis of authentic documents." In the *New York Times* Herbert Gorman found Fuller "brought to life again" and congratulated the author.

In addition, publication was followed by several requests to speak. Dutton's publicity department informed me that the Women's National Book Association had invited me "to speak before the lady booksellers of New York City at their monthly dinner . . . at the Hotel Pennsylvania." This I did, recalling for the group of "lady booksellers" how, before our first visit to Concord, Leona Rostenberg had said to me, "You know, Margaret Fuller would make a fine subject for a biography . . . Why don't you try it?"

Then too Adelaide Hawley, who conducted a WABC radio program, "Woman's Page of the Air," asked me to "guest" and gave me a fine opportunity to air my biographical purposes and intentions. And in October of 1942 Professor Harry R. Warfel, of the University of Maryland, asked me to join a panel at the next meeting of the Modern Language Association. "We all would like to hear something," he wrote, "about your magnificent *Margaret Fuller* or about any other ideas you wish to give away on the subject of biographical writing." Two months later—one year to the day after the Day of Infamy—Professor Warfel wrote again: "MLA seems to have been called off." The restrictions of travel necessitated by the war could make no exceptions for Margaret Fuller, Citizen of the World.

By that time I had already begun work on another biography. Both the *Times* and the *Tribune* carried my request for manuscripts and letters as well as personal recollections of another nineteenth-century woman, almost universally known as America's best-loved author of juveniles. Leona had made a second suggestion that would turn out to be even more fruitful than her first. Soon I would be in full pursuit of Louisa May Alcott.

LOUISA MAY ALCOTT'S MASK

Madeleine 📖 THE RE-construction of Margaret Fuller's life may have required the skills of a "trained historian" and even of "an expert writer of fiction," but it seldom if ever required the cerebration of a Sherlock Holmes. On the other hand, it appeared early on in my research on Louisa May Alcott that her restoration would demand the magnifying glass of a literary sleuth. Certain areas of her literary life, especially of her life prior to the creation of *Little Women,* seemed shadowy and hidden. To supplement the family income—for so long on the poverty level—she had at age nineteen become a domestic servant, but no one knew for whom she had worked or what the emotional results of the experience had been. She had, after her fame was secured, contributed an anonymous novel to her publisher's No Name Series, *A Modern Mephistopheles.* In that narrative, so unlike her customary fiction, such lurid themes as hashish and mind control had played a role. During her penurious salad days, had she perhaps written other tales that deviated radically from the pattern of sweetness and light with which she was identified?

I spent the early months of my research asking but not yet

answering those intriguing questions. On the subway my head was buried in nineteenth-century literary histories; even at my desk in school I leafed through the journals of Louisa's revered Ralph Waldo Emerson or the *Walden* of her neighbor Thoreau. In the crumbling pages of nineteenth-century weeklies and story papers at the New York Public Library I found Alcott's name or initials attached to tales previously unassociated with her. I planned articles on her addiction to the stage or her nursing work in the Civil War. As I wrote in my diary: "In my desperation to keep my desk cleared I go through many unimportant activities every day—keeping up with correspondence, checking bibliography, etc. All drops in the bucket—but a biographer's work necessitates such drops."

As the drops in the bibliographical bucket accumulated, my suspicion mounted that Louisa Alcott had indeed produced a corpus of deviational narratives. She might have hidden the details of her double literary life, but she had scattered through her letters and her journals and even in *Little Women* itself a plethora of clues. I needed to don my deerstalker, take up my magnifying glass, and embark on the hunt.

In that hunt her own clues would guide me. Among her letters was one she had written on June 22, 1862, to her young Concord friend Alf Whitman, who would be one of the models for the glamorous Laurie of *Little Women*. In it she had confided to him:

> *I intend to illuminate the Ledger with a blood & thunder tale as they are easy to "compoze" & are better paid than moral & elaborate works of Shakespeare, so dont be shocked if I send you a paper containing a picture of Indians, pirates wolves, bears & distressed damsels in a grand tableau over a title like this "The Maniac Bride" or "The Bath of Blood. A thrilling tale of passion."*

Had Louisa Alcott, author of the innocuous *Flower Fables* and future author of the domestic saga *Little Women*, actually "compozed" blood-and-thunder tales? If so, what were the titles she had concocted for them, titles like *The Maniac Bride* and *The Bath of Blood?* And if indeed she had written such narratives, where had they been published? Or was she simply exercising her bubbling sense of humor and teasing her young friend Alf Whitman?

Suspicion was heightened by the tantalizing clues she had jotted in her journals. Alcott frequently used initials in place of names in those diaries, which were, after all, not designed for publication. When, after her death, in 1888, her journals were made available to her large and enthusiastic public, they were edited by a family friend, Ednah Dow Cheney, who, in the interests of decorum, did not hesitate to remove full names and insert initials instead. What was left for an avid Sherlock Holmes was highly tantalizing.

In that very same year of 1862 when she had written her intriguing letter to Alf Whitman, Alcott had recorded in her journal:

> *Wrote two tales for L. I enjoy romancing to suit myself; and though my tales are silly, they are not bad; and my sinners always have a good spot somewhere. I hope it is good drill for fancy and language, for I can do it fast; and Mr. L. says my tales are so "dramatic, vivid, and full of plot," they are just what he wants.*

A few months later she added:

> *. . . Rewrote the last story, and sent it to L., who wants more than I can send him . . . I reel off my "thrilling" tales, and mess up my work in a queer but interesting way.*

Who was the Mr. L. who wanted more dramatic and vivid stories than the author could supply?

Firing my wonderment, increasing my perplexity, were other veiled remarks in those journals of Louisa's. A few years later she was receiving orders not only from L. but from a mysterious E., who "wanted a long story in twenty-four chapters, and I wrote it in a fortnight." There was no doubt in my mind that Louisa Alcott was writing vivid and dramatic tales in white heat, but what were they all about, where were they published, and what byline had she used?

Alcott's masterpiece offered even more exciting hints that its author had had a large clandestine literary output. Part I of *Little Women* contains an enchanting chapter entitled "Secrets," and one of Jo March's secrets is whispered to her confidant, Laurie. "I've left two stories with a newspaperman, and he's to give his answer next week." That suggestive whisper resounded thunderously in my ears by the time I reached Part II of *Little Women* and the chapter called "Literary Lessons." There, Jo sees "a pictorial sheet" with a "melodramatic illustration of an Indian in full war costume, tumbling over a precipice with a wolf at his throat, while two infuriated young gentlemen, with unnaturally small feet and big eyes, were stabbing each other close by, and a disheveled female was flying away in the background with her mouth wide open." And in that gaudy sheet Jo reads a tale that is a "labyrinth of love, mystery, and murder" belonging to "that class of light literature in which the passions have a holiday, and when the author's invention fails, a grand catastrophe clears the stage of one half the dramatis personae, leaving the other half to exult over their downfall." Moreover, Jo March boldly resolves "to try for the hundred-dollar prize offered" in the paper's columns "for a sensational story," and her manuscript actually does win the prize. Her $100 check is followed by others as, "by the magic of a pen, her 'rubbish' turned into comforts" for her needy family. *"The Duke's Daughter* paid the butcher's bill, *A Phantom Hand* put down a new carpet, and the *Curse of the Coventrys* proved the blessing of the Marches in the way of groceries and gowns."

Later on, Louisa Alcott singled out the "facts" in *Little Women* "that are true" and she included in her list "Jo's literary . . . experiences." Why should they not have been true? Certainly Louisa Alcott needed the money that sensation stories could earn; her family was habitually in need of "groceries and gowns." In addition, she was, in her early career especially, searching for genres, eager to experiment. Why not a foray into the sensational genre? Fearful to shock, she would surely have kept such ventures secret, but just as surely she would have enjoyed them. But the questions persisted, for, despite the scattering of clues, not one of them led to any certain identification of title or of any pseudonym she may have used.

Yet another chapter in *Little Women* did provide a colorful, if covert, description of Jo March's publishers. In the chapter entitled "A Friend" the avid reader is informed that Jo March "took to writing sensation stories, for in those dark ages, even all-perfect America read rubbish. She told no one, but concocted a 'thrilling tale,' and boldly carried it herself to Mr. Dashwood, editor of the *Weekly Volcano* . . . she dressed herself in her best, and . . . bravely climbed two pairs of dark and dirty stairs to find herself in a disorderly room, a cloud of cigar smoke, and the presence of three gentlemen, sitting with their heels rather higher than their hats, which articles of dress none of them took the trouble to remove on her appearance." Jo's interview with Mr. Dashwood follows and in the course of it she tells him that she is far from a novice, having won a prize for a tale in the *Blarneystone Banner*. When Mr. Dashwood accepts her story, Jo "rashly" takes "a plunge into the frothy sea of sensational literature" and "eager to find material for stories . . . she searched newspapers for accidents, incidents, and crimes; she excited the suspicions of public librarians by asking for works on poisons; she studied faces in the street, and characters, good, bad, and indifferent, all about her . . . and introduced herself to folly, sin, and misery."

Certainly Jo's—Alcott's?—publishers seemed a trio worth searching for, but no number of questions I might ask public librarians would identify the *Weekly Volcano* or the *Blarneystone Banner* or Mr. Dashwood and his two partners.

One interview Alcott gave later in life did offer further suggestions about the nature of the wild and melodramatic stories she may
have contributed to such sensational sheets. She had remarked to her
interviewer:

> *I think my natural ambition is for the lurid style. I indulge in gorgeous*
> *fancies and wish that I dared inscribe them upon my pages and set them before*
> *the public . . . How should I dare to interfere with the proper grayness of*
> *old Concord? The dear old town has never known a startling hue since the*
> *redcoats were there. Far be it from me to inject an inharmonious color into the*
> *neutral tint . . . To have had Mr. Emerson for an intellectual god all one's*
> *life is to be invested with a chain armor of propriety . . . And what would*
> *my own good father think of me . . . if I set folks to doing the things that I*
> *have a longing to see my people do? No, my dear, I shall always be a wretched*
> *victim to the respectable traditions of Concord.*

But had she indeed been such a victim? I did not think so. She
knew too much about graphic nineteenth-century story papers and
their publishers. Surely she had indulged in that "lurid style" for
which she had a "natural ambition." It was essential for Alcott's
biographer to uncover the truth of her literary life and identify
whatever stories she had written but never acknowledged. What was
in those narratives that pictured her characters "doing the things"
she had "a longing to see" her "people do"?

A visit to an Alcott collector in early 1942—one of many visits
Leona and I paid to family descendants and scholars in the natural
course of researching a biography—propelled us on the rosy path to
discovery.

Carroll Atwood Wilson lived on Horatio Street in Greenwich
Village. Urbane, handsome, he was distinguished in every way, in
the law that was his profession and in book collecting that was his
hobby. His collecting interest embraced thirteen authors, ranging
from Emerson to Hawthorne, from Trollope to Hardy. Among his

"representative men" was one representative woman—Louisa May Alcott. Greeting us cordially, he enthusiastically showed us his signed volumes, his first editions, his presentation copies, his manuscripts and letters. Among the last was a remarkable one written by Aaron K. Loring around 1864 to Louisa. In it, publisher Loring outlined his standards for popular literature:

> *A story that touches and moves me, I can make others read and believe in . . . I like a story of constant action, bustle and motion . . . I like a story that . . . goes steadily on increasing in interest till it culminates with the closing chapter leaving you spell bound.*

Surely Jo March had followed such standards for the *Blarneystone Banner* and the *Weekly Volcano,* and if Jo March had done so, had not Louisa Alcott?

All three of us mused aloud about that arresting letter, and our musings prompted our host to say to me, "Really, Miss Stern, you should devote all your time to your biography and get it written and published. Why don't you apply for a Guggenheim Fellowship so that you can stop teaching and work on Louisa?"

Then he turned to Leona. "All of us know that Jo March wrote sensation stories and published them in secret. The three of us suspect that Louisa Alcott did the same thing over some pseudonym. Maybe her publishers might throw light on her literary career. Miss Rostenberg, I know from your articles that you are interested in publishing history. Why don't you go ahead and discover Louisa's pseudonym and the thrillers she wrote?"

We did not forget Carroll Wilson's injunctions. During spring vacation of 1942 we visited Harvard's Houghton Library, recently opened and as elegant as its holdings were extraordinary. Its manuscript room was presided over by Carolyn Jakeman, to whom we presented our requests for Alcott material. In due course a page brought four boxes of letters and manuscripts to our table. We began to sift through the family papers and memorabilia.

In 1942 neither computers nor word processors existed. In the profound silence of the Houghton Library manuscript room not even a portable typewriter clattered. The pencil was the soundless tool of transmission from original manuscript to twentieth-century notebook. Leona vividly recalls both the scene and the action in the drama that followed:

> *I busied myself with Box II of the Alcott manuscripts. After contemplating a brief dossier from an Alcott third cousin in Syracuse referring to inflated prices, I tossed it aside and espied a small clutch of letters that seemed to belong together. As I picked up one of them, I immediately felt hot and cold and strangely faint. The letter was dated January 21, 1865; it was addressed to "Dear Miss Alcott," and it said: "You may send me anything in either the sketch or Novelette line that you do not wish to 'father,' or that you wish A. M. Barnard, or 'any other man' to be responsible for, & if they suit me I will purchase them . . . Let me hear from you. Very Truly Yours J. R. Elliott."*
>
> *My wild warwhoop shattered the dignified silence of the manuscript room of Houghton Library. Miss Jakeman stared reprovingly. Mady dropped her pencil. I scarcely believed my eyes. I had fulfilled Carroll Wilson's injunction. Now I knew the pseudonym. I also knew the name of the publisher. Mr. Elliott was surely the E. of Louisa Alcott's diary.*
>
> *After an intermission of congratulation, hilarity, and several cigarettes, we returned to our seats, and I meticulously copied every word of every one of the batch of five letters written by J. R. Elliott to "Dear Miss Alcott."*
>
> *The first letter was dated January 5, 1865, and it included the name of one of Miss Alcott's—A. M. Barnard's?—clandestine stories, "V.V." It also provided the name of the periodical that had carried it,* The Flag of Our Union. *And its letterhead identified Mr. Elliott's firm, "Office of Elliott, Thomes & Talbot's Publications, Journal Building, 118 Washington Street, Boston, Mass." Mr. Elliott's partners were Wm. H. Thomes and Newton Talbot. The disguise of Mr. Dashwood and his associates had been penetrated. The smoke-filled room of Jo March's publishers had been entered.*
>
> *The three other letters filled out the picture of the Concord writer in a*

vortex *of secret literary creativity. A letter of June 15, 1865, mentioned
another title, "The Marble Woman," and informed author A. M. Barnard
that Mr. Elliott's friends thought it "just splendid" and he thought that "no
author of novels need be ashamed to own it for a bantling." At the same time,
J. R. Elliott assured Miss Alcott that he had "not given currency to the idea
that 'A. M. Barnard' & yourself were identical." The final letter in the
precious group of letters was dated August 11, 1866, and it referred in
glowing terms to yet another product of A. M. Barnard's racy pen: "The story
entitled 'Behind a Mask' is accepted. I think it a story of peculiar power, and
have no doubt but my readers will be quite as much fascinated with it as I was
myself while reading the Ms. I will give you $65. for it . . . I should like
another by the 20th of September."*

In a state of overwhelming euphoria we returned home, determined to trace the thrillers contributed by A. M. Barnard in the
mid-sixties to James R. Elliott's *Flag of Our Union*. At any other time
but the early 1940s this would have been a comparatively simple
matter; but in 1942 the exigencies of war intervened and blocked
our purpose. Leona journeyed to Washington to examine *The Flag of
Our Union* at the Library of Congress, where the best run of the
periodical was deposited. The journey was fruitless. All issues of the
Flag had been placed in safekeeping for the duration; their location
was as well kept a secret as Louisa's thrillers themselves.

We did find at the Boston Public Library some issues of the *Flag*
containing the effusions of A. M. Barnard. Then, too, to our delight, checking the author's pseudonym in the card catalogue of the
New York Public Library, we pounced upon the following entry:
V.V./ BY A. M. BARNARD/ COMPLETE. The story, a narrative of a vindic-
tive and malevolent femme fatale, had been reprinted as a dime
novel and bound up by the New York Public Library in a nondescript
volume of "Pamphlets Various." We immediately enlightened the
Reference Division that, as the anomalous and pseudonymous offspring of Louisa May Alcott, *V.V.* should be removed to a more
exalted location in the library's Rare Book Division.

In addition to all this, a letter deposited in the Orchard House at Concord revealed still another market for the tireless spinner of tales. That letter, written in December 1862, had been sent to her while she was nursing in the Civil War and informed Miss Alcott that "Your tale 'Pauline' this morning was awarded the $100 prize for the best short tale for Mr. Leslie's newspaper . . . Allow me to congratulate you on your success and to recommend you to submit whatever you may hereafter have of the same sort for Mr. Leslie's acceptance."

Now we had identified not only the *Weekly Volcano* but the *Blarneystone Banner,* not only the E. of Alcott's journal but the L. The L. was Frank Leslie, newspaper magnate, lord of a journalistic empire on New York's Publishers' Row, whose star vehicle was *Frank Leslie's Illustrated Newspaper.* In the graphically illustrated folio pages of that gaudy weekly we found Jo March's prizewinner, a two-part serial entitled "Pauline's Passion and Punishment" by "a lady of Massachusetts." In that startling story of feminist anger, violent revenge, and the sexual power struggle, the unnamed "lady of Massachusetts" had let down her literary hair.

Leona, I felt, should announce her discovery to the scholarly world. She certainly had ample material for an article that would reveal the secret of Louisa Alcott's pseudonym and hint at the nature of the stories for which she had used it. She agreed, and began with a reference to Jo March and the *Weekly Volcano* and from there moved on to Louisa Alcott and *The Flag of Our Union.* She gave considerable attention to the firm of Elliott, Thomes and Talbot—a colorful trio—and touched upon the type of story A. M. Barnard had written for them—"tales of violence and revenge peopled with convicts and opium addicts." The article concluded with the printing of the five explosive letters.

Leona's study, "Some Anonymous and Pseudonymous Thrillers of Louisa M. Alcott," appeared in the summer 1943 issue of *Papers of the Bibliographical Society of America.* Not long after, it was reviewed in the *New York Herald Tribune Weekly Book Review,* where the eminent bookman Lawrence C. Wroth conducted a column, "Notes for Bibliophiles." In it he wrote:

> *Miss Leona Rostenberg gives most of us something of a shock by her revelation of a well concealed literary activity . . . From Miss Rostenberg's discoveries we learn that the author of "Little Women" wielded a purple-tipped pen when, hiding behind the name "A. M. Barnard," she released her inhibitions and in the 1860's wrote various tales for "Frank Leslie's Illustrated Newspaper" and for the Boston penny dreadful "The Flag of Our Union."*

Along with Lawrence Wroth, Carroll Wilson sensed the important implications of the discovery. But, perhaps because of the restrictions imposed by the war, perhaps because of the limited circulation of the Bibliographical Society *Papers,* those implications were not picked up by any scholar-detective. At the time, no one made the attempt to unearth further stories scribbled by a masked author with a "purple-tipped pen." The magnifying glass would not be applied to the corpus of Louisa Alcott's sensational narratives until three decades had passed.

Meanwhile, I had not forgotten Carroll Wilson's suggestion, recommending that I apply for a Guggenheim Fellowship, and I acted on his advice, in the wake of our discovery, preparing a seven-page single-spaced prospectus elaborating my "Plans for Work":

> *My purpose is not only to integrate the life of Louisa May Alcott with her times but to trace her literary development from the witch's cauldron to the family hearth . . . I am convinced that such a biography . . . will be a contribution to knowledge, first because there exists a bulk of heretofore unused material; secondly because none of the existent biographies of Louisa Alcott has attempted the integration of background with character that I hope to accomplish; and finally because no critical study of Louisa Alcott's work has ever been made.*

Along with my bulky proposal, I submitted letters from my sponsors.

On Sunday, March 14, Henry Allen Moe, secretary-general of the John Simon Guggenheim Memorial Foundation, telephoned, asking me to visit his office the next day at 4:30. Much excitement, discussion, and wonderment followed, and directly after school on Monday I bused to 551 Fifth Avenue. My diary records the ordeal of interrogation:

> *I sat at a long table & was pelted with questions from the two elders [Dr. Adlon and Mr. Moe]: "What did Margaret Fuller write about 'The Raven'?" Couldn't answer well. "What about your method of note-taking?" Long, heavy pauses. I know I left them with a poor impression. Came home exhausted & my darling Leona popped in to surprise me & hear my tale.*

My diary also records the sequel to that interview. On March 24, 1943, I wrote:

> *Day of Days. I heard this morning that I have been awarded a Fellowship by the JSGuggenheim Foundation. 12 months. $2000. Hurray!!!!!!!! . . . Leona called for me at school . . . Lil shook all over from excitement—a real palsy de delirium exquise . . . Wrote to thank all my "sponsors."*

Half a century ago, the Guggenheim was sufficiently distinguished to merit a listing of Fellows in the newspaper. I would be in very good company. My corecipients included not only those who would become illustrious in my own field—Randall Stewart, biographer of Hawthorne; William Charvat, student of professional authorship—but Martha Graham and Vladimir Nabokov. I arranged for my fellowship to begin in September, and on August 31 I wrote in my diary: "Tomorrow I start my Guggenheim-ship. May this be a fruitful year." By September 9 I was even more exuberant: "The night before school—therefore a night to celebrate my release . . .

I hope I shall make some interesting discoveries & do a good job." By the following month I would write: "My life is pleasant—almost, I fear to say—charmed. I spend most of my days digging at the library with the ultimate aim of revivifying the past."

Both before and during my "Guggenheim-ship" I worked as such a digger. Now, emancipated from teaching, I could give myself up completely to the shaping of another life, another career. Louisa Alcott presented far more hidden secrets and unsolved enigmas than Margaret Fuller. To trace the full course of her life, I searched out sources, found and followed clues. She had led many lives and presented many contradictions. She had transcended the New England that had spawned her. She had been a domestic servant in her youth; she had become, by self-appointment, family breadwinner. She had served as a nurse during the Civil War; she had taught and sewed and traveled. But especially she had written. And in writing she had revealed and masked many differing creative personalities. I knew I had to seek them all out, from the hints in her euphemistic narrative "How I Went Out to Service," and from the lurid ingredients of "A Marble Woman," whose heroine indulged in opium, from the malevolence of the vengeful Virginie Varens of "V.V." to the family love of *Little Women*. Louisa Alcott was a far more complex personality than had been imagined.

Now I could stalk her, and this I did. At Columbia, where Navy cadets paraded and military commands reverberated, I searched the stacks for sources that would yield up the secrets. At the New York Public Library I tried to identify the employer who had pursued and overworked her when she had been his servant in Dedham, Massachusetts. At the New York Public Library's warehouse on Twenty-fifth Street I delved through nineteenth-century Boston directories to trace the whereabouts and advertisements of her publishers. If she wrote about opium in "A Marble Woman," had she tasted opium herself? How available had it been? I examined the pharmacopoeias of her day at the New York Academy of Medicine.

In Philadelphia I located the site of her birthplace, now a Masonic temple. In an interview with Frederika Wendte I learned much about her last years, for Ms. Wendte remembered Louisa when toward the end of her life she had lived in Louisburg Square. In a packet of letters sent to me by Percy Whiting Brown—letters written by Louisa to his grandmother Laura Hosmer, a physician—I found a mine of homey details about her later life.

From time to time Leona and I journeyed to Boston, tracing the Alcott homes from Beacon Street to Groton Street, from Cottage Place to Louisburg Square. At the Colonial Inn in Concord we interviewed an elderly woman who recalled that Louisa's sister May had taught her drawing, but who warned me that anything else she recalled would be wrong. There too the charming Zoltan Haraszti, Keeper of Rare Books at the Boston Public Library, came to dinner, hoping to lure Leona to Boston to work with him, and discussing with me the tangled relationship of Hawthorne and the Alcotts.

In Concord I received my first sharp lesson in skepticism. At the Orchard House the curator pointed to a large copper teakettle that, she informed me with pride, was the teakettle Louisa had taken with her to Washington when she was a nurse in the Civil War. Later the same day I dropped in at the Concord Antiquarian Society, where I was shown a somewhat smaller teakettle that, the curator informed me with pride, Miss Alcott had taken with her to Washington when she was a nurse in the Civil War. When I objected, "But they showed me that teakettle at the Orchard House," the curator replied with some annoyance, "Did they! We had an understanding that this year it was to be our teakettle!" If the identification of teakettles was questionable, how much more questionable would be the identification of anonymous and pseudonymous stories!

I was searching for clues to the persona of the author of "Behind a Mask," who herself had masked certain phases of her life. It was an invigorating and absorbing, if often frustrating, occupation. But in the fullness of time her identity began to manifest itself—the identity of a professional writer, an experimenter in the many genres of writing, from fairy tale to domestic drama, from sensational to philosophical fiction. She had written more than anyone had imagined. And she had seldom repeated herself. I sought to track down the changing episodes of her life and the changing aspects of her work in a sequence of articles that were invariably read aloud to my perceptive mother and—usually over a table at Schrafft's—to my perceptive friend.

My Guggenheim days were charmed indeed. At the end of the first year, my fellowship was renewed for six months, and I started writing my biography. In between there were performances of *The Skin of Our Teeth* and *Tomorrow the World,* a drama in which Skippy Homeier played a brutal Nazi child. There was no escaping the war, what with intermittent blackouts and sirens and fundraisers staged by the Anti-Nazi League or Russian War Relief. Details of what would later be called the Holocaust had begun to penetrate over here, although they were often received with disbelief. At the time, those who shared a German-Jewish heritage, as I did, could find nothing believable in what would be known to the future as "the final solution." For the most part, I buried myself in a nineteenth-century life that engrossed and intrigued me. I knew that my return to teaching would cast a blight after my prolonged taste of freedom.

Leona too was finding her lengthy apprenticeship to a book-dealer intolerable. How often she confided in me her desire to become an antiquarian bookseller herself. Her family gave her no encouragement. Her father believed business was not meant for a woman, and her beautiful New Orleans mother declared, "My darling, no woman in our family has ever engaged in commerce." No doubt such comments merely increased Leona's desire. Although she was absolutely certain of her interest and her ambition, she constantly vacillated. In addition she had no capital, and in the rejection of her dissertation she had tasted failure and still feared it.

Yet had not Thoreau written in *Walden:* "If one advances confidently in the direction of his dreams, and endeavors to live the life which he has imagined, he will meet with a success unexpected in common hours''?

I decided that I had it in my power to end Leona's ambivalence. I planned a gift that would at once excite and encourage her and—I was sure—advance her confidently in the direction of her dreams. As soon as the gift was delivered I would pack it in a large box and present it to her for Christmas.

LEONA ROSTENBERG
—RARE BOOKS

Leona ' ' 'Christmas won't be Christmas without any presents,' grumbled Jo, lying on the rug." Her unforgettable complaint rang up the curtain on *Little Women*. Christmas of 1943 was indeed Christmas for me, and it rang up the curtain on my future.

I spent the holiday with Mady and her wonderful mother, Lil. My parents had gone south and my brother, now married, lived in Washington. The Stern home had become my second home. For the occasion I lugged a lamp for Mady's Guggenheim desk, and for Lil a copy of Marquand's new best seller, *So Little Time*. Before she would unwrap her gifts Mady handed me a large wobbly package, and Lil remarked, "I want to see your expression when you open this."

"It's a puppy!" I shrieked.

"As if I would wrap up a puppy. Open it up," Mady commanded.

As I unwrapped the package five boxes fell out. I opened them one by one, becoming fainter, more hysterical as I proceeded. Box Number One produced correspondence paper, typewriter size. Box

Number Two produced half-size correspondence paper. Box Number Three produced a batch of shipping labels. In Box Number Four there was a pile of small business cards. All of them were gloriously engraved with the following staggering words:

LEONA ROSTENBERG——RARE BOOKS
152 East 179th Street
New York 53, N.Y.
Telephone TR. 8–2789

In the upper lefthand corner was embossed the picture of a Renaissance printer and his apprentice.

By this time I was so emotionally overcome that I could scarcely speak. The last box undid me completely. It contained one hundred billheads with the same magnificent letterhead and device. I threw myself on the couch, screaming and moaning, "But I'll never have a hundred books!" Surrounded by these Christmas trophies, I experienced a mixture of emotions—excitement of course, gratitude, and, inevitably, fear. The die had been cast. I could not waste all this marvelously engraved paper.

Recovering my senses somewhat, I examined the stationery more carefully. The device of the printers had been taken from Jost Amman's *Book of Trades,* but unlike the original sixteenth-century woodcut, it bore a twentieth-century inscription:

LEONA ROSTENBERG——
RARE BOOKS

Leona Rostenberg had no choice. She had to go into business. And thirty years later, when Leona Rostenberg—Rare Books was interviewed by the *Times,* the article would be captioned: "How Stationery Started Two Women on a 30-Year Partnership."

Despite Mady's munificent gift, I was still Herbert Reichner's apprentice, and, being Leona, I still lacked not only confidence but cash. Over further Schrafft's lunches I still voiced my doubts at which Mady remarked: "Don't be an ass. Try it. And after my Guggenheim we can become partners. I'll lend you a thousand dollars."

"But suppose I lose it."

"You won't, and if you do . . ."

"Then you think I might."

"I don't think you will. You really are a fool. What about dessert?"

It was not until late May 1944 that I actually burned my bridges. I informed Herbert Reichner that I would not return in the fall. "I am not surprised," he replied, somewhat shaken. "I knew it would happen one day. You are of course going into business for yourself. But let me tell you that if you change your mind I will increase your salary. Remember, it is not easy. You must have what I call *Finger-Spitzengefühl*—you must have it in your fingertips, to know a rare book when you see one. Besides, the book business is not all pleasure; there are many problems with books and customers."

As things developed, Herbert Reichner would indeed have many problems. In the year that followed, he would endure a succession of seven secretaries. As for me, I set the stage for Leona Rostenberg—Rare Books.

The initial steps were taken in Sunnybank, the Maine house we rented during the summer of 1944. Unlike our primitive pagoda, this was a civilized dwelling with all the amenities, pine-paneled walls, and a view of the ocean. It also boasted four additional incumbents, named Meg, Jo, Beth, and Amy. These were a quartet of Rhode Island Reds, laying chickens that Mady had for some unknown and incomprehensible reason desired as a birthday gift.

I had tried to purchase them at Macy's, which at that time devoted its ninth floor to "Barnyard," where livestock could be purchased. My conversation with the knowledgeable salesperson was fruitless but quotable:

LEONA: I'd like to purchase four chickens.

SALESPERSON: Do you have a house?

LEONA: Of course I have a house.

SALESPERSON: Does it have electricity?

LEONA (fuming): Of course it has electricity. It has five rooms and a porch . . .

SALESPERSON (interrupting): I don't think *you* should have chickens.

When it finally dawned on me that the "Barnyard" expert had been referring to a chicken coop while I had been thinking of the lovely cottage we rented, I decided to order my livestock through our landlord. The result was interesting, but, unlike their namesakes of *Little Women,* our New Englanders proved troublesome denizens. The squawking from Mady's roost, not to mention four Reds flying the coop, frequently interrupted my attempts to get Leona Rostenberg—Rare Books rolling.

During my years with Herbert I had accumulated his discarded catalogues from foreign dealers. Now I began requesting them on my own, studying them and ordering a few sixteenth- and seventeenth-century items. At the same time, realizing that I would need customers for my stock, I assiduously copied the names of collector-members of such distinguished societies as the Grolier Club and the Bibliographical Society of America. These I supplemented with names of curators of Rare Book Departments in American libraries. While my three-by-five index card file began to mount, Mady devoted herself to the namesakes of our Rhode Island Reds, working on the chapter entitled *"Little Women."*

Since we could not prowl or book hunt along Piccadilly or Charing Cross Road, we prowled in the neighboring villages of Maine. Between Portland in the north and Portsmouth in the south, we drove, Mady at the wheel of her Plymouth, Chimpie sniffing the scents of summer, all of us keen for adventure. Would we find what the trade called a "sleeper," a book whose glories were unknown to the seller but old hat to us, the buyers? And so, from time to time, we ventured to Berwick and Biddeford, Kennebunk and Kittery, Sanford and Salmon Falls—to the House of the Thousand Chairs and the Old Grange, the Crow's Nest and Grandma's Attic, exploring jumble and dust, mustiness and broken crockery, armless dolls— and books.

Among the piles of old incomplete periodicals and copies of books without covers—the *Language of Flowers,* the *Girl of the Limberlost*—we pulled out a few possibilities to add to the meager stock of the future Leona Rostenberg—Rare Books. From the debris Mady extracted a folio volume compiled by Elizabeth Peabody, friend of Margaret Fuller, teacher in Bronson Alcott's school, hence well known to biographer Stern. Peabody's *Polish-American System of Chronology* was ours for twenty-five cents. Jackson's *Second Report of the Geology of the State of Maine,* published in 1838, bound in its original wrappers, and also priced at twenty-five cents, seemed to me an appropriate purchase. Although I preferred sixteenth-century European imprints, the firm of Leona Rostenberg—Rare Books would always find room for interesting American rarities. One such rarity, also tagged with the popular price of a quarter, was snatched up by Mady—the poems of Thomas Holley Chivers in first edition, entitled *Nacoochee; or, the Beautiful Star,* a work that had strongly influenced his friend Edgar Allan Poe. We would return to Sunnybank from our explorations with an early Webster *Speller,* a Pitman *Phonography,* a Christy *Melodies*—and with high hopes for the future of my budding business.

In between our field trips we combined swimming with desk work. Mady continued writing and rewriting her biography of Alcott while I continued shaping my business plans. We interrupted our sedentary labors to attend a local auction. When we learned that all the contents of a house and barn would be offered at public sale, we immediately made a preliminary tour of inspection. We wandered through rooms filled with piled-up mattresses and bedsprings, an array of chamber pots and flatirons, lampshades and antimacassars, and at last came to a dark corner of the barn, where we spied some books. We found an early Bible, a few hymnals, some indifferent novels, and then the *Finger-Spitzengefühl* kicked in. Scattered about the area I saw a number of what looked like pamphlets in printed wrappers. I picked one up. I had in my hands an installment of Charles Dickens's novel, *Master Humphrey's Clock*. We knew that Dickens's novels had been published in parts, or installments, before they were published in book form, and I knew that a Dickens in parts was of far greater value than a Dickens bound in hard covers. But were all the parts there? We scurried around, picking them up one after the other—a literary mouse had nibbled away part of the title page of one installment—but, sure enough, all twenty parts of *Master Humphrey's Clock* were spread around the barn. We gathered them together, made a bundle of them, threw in the Bible, and sought out the auctioneer. Would he kindly offer the lot at the upcoming auction?

He not only offered it at auction time; he waxed eloquent about it. After he had disposed of the mattresses and lamps, the chamber pots and cooking utensils, he held up the bundle we had put together. "And now, folks, we come to some mighty elegant literature. It ain't by no American, folks. It's by an English gent named Dickens. You all heard of Mr. Dickens. Now what will you offer for Mr. Dickens?"

The audience was unimpressed by what looked like a bunch of unbound papers. After I waited a moment breathlessly, I called out, "Fifty cents!" to which the auctioneer responded, "The lady with the glasses says fifty cents. Ain't I got no higher bid for Mr. Dickens? Can't let him go on one bid, ladies and gentlemen."

I poked Mady in the ribs and she quickly shouted, "Sixty cents!"

"The other lady with the glasses bids sixty cents. Sixty cents, folks. Mr. Dickens goin', goin', gone to the other lady with the glasses. Sixty cents!"

I had found my first sleeper. Leona Rostenberg—Rare Books

would be able to offer not only some unusual Americana, but a true nineteenth-century English literary rarity—a Charles Dickens in the original parts.

My *Finger-Spitzengefühl* had only just begun. It operated especially well one day when I was studying a catalogue just received from the English firm of McLeish & Sons, located on London's Little Russell Street. Mady was deep into Louisa Alcott's grand tour abroad in 1870; Chimpie was dozing on the front porch; I was turning the pages of the McLeish catalogue, which had just been forwarded to me by my temporary secretary, my mother. I had been uninterested in most of the items listed until my eye lighted upon number 188. Then the *Finger-Spitzengefühl* became an electrical conductor. My scalp pricked. And I shrieked aloud.

All those signs and symptoms had been activated by something that had taken place several months before. While still working for Reichner, I had studied one of his cast-off catalogues, a posh production listing superb antiquarian rarities sent by the firm of Lionel and Philip Robinson, Pall Mall, London. There I had read a glowing description of a volume to be lusted after: [CALDERWOOD (David),] Perth Assembly. [Leyden: Pilgrim Press,] 1619. At first glance, the work meant nothing to me. I had never heard of Calderwood or his *Perth Assembly,* and I knew enough from my association with Reichner to realize that Leyden had been a beehive of publishing activity in the early seventeenth century and that very few items issuing from that place and period were especially valuable. But it was the bracketed words ''Pilgrim Press'' that made the item a prize, and I learned why from the Robinson description.

The Pilgrim Press—so called by later historians—had been founded clandestinely and operated in Leyden between 1617 and 1619 by William Brewster. Brewster would issue only twenty titles from his secret press before he and his fellow Pilgrims immigrated to New England aboard the *Mayflower.* They were all not only evidence of the group's fervent anti-English-establishment attitude, but, in a sense, the earliest printed Americana. They reflected the background of our Pilgrim Fathers and hence they were the earliest printed records of our country—American incunables, so to speak. Calderwood's work, printed in secret by the Elder Brewster, was really a sample of pre-Colonial printing. As such, it might be regarded as almost priceless. It had a price, however. The Robinsons had tagged it at sixty pounds. Sixty pounds in 1944 was the equivalent of three hundred dollars, enough to live on in New York City for several months. Surely no matter how roseate my future, I would never be able to afford that amount for a single volume and I would never, never own a Pilgrim Press book.

Now, in August 1944, I had the chance to acquire one. I had come to item 188 in the McLeish catalogue where I read: "Perth Assembly. 1619."

All the bracketed designations, including "Pilgrim Press," had been omitted. The McLeish firm was not aware that it was offering an excessively rare book that had issued from the secret press of the Pilgrim Fathers in Leyden. It did not know that it had listed a prize, and had priced the book at one pound fifteen shillings, or eight dollars.

Now, the real challenge was: Would I ever get hold of this book? My waterfall of explanation, excitement, and concern poured over Mady and ended in a deluge. "It's one of the twenty books printed by the Pilgrims at their secret press in Leyden before they came to America! It's worth a fortune! But how will I get it?—how, how, how? I'm an unknown—surely a good London dealer will grab it!"

Mady was more controlled. She left Louisa Alcott at 2 Piazza Barberini in Rome and announced, "We'll take immediate action. We'll drive to the Ogunquit Western Union office and send a cable to McLeish." Deviously, I cloaked my discovery when I ordered item 188 by adding a few other items, and my cable was sent to 22 Little Russell Street, London. In days when international telephone calls were almost as rare as Calderwoods, all I could do was wait in alternating hope and despair, in constant suspense, for the outcome. Would I launch Leona Rostenberg—Rare Books with a great, great find or not?

Meanwhile, I performed the final task in my preparations. I formulated the announcement that would bring the existence of a brave new firm to the attention of a breathless book-buying public:

LEONA ROSTENBERG

takes pleasure in announcing

that she will engage in the sale of Rare Books

at

152 East 179th Street

New York 53, N.Y.

Tremont 8—2789

At a slight extra charge the Portland printer included my stationery device in the upper left corner. I had two thousand copies printed. We mailed them all and, after donating the now brooding Meg, Jo, Beth, and Amy to our landlord, we departed the lovely house facing the sea in early September.

My business filled one requisite for the antiquarian book trade: it was located on the East Side. It was a bit high up, however: 152 East 179th Street, the Bronx. There, in the three-story house where I had grown up, I converted my brother's abandoned bedroom into my office. There I installed my magnificent stationery, my full sheets, my half sheets, my cards, my labels, my one hundred bill-heads. As for my stock of antiquarian books, it fitted easily into a small bookcase that originally housed the *Encyclopaedia Britannica*, acquired by my parents when their son entered high school. My flat-top desk—once my father's—was placed in a recess facing the window. On it reposed my typewriter—my junior typewriter, which had never been equipped with a backspacer. My walls were adorned with reproductions of fifteenth-century woodcuts purchased in Strasbourg. My wirehair, Chimpie, curled up on the rug. My telephone sat waiting on a ledge. Leona Rostenberg—Rare Books was poised to begin.

A letter dated September 14, 1944, helped break ground. In response to one of my two thousand announcements, the noted columnist for *Publishers Weekly,* Jake Blanck, wrote:

Dear Leona Rostenberg—

All good wishes! I know that with your expert knowledge you'll make a great success of bookselling.

How about writing 3 or 400 words on what you plan to do? Your specialties, etc.? A list of your writings etc., etc.? I'll run it in PW.

And don't be modest!

Yrs—

Jake Blanck

A month later *Publishers Weekly* reported to the book world the launching of a new antiquarian book business:

LEONA ROSTENBERG, *who has been connected for five years with Herbert Reichner, rare book dealer in New York, has opened her own shop at 152 East 179th Street, New York 53, N.Y. Miss Rostenberg tells us that though her interests are not confined to any one period, she will specialize in literature of the Renaissance and the Reformation and the history of printing.*

Miss Rostenberg received her M.A. from Columbia University in 1933 and then spent the following five years doing graduate work in mediaeval and modern European history, specializing in early 16th century printing. She lived for some time in Strasbourg where she studied incunabula and 16th century Strasbourg editions. Miss Rostenberg has written many articles on the subject of printing, among them "The Printers of Strasbourg and Humanism," "The Libraries of Three Nuremberg Patricians."

Miss Rostenberg was gratified by the public recognition of "her own shop." Miss Rostenberg, however, had still to make her first offer, had still to hear the telephone ring with her first order. The majority of books in the *Encyclopaedia Britannica* bookcase were being saved for what I hoped would be my Catalogue One. To expand my meager stock and activate the process of supply and demand, I returned to Morningside Heights.

The balcony shelves of the Columbia University Bookstore were lined with dull cloth-bound sets of forgotten English literary lights. A calfbound volume caught my eye until its missing title page replaced hope with disappointment. Surely there must be some duplicate—even some discard—not wanted by Columbia but ardently desired by another university library. And then I spied it. It was a quarto, beautifully bound in polished calf, and its glitter was enhanced by a gilt-impressed crest on the covers. I took it carefully off the shelf, and when I looked at the title page I nearly fell off the balcony. I had seen another copy of the very same book at Herbert Reichner's: *A Six Weeks Tour through the Southern Counties of England and Wales* by Arthur Young. Herbert had raved on about its importance; it was a treasury of information about eighteenth-century English economy, from soil cultivation to labor prices, from farming to the working poor. Herbert had had it in first edition of 1768, and this too was a first edition, but an even better copy than his; this one had come from a great library, the Camperdown, and had its arms embossed on the covers. Why Columbia had discarded it was a conundrum to me, but I had more important things to do than worry about that. I had to check the book to make sure it was complete, and then I had to avail myself of the facilities of my alma mater's library and check references. I spent some time looking up the catalogue of Harvard's Kress Library of Business and Economics, and reassured myself that that great library boasted only the second edition of the work. This was not only the first, but the Camperdown copy. Its price was three dollars. I quickly took my find to the cashier and exchanged it for three singles. Young's *Six Weeks Tour* was the handsomest book in my small stock. In addition, it was rare, and, to cap it all, it was in English and so would appeal even to librarians without Latin and Greek. It would be the first formal book offer of Leona Rostenberg—Rare Books.

For this purpose I selected not a half sheet but a full sheet of my splendid stationery. The description I wrote almost rivaled the book in length. It elaborated every detail of the six weeks' tour and ended with the encomium: "It is both an economic and social survey of a good portion of England during the second half of the eighteenth century. Rare First Edition." In days that boasted no Xerox, I made eleven copies of my offer and circulated it among eleven libraries.

I reported my results to Mady: "My Arthur Young is taking his first American tour. What do you think?" Mady, trying to forestall any possible disappointment, cautioned me, "Try to be patient. It could be that you might not have an order before Christmas."

Dejected, I returned home to find a household uproarious with excitement. In my absence, my telephone had rung. It had been answered by my father's receptionist, Miss Kerry, who had jotted the message down on a prescription pad. What a prescription! "Please send the Young on approval. John Fall, Acquisitions Department, New York Public Library."

Arthur Young had traveled a good deal. He had crossed the Channel several times. Now, well packed in numerous layers of tissue and corrugated paper, he crossed less turbulent waters—the East River—transported to Manhattan by his temporary owner. John Fall greeted both of us with amusement.

"He's sure well wrapped."

"He had quite a trip," I replied.

"A nice copy," he commented after disgorging the smothered Mr. Young from his many-layered wrappings. "We'll let you know."

It was my first sale. Moreover it was followed two days later by my first duplicate order from the Kress Library of Business and Economics, Harvard University. My mother was so overwhelmed that she made a long-distance call to her sisters in Cedarhurst, Long Island. Business had begun.

To the amazement of my family, and indeed to my own, business continued. From foreign catalogues I selected books of earlier centuries that seemed to have some bearing on ours, and librarians apparently agreed with me, for they were purchased: Rousseau's *Treatise on the Social Compact,* which had had some influence upon our Constitution; the *Correspondence* of Lady Mary Wortley Montagu, an early feminist who had introduced to the West the practice of inoculation against smallpox. A slim English catalogue, delivered shortly after our return from Maine, introduced me to what were designated as *"petites histoires,"* published in the seventeenth century, brief histories of great events and great people. I delighted in those little calfbound volumes—a history of Dunkirk, still timely; a life of Christina of Denmark; a violent invective against an earlier dictator, Louis XIV. These unimposing mementoes of another age crystallized for me the bits and pieces of seventeenth-century fact and fancy. Individually they might be unimportant, but together they reflected a time gone by. For me they offered *multum in parvo,* and again the curators of university libraries agreed. The *"petites histoires"* departed 179th Street almost as soon as they came in.

Not all my purchases had such a halcyon fate. An atypical purchase for me was a volume by Arthur Conan Doyle. Having killed off Sherlock Holmes at the end of 1893, the author had experimented with stories unrelated to the great detective, and in 1894 Doyle published *Round the Red Lamp,* consisting of narratives recalling his medical practice. This I described at length, beginning my offer with an account of the author's medical education and ending with a critical analysis. Naturally I sent my voluminous offer to the Sherlockian expert Christopher Morley. His reply was disheartening: "Many thanks, but I have it already—am sending on your memo to another connoisseur.'' This was cold comfort, since I never heard from the other ''connoisseur.''

Around the same time, I decided to offer to another expert Jackson's *Second Report of the Geology of the State of Maine* which I had found at the House of the Thousand Chairs in Salmon Falls. The description of Jackson's *Report* was even more voluminous than the description of Doyle's *Round the Red Lamp*. It began with Jackson's background, proceeded to his appointment as state geologist, and recounted the contents of Parts 1, 2, and 3 of his *Report*. In 1944, the most popular novelist associated with the State of Maine was Kenneth Roberts, author of *Oliver Wiswell*, and a familiar of its rocky coast. To Mr. Roberts of Kennebunkport, therefore, I dispatched my Jackson offer. His reply, like Christopher Morley's, was disheartening:

> *Thank you very much for your letter . . . and the kind things you say.*
>
> *I'm a little doubtful as to whether Jackson's book would be of much help to me in writing novels—Cap Huff only needed to distinguish between two sorts of rocks: the sort he could pick up and throw, and the sort big enough to fall down on.*

Such disappointments were, I knew, part of being in business. Moreover, they were completely eclipsed by the arrival of a small package from Little Russell Street, London. When I saw the label of McLeish & Sons, I almost feared to open it. Would the package contain just those few items I had ordered to cloak the Pilgrim Press prize, or would the great rarity be there? I conquered my hesitation, tore off the wrappers, dislodged the corrugated paper, and with pounding heart found two books. One was an eighteenth-century work on Spanish painters. The other was an octavo bound in sheepskin. I opened to the title page: *Perth Assembly*. 1619. In my hands was one of the twenty titles published by the Pilgrim Father, the Elder Brewster, at his secret press in Leyden before he boarded the

Mayflower. *"Petites histoires"* were all very well, and so too were Jean-Jacques Rousseau and Lady Mary Wortley Montagu. But now I owned a monument, a landmark in printing history.

Tempering my excitement, I placed my Calderwood exactly where it belonged in my *Encyclopaedia Britannica* bookcase, right before a volume by Gasparo Contarini. I had bought the latter, *The Commonwealth and Government of Venice,* from another English dealer—the English translation of a Venetian history published in 1599 that William Shakespeare may have studied before writing *Othello.* Certainly there were details in the Contarini that punctuate the tragedy of the Moor of Venice.

During the next few weeks I exulted in my acquisitions: a Shakespeare source placed next to an American incunable. Having reveled especially in my prize showpiece, my Calderwood, I decided to do what all good booksellers must do, sell my wares. I wrote up both works and offered them together to my old friend John Fall, Chief of Acquisitions, New York Public Library. This time when I informed Mady what I had done, she did not caution me to wait till Christmas for a decision. Once again I carried my books wrapped in their protective layers to Forty-second Street, and once again John Fall admired their packaging. This time, however, he warned me that it would take some time for a decision, since the Calderwood would be no ordinary purchase. And once again I waited in suspense for the outcome.

A week later the Chief of Acquisitions telephoned. "I have good news and bad news."

I stopped breathing.

"We have the Contarini. But we are buying the Calderwood—delighted to acquire it."

Who cared about *Othello?* I had made my first really big coup. Another call was made to Cedarhurst, and this time I magnanimously permitted my awestruck mother to use my phone.

From time to time I noticed empty spaces on my bookshelf. For a beginning bookseller this was a situation that had to be remedied. The balcony of the Columbia University Bookstore where I had found my Arthur Young might yield more finds. Browsing through the shelves, whistling softly to myself in hopeful anticipation, I pulled out and replaced, contemplated and discarded, until I noticed a stout octavo volume. I opened it and saw an indifferent-looking title page: *Orationes IV*. The author of *Orationes IV* had an equally unenticing name: Johann Balthasar Schupp. Lackadaisically I leafed through his outpourings of 1704. Mynheer Schupp was apparently tireless. His *Orationes IV* was followed by another title page in Latin, a *Dissertation on Opinion,* penned in 1703. These verbose meanderings of nearly two and a half centuries ago would not command more than fifteen or twenty dollars. But something—perhaps *Finger-Spitzengefühl,* perhaps ESP, perhaps simply serendipity—lured me on. I turned the pages of Schupp on *Opinion* rapidly. And then I hit upon a third title page. My lack of interest was replaced by excitement, and my excitement by palpitations. Bound with Mynheer Schupp was another Latin work published more than fifty years before his bombast. It had been written by no Dutch orator but by the eminent French skeptic René Descartes. Moreover, it was his greatest contribution to the field of psychology. Tucked away at the end of two completely nondescript works was the first Latin edition of the supremely important *Passions of the Soul.* The volume was priced at five dollars. Here my profit would be enormous. The Descartes could fetch as much as two hundred dollars. (Today it would bring a minimum of ten times that.) Before making the purchase I naturally availed myself of the Columbia Reference Library, where I confirmed my belief that Columbia University had discarded a rarity. Now it was mine.

Descartes would go to the Sterling Library of Yale University, where it would introduce me to the extraordinary librarian Donald Wing, who would become a lasting friend. In a way, the second or duplicate order for the Descartes was even more interesting. It was incredible. It came from the Accessions Department, Columbia University Library.

As for the two boring compositions by Mynheer Schupp, I would place them in alphabetical order in my *Encyclopaedia Britannica* bookcase and try to forget them. Forgetting them, however, would prove impossible. Leona Rostenberg—Rare Books was about to be enlarged by admission of a partner who would enter the two indifferent volumes in an inventory, estimate their costs as zero, and, in time, proceed to sell them at what can only be described as total profit. On April 9, 1945, Madeleine phoned to me and said, "You have a junior partner. I'll be up tomorrow."

Madeleine 📖 THAT PHONE CALL WAS THE culmination of all my preceding life, but it was initiated by more immediate events. After my Guggenheim had ended, teaching was more repugnant to me than ever. On April 9 I was told that the teacher of a special class of below-average students had had a nervous breakdown and that I was to be her replacement. At that point I envisioned my own nervous breakdown. I rode the subway back from school, my inner turmoil gradually turning to decisive calm. I had long ago planned to join Leona in the fall; I would simply do so now, in the spring. I would burn my bridge to security as a tenured teacher and add my name to Leona's magnificent correspondence paper: Madeleine B. Stern, Associate.

When I reached home I phoned my principal and my head of department, informing them of my decision. I mailed back my keys. When my mother came home, I greeted her with the explosive statement, "I've resigned from school." She sat down quickly and then said, "Something terrible must have happened." Her mind was filled with protective impulses. Through the long Depression and the course of the war she had taken comfort in the thought that, as a tenured teacher, I would forever be secure, financially independent, able if necessary to walk alone. She must have been devastated, though she refrained from further comment. She would be, as she had always been, as supremely supportive as she was loving.

I often wonder what Leona's reaction—and her family's—was to my announcement. Now I think they may well have been as worried as my mother about the outcome. If they were, they did not show it. I polished my shoes, put on my red check suit, and on April 10, 1945, took the subway up to the large rambling house in the Bronx. I had been there thousands of times before. But this time it was not just the home of my closest friend, but a house of business with which I would be associated. And this time I found a WELCOME sign upon the door.

The senior partner escorted the junior partner to the office. A bridge table had been set up with a card labeled: M. B. STERN, ASSO-CIATE. I did not linger long at the table but scrutinized the stock, with which I was already familiar. Indeed, I had selected some of it. When I examined the stationery, I assured my partner, "You're soon going to need more billheads." At an executive meeting attended by both partners and wirehair Chimpie, we allocated departments to each other. Leona would specialize of course in early printed books; Mady, completing her biography of Alcott, would naturally head the literary and Americana sections, such as they were. Chivers's poems were still on hand, along with Elizabeth Peabody's *Polish-American System of Chronology,* and the Webster *Speller.* We would have to enlarge that Americana department to accommodate a department head. Barnard College was apparently unaware of the diminutive nature of our Americana section. A short time later the college's alumnae magazine announced, to our amusement, that *"Madeleine B. Stern* is consultant and manager of the research department in Americana for the rare book firm of Leona Rostenberg, New York City." As "manager of the research department in Americana" I took home for study the poems of Chivers and the *System of Chronology* of Elizabeth Peabody. My junior partnership had begun.

It was interrupted two days later by the sudden death of Franklin D. Roosevelt. We all wept for our idol and wondered whether America would ever be the same again. Roosevelt's death and our formal partnership marked a milestone in our lives. FDR epitomized the continuous flow of the past; our partnership chartered the future in the antiquarian firm of Leona Rostenberg—Rare Books.

Whatever doubts I may have had were soon dispelled. Leona's mother and father both welcomed me warmly; my mother's anxieties diminished; with every sale that was made their amazement grew. It took me a while to make my own first sale. Neither Webster nor Chivers nor Peabody seemed to attract the nation's rare book librarians. I persevered, however, and was finally rewarded. My two-page single-spaced description of Elizabeth Palmer Peabody's *Polish-American System of Chronology* at length found a buyer. Having described the physical details of the book, I elaborated on the life of Miss Peabody from her work in Bronson Alcott's Temple School to her kindergartening. In between I discussed her acquaintance with the Polish exile General Joseph Bem and his curious system of historical charts. I concluded with the incontrovertible statement: "The volume is of great importance in any collection of pedagogical works." And one institution—the University of Alabama—concurred. It purchased our Peabody, which had cost us a quarter in Maine, for $6.75. With the arrival of the small printed library order form requesting my offer, I reached a state of joyful hysteria, which was not diminished when other orders followed. Chivers's *Nacoochee,* a work of "literary significance," Poe's stories in Baudelaire's translation, the *Poems* of Phillis Wheatley, an eighteenth-century former slave—all passed through my eager hands before entering a research library. The excitements of cerebration brought us mutual joy. Despite a friend's dire prediction that business and friendship do not blend, ours was the exception. Our blend would endure.

Together we examined and assessed our stock. What remained on the shelves of the *Encyclopaedia Britannica* bookcase were primarily books selected by Leona for Catalogue One. It would present, she explained to me, a history of the book as a physical object and as a medium of expression. It would encompass the art of printing and the great printers; the collectors of books; the binders of books; the craftsmen of books; the lovers of books; even the forgers of books.

"But isn't that terribly limited?" I asked. "There's no literature, no history, no science, no art. Will there be enough interest in such a specialized subject?"

Leona reassured me, "To librarians, booksellers, and collectors there is nothing limited in the subject of Books about Books." And so we began.

The concerns and problems associated with the production and publication of any catalogue are not completely dissimilar to the bearing and delivery of a child, and the first catalogue is surely comparable to a firstborn. In the case of our Catalogue One the period of gestation took longer. It was not until the end of 1945 that we had assembled the hundred books it would comprise. The former apprentice Leona Rostenberg could identify closely with nineteenth-century French verses on the misery of apprentice printers; the discoverer of the Alcott pseudonym would not be loath to include a seventeenth-century French volume on pseudonymity entitled *Auteurs déguisez.* Just so her interest in seventeenth-century printing was reflected in Clavel's *General Catalogue of Books printed in England since the dreadful Fire of London 1666.* The first catalogue of American first editions, issued in 1885 by the mysterious Leon & Brother of New York, who turned out to be refugees from Poland, fascinated detective Stern, while other items, relating to a famous or infamous book thief named Libri and an erudite and outrageous forger named Thomas Wise, intrigued both of us. Censorship was represented in Catalogue One by an edict on prohibited books promulgated in 1570 by Philip II of Spain; and the answer to censorship was represented by the catalogue's hundredth entry: the libel *Trial of John Peter Zenger,* whose acquittal marked the cornerstone of American liberty of the press.

We studied and pored over our hundred books, not only their content but their appearance: their format and binding, their paper and typography—and we delighted in all of them. But would our potential customers share our delight? We were not sure.

Before we could find out, we had to have our catalogue printed. Our funds were severely limited; we could not afford the posh Southworth-Anthoensen Press. The printer we selected—one Mr. Rapp—was a patient of Leona's father and had his office on New York's Hubert Street. When the galleys were ready, we rushed there, finding the area redolent with a delicious aroma from a nearby chocolate factory. The galleys, which had been carefully printed, were as sweet to us as the air, and as we corrected the few errors we breathed in the delicious fumes of Hubert Street.

Our excitement mounted when Mr. Rapp telephoned to say that the two thousand copies would be delivered within the week. When they arrived, we gazed with rapture at our first-born: *A Catalogue for the Easter Term containing divers matters relating to the History of the Book.* Our pals from the local post office provided us with a dozen mailsacks. Weighed and stamped, our precious burdens were loaded into a taxi bound for the Forty-fifth Street Post Office. Once they were piled on the ramp—"Take good care of them!" we implored—we stood together on the loading platform and embraced each other hysterically. Our first collaboration was on its way. What would its future—our future—be?

Almost immediately the future became the present. Within a week, more than half the catalogue had been sold, and many items could have been sold several times over. Item 42 was ordered by eight collectors, including Harvard and the Newberry Library, at which Leona tore her hair out and her puzzled mother commented, "Darling, I don't understand you. Why don't you buy several copies of your books at once?"

"Several copies" of Item 42 would indeed have been miraculous. Item 42 was an ephemeral article on "the Art of Paper War," written for a periodical, the *American Museum,* in May 1787. The article was illustrated by different contemporary type specimens, and its author, Francis Hopkinson, had made the curious suggestion that the emotions of joy, passion, and earnestness could be expressed by various type sizes and type faces. "The Art of Paper War" attracted so much attention that we ardently wished we could have supplied eight copies. As it was, the copy we sold had cost Leona nothing. Late one evening she had studied a catalogue issued by a New York dealer and found the Hopkinson listed. Despite the lateness of the hour, she had telephoned for it, only to be admonished for having interrupted a weary and irate bookdealer trying to enjoy a concert on the radio. She never expected to receive the Hopkinson. Much to her amazement, he posted it to her minus an invoice but with apologies for his impatience.

In ordering Item 42, along with four other items from Catalogue One, the distinguished Harvard librarian William A. Jackson wrote, "Congratulations on a very interesting catalogue—well written and with many unusual books in it . . . Keep up the good work."

Others, even those who did not order books, responded with praise and enthusiasm. Dr. R.W.G. Vail, Director of the New-York Historical Society, softened the blow of not ordering with a generous sprinkling of praise for a "very charming catalogue," its "valuable collection of material on the history of book making through the ages," and its "historical notes." Congratulations came from Leona's old friend John Fall of the New York Public Library and from the head of the John Crerar Library, who singled out for comment "the excellence of your cataloguing, your descriptive notes and your evaluation of the books presented. You deserve the best of success.'' Perhaps the most exciting letter came from the great type designer Bruce Rogers: "I have read your Catalogue . . . with great pleasure and profit. It throws many interesting, and to me, new, sidelights on bookmen that have long been familiar and others whom I had never heard of before . . . I congratulate you on issuing one of the most interesting catalogues I have ever seen."

We had savored the sweet taste of success. We had more than doubled our investment. But, more important, Catalogue One had earned for us the best of possible audiences for a bookseller— appreciative collectors, both institutions and individuals. Catalogue One also earned for us—shaped for us—our Catalogue Two.

One of the very few unsold items in our first catalogue was number 29, the 1674 stocklist of the House of Elzevier, a family firm of Dutch publishers who dominated the book production of seventeenth-century Europe. Our unsold stocklist cited twenty thousand items, from extravagant folios to small neat pocket editions of the classics and histories of European "republics." Our Catalogue Two would include 165 Elzevier publications that reflected political, historical, and literary aspects of the seventeenth century—the Age of Louis XIV, the Sun King, and the attitude of the Dutch against his aggression and conquest.

To obtain those books we expanded our sources of supply. We bought not only from foreign catalogues but from American auctions, notably the Freeman Sale in Philadelphia. In 1946 we made two trips to the City of Brotherly Love, the first to inspect several lots of Elzeviers to be auctioned by the firm of Samuel Freeman, the second to buy.

Item 29 in our Catalogue One now became item 45 in our Catalogue Two. Once again we studied our wares, sent our descriptions to Hubert Street for printing, and sent our catalogues forth upon the world. Within a week of distributing Catalogue One we had sold half the items. Within three weeks of distributing Catalogue

Two we had not even a single telephone order. What was wrong? Had we lost our touch? Had the seventeenth century no impact upon the twentieth? Or had something unforeseen happened? After a few phone calls to faithful customers, we learned that *The House of Elzevier* had never been delivered. We made our way once again to the Post Office at Forty-fifth Street and Lexington Avenue, where our catalogues had been deposited. The postal chief led us to a dark third floor and pointed to a pile of sacks in a particularly dark corner. "Yours?" he queried. We looked into the sacks. There, in utter and complete repose, lay *The House of Elzevier,* for reasons unknown completely overlooked by the United States Post Office. Our carefully prepared catalogues had all been given a long and unanticipated Poste Restante. Finally, they were distributed. When Catalogue Two reached its divers destinations, the phone began to ring again, telegrams and letters arrived, and life for Leona Rostenberg—Rare Books was up and running.

With the renewal of activity—the shipping of many packages to customers, the arrival of a few packages from foreign booksellers— we realized that our shelves were beginning to show too many empty spaces. When I entered the firm I had said, "You're going to need more billheads." The consensus now was that we were going to need more books as well.

The English catalogues from which we had bought whetted our appetites for early printed books. At the same time, many of the foreign booksellers with whom we had dealt during the last three years now sent "warm personal regards." We wondered about them. Had the time come for us to give them *our* regards in person? It is true that the newspapers painted a sorry picture of postwar England, with its food shortages, torn-up streets, lack of amenities. Very few if any American dealers had ventured abroad to buy books. Were we two spoiled Americans prepared for the grim reminders of war, the rationed food, the rationed comfort? The foreign catalogues we studied outweighed the newspapers we scanned.

We had both gone abroad several times before, separately; together we had worn glengarries and carried alpenstocks. Now, despite parental concern, we decided to embark upon what would be our first professional trip abroad. In April 1947 we visited the Holland-America Line on lower Broadway and purchased two tickets on the S.S. *Veendam*—destination Southampton.

BOOKS
AFTER THE BLITZ

Leona and Madeleine  Despite the excitements of the midnight sailing on July 29, 1947—the crowds of well-wishers, the cries of bon voyage, the band playing, the foghorn booming—our voyage aboard the S.S. *Veendam* was no luxury cruise. We were aware of this as soon as "All ashore that's going ashore" signaled the departure of our parents and friends. Our cabin on D deck was not only an inside one far below water level; it had no facilities. To reach the john, we had to climb a ladder to C deck. We also discovered that we were sharing the cabin with a third occupant, who turned out to be the friend of a friend, a woman who embodied for us the disruptions wrought by the war. Valerie Kunreuther was a refugee from Nuremberg. The daughter of wealthy German Jews, friends of Bismarck, she had been brought up by a governess. To escape the Nazi terror she and her husband had fled aboard the ill-fated *Navimar,* which was forced to land in Cuba. By the time she reached the States she had lost her husband and was compelled to earn her living by domestic service and catering. Now she was on her way to visit her daughter, who had settled in England and whom she had not seen in eight years. She made the war and its aftermath very real to both of us.

The effects of the war were reflected everywhere on board ship. There were no tourists or teachers but rather refugees returning to

locate Holocaust survivors. Queues formed everywhere for everything, from deck chairs to writing paper. The food was atrocious
and we spoiled Americans disposed of much of it through a port-
hole. Cream was available, but only in first class.

All this became insignificant when, after ten days, the *Veendam*
anchored off Southampton. A tender carried us to Southampton
Docks, now a temporary shelter that replaced the bombed original
and set the stage for what was to follow. The port's gaping holes,
shells of buildings, and glassless windows stunned us. On the train to
London we read the slogans designed for the war-weary: "Work or
Want"; "DON'T GROUSE!/When you miss your 'Roasts & Gravies'/
Give thanks for the Royal and Merchant Navies."

The capital of the British Empire was a dilapidated, bomb-
stricken city, a city in decay that formed the architectural backdrop
of our first professional quest for books. The boat train took us to
Waterloo Station, and from our corner room at the Cumberland
Hotel we looked out on the Marble Arch and Hyde Park. Southampton Docks had given us a foretaste of physical London. Our first
breakfast at the Cumberland gave us a foretaste of the trials of
postwar dining. In between the moldy cereal and the tea all the
waiters, clad in their fraying tailcoats, abandoned their tables, strik-
ing for higher wages than their ten shillings (two dollars) a week.
Actually, they had practically nothing to serve. We learned immediately that only three courses were allowed, and a roll constituted a
course. We were not permitted to spend more than five shillings
plus house charge for a meal. English weekly rations included one
ounce of lard, two of butter, and one rasher of bacon. Milk, except
for children, was not pasteurized. Horsemeat and whalemeat were
served instead of British beef. Fish was available, but we learned to
eye it with suspicion once we saw it in the markets—an iceless host
for hungry flies. The natives, threatened constantly with meatless
days, lived on their specialty: "bits and pieces."

In between the meals of postwar London, we wandered its sorry

streets in pursuit of our booksellers. In a letter home Leona characterized those highways: "There is not a spot in this great battered
city that has not been hit in the poorest section & in the best—just
gaunt walls to recall the Teutonic fury—and the buildings that do
stand are grey, splintered, ill kept." On our way to Charing Cross
Road, London's Booksellers' Row, we walked into a bombed-out
home and looked at its hanging rafters, singed boards, the plaster
and glass littering the ground. We saw with horror a bathtub hanging precariously on a third-story floorboard. At 118 Seymour Street
near the Cumberland we saw a walled-in garbage dump that had
once been a palatial home, and on the ground there was a single
square of old black-and-white tile still intact. "We entered a blitzed
building," Mady wrote to her mother, "finding broken glass and
rubble and gaping holes everywhere. In many places there is nothing
but emptiness, except for the red weed that grows up to cover the
emptiness." For us they became three almost obscene indicators:
the bathtub in midair, the bit of black-and-white tile, the red weed
encroaching.

We walked past gutted buildings and cluttered debris at which
only visitors stared. The Londoners no longer saw them. They were
far more concerned with muddling along as best they could, spending much of their day queuing for buses and theaters, queuing for
everything, especially food. They did not queue for clothing, for
everything in that category was so strictly rationed and so overpriced
that it remained unsold. If you had the necessary coupons, you could
buy a blouse made of parachute silk, worth three dollars, for six
times that amount. Whatever was coupon-free had a 100 percent
purchase tax added to the price. One hefty London woman informed us indignantly, "I need a permit from the Board of Trade to
get a bust supporter!"

The British seemed to us to be well equipped with grit but less
so with ingenuity. They persisted with their traditional forms. Waiters' coattails swished around sparse tables. Monocled gentlemen sat

at napkinless dinner places manipulating fish forks with languid elegance. Having suffered rockets and buzz bombs as well as points and rations, they somehow listened imperturbably to Clement Attlee's warnings over the wireless that things could be worse.

Although all of England seemed to want to flee to America, most of its countrymen had turned anti-American. In Hyde Park the orators targeted America in general and Wall Street in particular. Yet despite their distrust, they still looked to us for help. We were also reminded, at a tea party given by the British in-laws of Leona's cousin, that the poor Germans cannot be allowed to starve. We must forgive and forget.

At the bookshops it was easy for us to forget not only the "poor Germans" but the devastated English. For us two, prowling together through the pitted streets of London, climbing to the attics or basements of London's bookhouses, there was an abiding enchantment. In this worn and war-weary city we found our books and began to know our booksellers.

We started our book hunt in earnest on August 9, 1947. "Tuppence ha'penny, love." The conductor's voice was shrill, cheery, and warmly Cockney as the number 12 bus lunged down Oxford Street. We scrambled to the upper deck, secure in the knowledge that we had all of $2000 to spend on books, a world of dealers to meet, and treasures waiting for us in Mayfair and Bloomsbury, Soho and Holborn, Wimbledon and Golders Green.

Our first stop was on Berkeley Street. In the absence of the proprietor, Thomas Thorp, we were greeted by his associate, one Mr. Harris, bulbous-domed, stocky, who told us that the firm had lost forty thousand books in the Blitz. It seemed to us that they must have another forty thousand left, and among them we found a prize, an Italian architectural work by Domenico Fontana, published in Rome in 1590. Just a few years earlier, Signor Fontana had accomplished the remarkable feat of engineering described in the book. Back in the reign of Caligula, a great Egyptian obelisk had been brought to Rome. Centuries later, the Pope wished the obelisk moved from its ancient location to the front of St. Peter's, where all the world could see it. This triumph of engineering Fontana accomplished, and the book describing the transportation of the obelisk became an architectural landmark. We found it on Thorp's decimated but still crowded shelves and ordered it to be transported to East 179th Street in the Bronx.

Just so we found other exciting sixteenth-century books and met the colorful British dealers who had been no more than names on catalogues to us. It was only natural that the McLeish firm should have been among our very first targets. Had not the Pilgrim Press book that gave Leona Rostenberg—Rare Books its first coup come from 22 Little Russell Street? And so we bused, one of our first mornings in London, to the bright and comfortable shop, introduced ourselves to Mr. McLeish, and headed for his irresistible shelves. At the time we did not know he had a brother, and when we recorded our visit in our journals we described the proprietor as the affable Mr. McLeish. Later, when we published an article based on our 1947 European book hunt and referred to the affable Mr. McLeish he would twit us about which of the two brothers we had meant. The term covered both of them, as it turned out. They were affable, voluble, full of welcome and book talk. Their rooms were comfortable, and we decided that if ever we had an open shop we would also provide chairs and tables for scanning books and ash trays for the inevitable cigarettes. Now, in 1947, we found no Pilgrim Press book on the enticing shelves but we did find a few interesting rarities, including a 1508 legal discussion of whether or not hanged criminals should be buried, a 1511 first edition of the *Ship of Penitence* by a preacher at Leona's Strasbourg Cathedral, and a 1550 *Decameron,* adorned with a portrait of Boccaccio and ten large woodcuts. We were happy indeed with our first encounter with McLeish, though it would not be until a year later that we would be served tea and cake for "elevenses" in the room overlooking Little Russell Street.

Another bookshop nearby, Grafton's on Great Russell Street,

would be as unforgettable to us as McLeish, though for quite a different reason. The proprietrix, whom we assumed to be Mrs. or Madam Grafton, turned out to be neither. When we first met her, she was seated in a corner of the shop arrayed in a black silken cloak adorned with a garnet brooch, a wide-brimmed hat on her head, and a cup of tea in her hand. As a result of our later visits to her domain, we came to believe that she never moved from that location and almost never changed her attire. Certainly the hat would be a constant. Now, from her command position, she issued orders to her two assistants, the bibliographer Robert Peddie and the authority on the Elzeviers, H. B. Copinger. These two eminent scholars, advanced in years, were visibly cowed by their termagant employer. Before we could even glance at the shelves, she voiced the admonition, "You can buy the books, gels, but don't touch them!" We paid no attention and proceeded to remove from her shelves a most appropriate volume, the life of another more famous termagant, Catherine de Medici. Meantime the Grafton proprietrix expostulated about consular invoices and the difficulties of shipping to the States. She would greet us annually with her admonitions and complaints, to which we scarcely listened. Besides finding books at Grafton's we would learn more as the years passed about the cloaked and hatted proprietrix of 52 Great Russell Street, who turned out to be "Frank Hamel," author of popular historical novels.

During our first two days in London we bought fifty-one books. Some had been brought back to the city from safekeeping in warehouses; some had endured the Blitz in cellar hideouts; some bore traces of flame and damp; but all were survivors—survivors of Renaissance battles, survivors of twentieth-century devastation. At the palatial quarters of Maggs Brothers, at 50 Berkeley Square, we saw few signs of the war. The place breathed elegance. Its showcases displaying gleaming calfbound volumes intimidated these two novices. In 1947 we bought nothing from Maggs, but we carried away its essence. Maggs was, we decided, a champagne dealer.

We fared a little better at the great house of Bernard Quaritch, on Grafton Street, next to the Medici Galleries. The huge circular display cases lured without intimidating, and we carried off two trophies from the somewhat amused chief of staff, Mr. Edmund Dring. One was a discourse on peace of mind by a noble Renaissance lady, Isabella Sforza; the other was the first biography of the Queen of the Nile, who antedated Isabella by more than a millennium. When we returned home we would offer our Cleopatra to Katharine Cornell, who was impersonating her at the time on Broadway. The resulting phone call from her office declined our offer, but what did that matter? We had been in close contact with the greatest of all actresses—greater even than Cleopatra herself— whom we had long worshipped from afar.

On our first bookbuying trip to London we came to know two other legendary dealers, at least to begin to know them. Irving Davis, of the firm of Davis & Orioli, was more Italian than he was English. He was surely the Italianate Englishman incarnate. He scurried off to Italy at the slightest provocation and returned to London with his finds—all Italian, all sixteenth century, all, to us, magnificent. He looked like a keen-eyed elf, with goblin-like wisps of hair sprouting from his dome. He was a kind of literary hobgoblin. He talked incessantly, despite the omnipresent pipe he sucked on. And he introduced us to a world of Italian Renaissance books that we fell in love with. From his rooms on Maddox Street we carried off not only a Vasari life of Michelangelo but an indelible image of a personality, a character inextricably connected with the books that surrounded him.

Not far away was the domicile of the greatest scholar-dealer in early printed books. To us E. P. Goldschmidt, of 45 Old Bond Street, was the apex of learning, the nonpareil of booksellers, the patron saint of humanism, as well as the author of the definitive *Gothic and Renaissance Bookbindings*. Born on the continent, he had settled in London in his youth. We came to him as worshippers, but we also came to him with some trepidation. A homosexual, he had the reputation of not taking kindly to women. Besides, his schedule was a rigid one and had to be complied with. Since he worked at his books all night and never rose before noon, any appointment with him had to be set for after 4 P.M.

We conquered our fears and after 4 P.M. on an August afternoon followed Mr. Goldschmidt's assistant up the stairs to his book-lined sanctum. Leona's excitement was such that she missed the chair proffered by the elegant young man, Randall, and almost flopped on the carpeted floor. We recovered sufficiently to look around us. E. P. Goldschmidt sat like a deity at his desk. Behind him was a drip coffee pot, brewing and aromatic. Within easy reach was the fireplace, littered with his discarded cigarette butts. The smoke-filled air was dense. All around us were bookshelves holding magnificent bindings, folios in calf, pigskin, and vellum, pocket editions in tooled morocco, books that combined beauty and knowledge. In addition, wonder of wonders, E.P.G. seemed to take most warmly to us, chatting on about his books as easily as if they were friends. Year after year we were to return to 45 Old Bond, listening, telling our book stories, discussing bookish points with him. When he died a few years later, Leona wrote a brief recollection of him for *Antiquarian Bookman* that evoked a poignant response from a London colleague, who commented on her "flavored memory of E.P.G.," adding that "It brought back memories of his inimitable little anecdotes in that first-floor room . . . He used to tell me how you were his favourite 'in statu pupillo.' " Now, on our first visit to the Goldschmidt shrine, we were both enchanted, enchanted with his stories about his finds in Austria, his purchase of books from the famous Abbey of Melk, enchanted with him. Our only problem was—what to buy? "How much would this be, Mr. Goldschmidt?" we asked timorously, holding up a slim volume. "Oh, I should say only $75." "Would there perhaps be something a trifle less expensive?" He seemed to understand our predicament, and we were actually able to purchase from the god of our idolatry a Renaissance pamphlet for $11. Bemused, exalted, we walked back to the Cumberland on air.

Cecil Court was a far cry from Old Bond Street. It resembled to some extent New York's Fourth Avenue, lined then with small second-hand bookshops. A short alley intersecting Charing Cross Road, it was tenanted by antiquarian dealers whose cluttered stores were filled with promise. We might not be able to make a find at Quaritch or Goldschmidt, but here surely, in this warren of books, we might sleuth and make a discovery. The shop of E. Seligman was not easy to enter—books were piled on the floor and the bookshelves reached to the ceiling. There was a table in the center, but it too was so covered with books that it was scarcely discernible. In the back was a tiny office all but impossible to penetrate. There, at a cluttered desk, sat the proprietor. E. Seligman was a German refugee, a short man of short temper. When we tried to extricate a volume from a pile, he became quite irate, stamping his foot. We had the temerity of youth, however, and even ventured up a swaying ladder to his topmost shelves. A volume bound in pigskin caught our eyes and we descended the ladder to examine it. In our hands was a collection of sixteen sermons delivered by Martin Luther between 1519 and 1522. As we flipped the pages we noticed that one of them—the earliest, published in 1519—bore on the title page a woodcut portrait of the Reformer. We eyed each other. Was this the sleeper we had been hoping for? We knew that there was a portrait of Luther by the German artist Lucas Cranach, but we were sure that was done later. Was it possible that we had found Luther's first portrait? Seligman glanced over our shoulder. *"Ein schöner Sammelband,"* he commented. We agreed. The *"Sammelband,"* the collection, might be even *"schöner"* than Herr Seligman believed. We would have to make sure, of course, but our instincts were already quite certain. The 1519 sermon showing Martin Luther in his monk's habit just might be a landmark portrait. We bought other books that day from E. Seligman, all of which we had shipped to the Bronx. But the *"schöner Sammelband"* we carried carefully with us when we departed the haunts of Cecil Court.

The refugee from Germany was part of the postwar London scene, along with the battered buildings and the empty spaces where weeds grew. Several joined the rare book trade, and we met a few of them in 1947. Heinrich Eisemann, who lived in a rambling flat in Maida Vale, resembled an aging Mephistopheles. He would set a price only after he had consulted his "bible"—his huge inventory book—and had done the necessary mathematics aloud to himself in German, which he assumed we did not understand. With another refugee dealer we became far closer. Ernst Weil of Munich had become Ernest Weil of Golders Green, where he lived with his mother, his wife, his housekeeper, and his cat. He welcomed us with warmth, sold us a few books as he sat in his study with a fire going, and then marshaled us into the drawing room for *Kaffee und Kuchen*. There, overlooking the garden, we talked of the war and its aftermath, of America, and of books, while his mother coughed, his cat purred, and his wife urged us to eat more of the open sandwiches and the homebaked *Kugelhopf*.

It was still another dealer who epitomized for us the ravages of war. He was a refugee, not from Germany, but from life. A German bomb had found its target. During Francis Norman's absence, his wife and child had been killed, much of his stock destroyed. He lived alone in a cellar on Gower Street, where we searched through his dust-laden, fire-singed books while he played the piano. He lived and would continue to live in a private world, diffident, remote, unsure. Eventually he would move from Gower Street, but the grime and debris that surrounded him would always accompany him. He would remarry and have a new family, but essentially he would never change. He would carry with him, wherever he went, whatever he did, the unforgettable scars of war, and through him we would catch a glimpse of them.

In 1947 the journey from London to Paris was an all-day affair. It included several de luxe elegancies after the rigors of Britain. We boarded the *Golden Arrow,* a luxurious train well named, and at Dover we embarked on the *Invicta,* crossing the choppy waters of the Channel for Calais. There, the French alter ego of the *Golden Arrow* awaited us, the *Flèche d'Or.* The fancy waiters flying up and down the aisles introduced us to luxuries unknown to London tables—supplements of beef, melon, and creamy pastries. We were already not only in France but in another world.

More of that world became familiar to us, and we realized that, while England addressed the problems of postwar economy by rigorous official regulations and restrictions, France resorted to the black market. A luscious peach could be had for the outrageous price of fifty francs. Black market, however, did not control our breakfasts at the Hôtel Lutétia. There, ersatz dominated—ersatz coffee or ersatz tea—supplemented by a *confiture* from Africa and, as the maître d'hôtel put it, it was *"pas fameux."* The books in Paris were not *"fameux"* either. The bookstalls along the Seine offered postcards or modern paperbacks. Many of the antiquarian dealers were still closed for the *congé annuel.* We learned in 1947 to date our future Paris bookhunts with reference to unchanging French customs. There was little purpose in extending our stay in the city.

Instead, we revisited Strasbourg on the Rhine. More than ten years had passed since Leona studied there—ten appalling years. The bookshop where she had gazed upon Renaissance folios in pigskin bindings had nothing left of *livres anciens.* At the library, François Ritter greeted his erstwhile inamorata with deep affection and warmth, but his face betrayed the agonies that the Alsatian city had endured. We had carried our Luther *Sammelband* with us and we showed it to him. When he saw that vignette of Martin Luther on the title page of the 1519 sermon, he looked at it from every angle, took a deep breath, and made his judgment: *"C'est inconnu;* it is unknown. You have made a great discovery."

The city itself was a symbol of the war that had ended. The stained glass was gone from Strasbourg Cathedral. To us this became the hallmark of postwar Europe. Europe had lost its vibrancy, its *élan,* its color—Europe had lost its stained glass.

We two spoiled Americans, already war-weary, fled to Switzerland for rest and comfort. After the balm of white rolls and fresh eggs, the view of the Jungfrau from our windows, the familiarity of the sparkling Hoheweg, we were refreshed. Interlaken restored us, and en route to The Hague we took time off to visit Basle. There, we rushed forth to the Haus der Bücher, a bookshop on the Bäumleingasse, also known as the Erasmushaus. In that very building the great sixteenth-century Dutch humanist Desiderius Erasmus, author of the *Praise of Folly,* had lived for a time as the guest of the printer-publisher Froben. The stock room still had the original timbered ceiling of 1534, blackened now by age. Appreciating our deep interest, the proprietor, Herr Doktor Seebass, showed us around the domain of the "Stupor Mundi" Erasmus. He showed us books too, and to our delight we purchased some Renaissance beauties. The jewel that crowned our joy was a copy of Erasmus's *Praise of Folly—Moriae Encomium*—published in Paris in 1524 by the celebrated printer Badius and bound in blind-stamped morocco. A jewel in any crown.

The S.S. *Veendam* was to depart from Rotterdam in late September. We would stay in The Hague to be ready for our exodus. And in The Hague we would do our last-minute book hunting. We arrived by overnight train to find a city as shabby and dilapidated as Switzerland had been bright and shining. At the long-established firm of Martinus Nijhoff, on the Lange Voorhout, we were received by an elderly gentleman, Mr. Kern, who introduced us to what would become one of the passions of our life in books.

We were seated together at a table in his office when Mr. Kern brought to us a little collection of fifteen octavo French pamphlets printed between 1604 and 1610. Most of them were anonymous or pseudonymous, some supposedly by one Maître Guillaume, a cook, who, under the protection of Henry IV, became court fool. These little ephemeral nothings, brought together in a collection, seemed to assume significance for us. Leona especially, flipping through the pages, sensed in these evanescent issues the newspapers of their day, recording the political intrigues, the foreign alliances, financial problems, Turkish threats, bitterness between Catholic and Huguenot, battles fought, the longing for peace. The whole age seemed to be here in these nutshells. One of the pamphlets had an engraved title page, depicting the French soldier in full armor. Surely this was *multum in parvo*—pamphlets designed to be read hastily and thrown away, pamphlets that reflected the age that had spawned them, pamphlets that were now treasures. It seemed to us too that those pamphlets encapsulated in a way the postwar world we were about to leave. We too had been eyewitnesses, three and a half centuries later, to a gray peace born of war. This history we had seen ourselves.

We paid for our French pamphlets in guilders and took them away with us. From our first European book hunt we had assembled 280 books, for which we had paid about $2000. Now the adventure was over. It had given us some slight insight into a postwar world whose stained glass had been shattered. On September 19 we boarded our ship, bound for New York Harbor. Our fellow passengers included a few Jews who had survived the concentration camps and many non-Jewish Europeans in search of a better world. Among them was a young boy with a constant craving for sugar, which he had been denied. He sat at the table next to ours with his parents, who told us also that he did not know how to tell the truth, because he had been taught to lie constantly to the Nazi invaders about his identity. We gave him all our sugar; but we could not give him a sense of truth.

We two had a sense only of happiness. We were on our way to our own country. We were on our way home. "God help poor sorry Europe," we wrote in our diaries. "We rejoice because we can leave it, and because we have all our wonderful books, and because we are together."

FINGER-
SPITZENGEFÜHL

Leona and Madeleine   📖   As far as we know, the word *Finger-Spitzengefühl* never made it to a dictionary. It was originally Herbert Reichner who passed it on to us. A tingling of the fingertips becomes an electrical current of suspense, excitement, recognition. In an artificially controlled voice one of us calls to the other, "Look! This may be something." And two heads look down upon the title page of a discovery. Sometimes the *Finger-Spitzengefühl* occurs on the spot as we scan the shelves of a foreign dealer. Sometimes it takes place only after the purchase has been made and we study our find. Whenever or wherever it occurs, it is an experience that makes the rare book business a hymn to joy.

Through the decades, from "books after the Blitz" to our most recent bookhunts abroad, we felt our *Finger-Spitzengefühl* explode from time to time. Always on the lookout for ephemeral material, we'd glance over a pile of English Commonwealth decrees at a small dealer's in the West End of London. We'd stare hard at a slim quarto pamphlet issued in London in 1652, and suddenly Leona's *Finger-Spitzengefühl* began to erupt. She had done quite some research on seventeenth-century English printer-publishers, and the printer-publisher responsible for this little item was well known to her. He was named William Dugard and he had been the printer of several world-shaking items by one John Milton. Could John Milton have had anything to do with the pamphlet before us? It had been published in 1652, when Milton was Latin Secretary to the Commonwealth's Council of State, and it was a declaration of war by the Commonwealth against the States of Holland. Nowhere in the course of this Latin text was John Milton's name so much as mentioned. And yet, the *Finger-Spitzengefühl* was sending its electrical currents, and Leona was rapidly making connections.

Not until she studied the pamphlet carefully would she be able to establish the connection she so strongly suspected—that John Milton, as supervisor of state papers for the press, had indeed been involved with this indifferent-looking tract. As Latin Secretary to the Council of State he had prepared the text and supervised its printing. This modest-looking *Scriptum* of the Parliament of England bore the stamp and the style of the second greatest poet in the English language. Moreover, it had never before been assigned to or associated with Milton. Leona's *Finger-Spitzengefühl* had pointed the way to an extraordinary discovery that was promptly added to the great Milton collection at the University of Illinois.

It was at a larger and far better known London bookstore, at the famous address of 84 Charing Cross Road, that Mady's *Finger-Spitzengefühl* began its thrilling vibrations. Although we seldom deal in manuscripts, she was immediately drawn to a ninety-five-page handwritten notebook bound in Italian vellum, dated 1820, and filled with pen-and-ink sketches. The notebook, she saw, had been kept by one William Paget, and it recorded a journey he had made to Italy between April and October. As Leona had immediately thought of John Milton when she saw the Latin *Scriptum,* Madeleine thought of Percy Bysshe Shelley when she flipped through the autograph pages describing the streets of Pisa, the sights of Genoa and Leghorn, Lucca and Florence. Had not Shelley visited the Italian villages and cities at the very same time as Mr. Paget? Had he not written his "Witch of Atlas," his "Skylark," and his "Sensitive Plant" there? Paget's notebook was filled with descriptions not only of vine and olive but of food and dress, theaters and carriages, the politics that followed the "iron reign of Napoleon." All this Shelley too had experienced at the same time.

And so the little notebook that William Paget had bought in Pisa to preserve his Italian impressions was a vicarious source for Shelley's life. Unknowing, the traveler had followed in Shelley's footsteps and seen the Italy that was enchanting the great poet. Paget's sketches and notes set the scene for Shelley's Italian drama. The *Finger-Spitzengefühl* had given its electrical signal. The link had been made. A previously unknown source in the Romantic movement had been uncovered at 84 Charing Cross Road. It can be viewed today in the renowned Shelley collection of the Pforzheimer Library.

We discovered more than a Romantic source in a bookshop at one end of the rue Bonaparte—actually, we discovered a continent. True, we weren't aware of all this when we found the sixteen-page French pamphlet printed in Paris in 1617. We were aware of enough, however, to set the *Finger-Spitzengefühl* in action. We had come upon a small group of eight unbound seventeenth-century French tracts, the kind of ephemera we had learned to love. One of them had a couple of words in its title that electrified the *Finger-Spitzengefühl*. The title read: *Copie de la Reqveste Presentee Av Roy d'Espagne . . . sur la descouuerte de la cinquiesme Partie du monde, appellee la terre Australle*—or *Copy of the Request Presented to the King of Spain on the Discovery of the Fifth Part of the World called the Austral Land*. Although Austral Land sounded to us very like Australia, we thought at the same time that this might have been a fiction or a hoax. How could it possibly be the report of the discovery of a fifth percent of the planet Earth, here at the end of the rue Bonaparte, here now in our hands?

We made a lot purchase of the eight pamphlets for the equivalent of $2.90, and calmed down. It was only when we returned home and studied our pamphlet that we realized, with mounting excitement, that we had indeed made a great discovery. Reading the pamphlet was for us like reading a serialized suspense page-turner. It had been written by Pedro Fernandes de Queiros, who, we learned, had been a Portuguese navigator in the service of Spain. In 1606 he had sailed from Peru and found what he believed to be a new continent. He named it Australia del Espiritu Santo, and he claimed it for the Spanish crown. When he returned from his explorations he wrote about his discovery, asking for funds and ships to colonize his newfound land. One of the requests he had circularized was on our desk. In it the enthralled navigator described the Terre Australle as a fifth part of the terrestrial globe. It was populated by Indians, he wrote, and its soil was fertile, its rivers and forests fruitful, its birds beautiful. It was rich, he said, in silver and pearls, spices and natural resources. It was comparable if not superior to America or Peru, Nicaragua or the Philippines. Whether or not our author had actually discovered Australia—a fifth part of the universe—he thought he had. And his memorandum, our *Reqveste,* was cited in scholarly bibliographies of books and pamphlets relating to Australia.

There are thousands of seventeenth-century French pamphlets on every subject imaginable, from the Huguenot wars to peace alliances, from the birth of a dauphin to the death of a king, from the price of wheat to the cost of a burial. Individually they did not command a great price when we began to forage for them. Indeed, many were tagged at no more than the paltry sum we had paid for our Fernandes de Queiros: thirty-seven American cents. During the decades that have passed since that purchase, its price has risen. At one time we saw our *Reqveste* listed in a dealer's catalogue for $2000. More recently, the English translation of our pamphlet was estimated not in four but in five figures. Fernandes had found, he thought, a new continent. We had found, we knew, a pot of gold. But—far more important—we too had adventured and explored, and, like our Portuguese navigator, we too had been discoverers.

In his way, Pierre Samuel Du Pont had also traveled widely. The distinguished French statesman and philosopher had, we knew,

helped implement foreign recognition of our United States, and in
1799 had voyaged to America, where he worked with Thomas Jef-
ferson. He had also fathered Éleuthère Irénée Du Pont, founder of
the E. I. Du Pont de Nemours Company. In 1947, when we were
looking for our books after the Blitz, we visited the Welshman Ifan
Kyrle Fletcher at his home in Wimbledon and there had taken from
a shelf a volume bound in boards, published in Paris in 1799, entitled *Philosophie de L'Univers*. It was the work of our pro-American
French philosopher Pierre Samuel Du Pont. Indeed, there was a
finely engraved portrait of the author in the book and there was also
an author's presentation inscription. *"À Myladi Davy,"* he had written, *"avec les respects de l'Auteur."* We knew who the author was, all
right, and we were fairly certain we knew to whom he had inscribed
his respects. Surely "Myladi Davy" must have been the wife of the
great English chemist Sir Humphry Davy. We added Monsieur Du
Pont to our little pile of Wimbledon purchases, and when we returned home decided to offer him straightaway to the current head
of the Du Pont empire, the bibliophilic Irénée Du Pont.

Irénée was receptive but also skeptical. Our *Finger-Spitzengefühl*
may have assured us that Pierre Samuel Du Pont had inscribed his
work to Sir Humphry Davy's wife, but our *Finger-Spitzengefühl* was
not trustworthy enough for Irénée. "I already have 35 copies of my
ancestor's disquisition," he informed us, but if we could *prove* that
the author had actually given this particular copy to Sir Humphry
Davy's wife, he would add it to his collection. We took up the
challenge. We would prove not only that the lady in question was the
recipient of Du Pont's gift, but that our sparkling *Finger-Spitzengefühl*
was to be trusted. The Davys themselves collaborated in our research. At the New York Public Library we learned that Sir Humphry Davy had not only conducted revolutionary chemical experiments but had kept a diary. Obligingly, he had recorded in it a visit
he and his wife had made in 1799 to Nemours. That was the year Du
Pont's book had been published. Nemours was the location of Du

Pont's home. We put two and two together, found they equaled *Finger-Spitzengefühl,* and made a little sale to Irénée Du Pont.

With happenings like these punctuating the early years of Leona Rostenberg—Rare Books, the partners rejoiced in the firm's expansion. It was appropriate for the Du Pont empire to play a small part in that process. By 1948 we felt a kinship with the family and therefore hastened to inform them that a forthcoming New York auction was featuring numerous items by the eminent French chemist Antoine Lavoisier, a close friend of their illustrious forebear. Our letter, which listed estimated prices, was immediately acknowledged by a telegram: "Letter with estimated prices received. Will take any one or all of collection at higher prices named by you . . . Total . . . amount may be used to acquire the total list regardless of price of individual items." The Du Ponts had placed such trust in us that we could not help wondering whether they were confusing the name Rostenberg with the renowned name Rosenbach. Years later, when the family asked us to appraise two Du Pont collections, we would be assured that no such confusion had occurred.

Yale University Library played a more important role than the Du Ponts in our development. We metamorphosed ourselves into itinerant peddlers and journeyed periodically to New Haven. Each of us carried a satchel of small, carefully selected sixteenth-century volumes, some of which we had "enhanced" with our own decorative wrappers. It was always a special day when we tripped aboard the New York, New Haven and Hartford Railroad or sped along the Connecticut Turnpike for Yale University, for at the end of the trip Donald Wing was waiting to receive us.

His office was crammed with books, fileboxes, shoeboxes filled with his bibliographical slips. An old folio volume supported one leg of his desk, and the desk itself was obliterated under a mass of catalogues, quotations, reports—and, of course, books. A library van stood in a corner, teetering under the weight of books. "If you can find a chair, sit down," Donald Wing remarked laconically in his gravelly, nasal twang. He was tall, gaunt, slightly stooped. He was enamored of his profession. When, years later, he was interviewed by the *New York Times,* he said of his lifetime in books, "It has been marvelous. I have actually been paid to read second-hand catalogues." After some small talk we opened our satchels and he placed the books on an empty van. "I'll check them myself right away." Then, as he eyed our homemade wrappers, he chuckled and commented, "Boudoir bindings?" Within an hour he returned. Our books were now in two sections of the van. "I want the books on the top shelf. Have the ones below. Nice to have you come. Visit me again."

Trips to Yale, Harvard, and Cornell swelled our income. No one confused us with Rosenbach, but from time to time we *felt* like Rosenbach, and soon we began the search for a downtown office.

In 1948 the *New York Times* carried our ads under "Business Places Wanted." What we wanted was a "Store, or first-floor front room, for rare book business between the East 40s and the East 70s." Periodically, we inspected possibilities, including one on Herbert Reichner's East Sixty-second Street. But our search was desultory. Although we might *dream* about some ideal open shop in mid-Manhattan that would attract the elite among collectors and librarians, we were always of two minds about implementing such a dream. For this ambivalence there was a powerful reason.

We did not wish to curtail our freedom with the nine-to-five schedule necessitated by an open shop. We were both working not only on rare books but on what we liked to call "our own books"— the books and articles we were researching and writing. Confined during business hours to an open shop, we could not go to the library whenever we wished and spend long days in research; we could not visit Concord or Cambridge whenever the spirit moved us. The double lives we had begun to lead would be in jeopardy if we had to keep tight office hours. And, to ensure the rent of a downtown office, those hours would indeed be tight and long. And so we continued as we had been, enhancing our Bronx quarters with magnificent glass-enclosed oak and mahogany bookcases and retaining the freedom of our double lives.

The midcentury was momentous for us. Nineteen-fifty brought us the worst and the best. For Leona it was the year of her father's death:

> *For a long time I had known of his heart ailment and I had dreaded the approach of finality. When it actually happened it was not only tragedy but melodrama. I customarily had dinner at Mady's on Tuesdays, and so I was not present when it happened. My uncle had been invited to the Bronx that evening, and he collapsed at the table. My father—ever the doctor, despite his weak heart—rose to help him and he too collapsed. Babette phoned and summoned me home. Mady and I confronted a house filled with police and a mother overwhelmed by tragedy and loss. I quickly realized that my uncle had had a fatal seizure, but I was not aware of my father's death until later. He had been stricken while trying to help his brother-in-law and had died immediately. The shock of the double tragedy soon gave way to unadulterated grief for my darling father. For months I was assailed with an obsessive selfish grief. I could no longer tell him about my little triumphs; I could not take delight in his delight with our growing success. Part of me was cut off.*

In contrast, that same year of 1950 held jubilation too, for it was the year when Mady's *Louisa May Alcott* was published:

Madeleine 📖 IN AN ARTICLE I HAD WRITten for *Publishers Weekly* on "The Mystery of the Leon Brothers"— two Polish refugees who had become New York booksellers and issued the first catalogue of American first editions in 1885—the editors inserted a biographical note about "Miss Stern," concluding with the statement that I had "recently completed, under a grant from the Guggenheim Foundation, a biography of Louisa M. Alcott.'' Aware that public interest was centered less in the career of Louisa May Alcott than in books about the aftermath of World War II, E. P. Dutton had waived its option on my second book. Unlike Dutton, Savoie Lottinville, head of the University of Oklahoma Press, responded enthusiastically to the note in *Publishers Weekly,* immediately asking me to send him my manuscript. The war had not stifled his interest in the Alcotts; moreover, he had recently accepted a biography of Louisa's mother, *Marmee,* by Sandford Salyer. Savoie Lottinville, as astute as he was charming, appreciated the chance of a companion piece for *Marmee* and contracted to publish my *Louisa May Alcott.*

He announced it as a reconstruction of Alcott's life ''as she lived it, integrated with the period in which she lived,'' and he also noted that it contained a bibliography of Alcott's writings, ''including the newly identified pseudonymous and anonymous stories.'' Advance sales were gratifying; reviews were appreciative, many of them emphasizing the breakthrough on Louisa Alcott and her pseudonym. Perhaps the highest compliment was paid by the *Book-of-the-Month Club News,* which stated: ''It is very nearly as absorbing to come upon this intimate, affectionate and detailed biography of Louisa May Alcott and her family as it was to read *Little Women* as a child.'' A British edition was published, and a film made by Encyclopaedia Britannica Films. The voluminous correspondence evoked by the biography included one letter that I found especially heartening. It was from the son of Louisa's young Concord friend Alf Whitman, to whom she had written that remarkable letter: ''I intend to illuminate the Ledger with a blood & thunder tale as they are easy to 'compoze' & are better paid than moral & elaborate works of Shakespeare.'' In it, John Pratt Whitman wrote to me, ''You are the first biographer to recognize fairly my father's part in the boy Laurie, and you have done it splendidly and convincingly. It is to be hoped an end has been made to a narrow kind of provincialism in Concord that grows irate at any suggestion that 'Alf Whitman' was the American half of the hero of *Little Women*." And he ended his letter with the request: "I hesitate, knowing Louisa's dread of autograph seekers, to ask you for yours to the son of Laurie, that I can paste in the fly leaf of this, my new and much prized book."

All this was sufficient to spur me on to my next biography and to apply the revelations of *Finger-Spitzengefühl* to yet another nineteenth-century American woman. As usual, one thing led to another: Louisa Alcott introduced me to Mrs. Frank Leslie, journalist, editor, publisher, and colorful combination of feminist and femme fatale. Mrs. Leslie may have inspired one of Louisa Alcott's blood-and-thunders; actually, her second husband had accepted Alcott's prize story "Pauline's Passion and Punishment," and it was his letter of acceptance that led me to the subject of my next biography.

The woman who became Mrs. Frank Leslie was then named Miriam Squier. She was known by several names during her long lifetime, some but not all based upon her marriages, of which she had four. Her last husband was Oscar Wilde's unstable brother Willie; her next to the last was the New York publishing magnate Frank Leslie, whose periodicals were nineteenth-century household words. His seductive wife became his irresistible widow, manager of his vast publishing empire, salon leader, woman of affairs public and private, feminist who bequeathed two million dollars to the cause of woman suffrage. Needless to say, such a woman prized public acclaim far above accuracy, especially in matters concerning her own life. If the arts of detection were recommended for the reanimation of Louisa May Alcott, they would be absolutely essential for that of Mrs. Frank Leslie.

And so, in the preparation of that life, one challenge after another demanded whatever detective skills I had come to possess. Ferreting out one very private fact was particularly challenging. By 1878 my heroine, in her early forties, had weathered two marriages,

The house on the hill, the Bronx.

A CATALOGUE
for the
EASTER TERM

containing divers matters
relating to the
History of the
BOOK

LEONA ROSTENBERG
Rare Books
152 EAST 179th STREET
NEW YORK 53, N. Y.

1946

*"*O*ur firstborn."*

*B*ound *for the hunt on the S.S.* Veendam, *1947.*

*M*adeleine *and Leona on the prowl, London, 1948.*

*T*wo *sleuths at work. Madeleine and Leona in the office, 1953.*

Catalogue 22

THE MAN OF THE RENAISSANCE

LEONA ROSTENBERG
Rare Books
152 EAST 179th STREET
NEW YORK 53, N. Y.
Tel.: TR 8-2789

The spirit of the Renaissance, 1954.

Madeleine and Leona at the
National Library, Vienna, 1954.
Old books and . . .

. . . new wine. Leona and Madeleine at the Heuriger, Vienna, 1954.

PERTH ASSEMBLY.

CONTAINING

1 The Proceedings thereof.
2 The Proofe of the Nullitie thereof.
3 Reasons presented thereto against the receiving the fiue new *Articles* imposed.
4 The oppositenesse of it to the proceedings and oath of the whole state of the Land. *An.*1581.
5 Proofes of the unlawfulnesse of the said fiue Articles, *viz.* 1. Kneeling in the act of Receiving the Lords Supper. 2. Holy daies. 3. Bishopping. 4. Private Baptisme. 5. Priuate Communion.

EXOD. 20. 7.

Thou shalt not take the name of the Lord thy God in vaine, for the Lord will not hold him guiltlesse that taketh his name in vaine.

COLOS. 2. 8.

Beware lest there be any that spoyle you through Philosophy & vain deceit,through the traditions of men, according to the rudiments of the World,and not of Christ.

MDCXIX.

Leona's first great find: A Pilgrim Press Book issued secretly by William Brewster, Leyden, 1619.

IL LIBRO DEL CORTEGIANO DEL CONTE BALDESAR CASTIGLIONE.

AL   DVS.

The Aldine device of the anchor and dolphin on the title page of Castiglione's Courtier, *1528— now the Doubleday colophon.*

Hassi nel priuilegio,& nella gratia ottenuta dalla Illustrissima Signoria che in questa,ne in niun'altra Citta del suo dominio si possa imprimere, ne altroue impresso uendere questo libro del Cortegiano per·x· anni sotto le pene in esso contenute ·

*D*ressed for dinner. An
English Association party at
Quaglino's, London, 1965.

*L*eona and Madeleine "on
tenterhooks" with a $25,000
bid, Streeter sale, 1968.

L<small>eona</small> *sits for her portrait*
as ABAA president, 1973.

M<small>adeleine</small> *sits for her*
portrait for the New York
Times, 1973.

*"D*r. *Leona Rostenberg: Columbia U reverses itself," annus mirabilis 1973.*

*A*s the New York Times *saw us, 1974.*

BOOKS PUBLISHED
DURING
SHAKESPEARE'S LIFETIME

Catalogue 84

LEONA ROSTENBERG & MADELEINE B. STERN

Members ABA-ABAA
Box 188 — Gracie Station
New York, N.Y. 10028
Tel.: [212] 831-6628
BY APPOINTMENT:
40 East 88 Street, New York, N.Y. 10028

1564–1616: Our 1980 catalogue honoring the bard.

At our booth at the first Bryn Mawr College Library bookfair, May 1976.

Old and Rare with dachshund Bettina, East Hampton, 1993.

and as the wife of Frank Leslie she was a decorative and useful adjunct to his publishing domain. She was also the author of a travel book, *California: A Pleasure Trip from Gotham to the Golden Gate,* in which she excoriated the Nevada mining town of Virginia City as the "god-forsaken" home of forty-nine gambling saloons with a population largely masculine, except for a few women "of the worst class." Virginia City took exception to her remarks. Its newspaper, the *Territorial Enterprise,* headed by a fighting editor, devoted the first page of its July 14, 1878, issue to an anonymous article, "Our Female Slanderer," including her "Life Drama of Crime and Licentiousness," with "Startling Developments."

Among those "Developments" was the following revelation about Miriam at age twenty-one: "About this time a Congressman from Tennessee put in an appearance . . . A house was bought in Seventh Street, in New York . . . and put upon the record in her name." This was a tempting allegation for Miriam Leslie's biographer, and I felt impelled to identify the congressman in question. Unfortunately for my purpose, Tennessee sent eleven representatives and two senators to Congress, and the task of identifying Miriam's particular congressman seemed hopeless.

The one distinguishing fact about the congressman was that he had purchased a house—not, to be sure, in his own name, but in Miriam's. Detection must center, then, on the conveyances of the Seventh Street property deposited in New York City's Hall of Records. Sure enough, I found an indenture dated April 29, 1857, indicating that one Miriam F. Follin (her maiden name) had paid $9000 for the ground and dwelling at 37 Seventh Street. I was probably the only living person who realized that, since Miriam Follin had been impecunious in 1857, the statement had to be spurious. My Tennessee congressman was definitely in hiding. I had to search for further relevant conveyances of the property.

The next indenture was of interest mainly for its date: September 15, 1857. Miriam had obviously not held "her" Seventh Street residence for long. On that day, I learned, she had sold it for $9000 to a merchant, one Perez D. Gates. The Tennessee congressman was laundering his property. He did not come out of hiding till I found a third indenture. On December 2, 1857, the house of assignation was sold by Perez D. Gates to William M. Churchwell of Tennessee. Mr. Churchwell turned out to be not only a citizen of but a congressman from Tennessee. The conveyances in New York's Hall of Records had turned into gossipy disclosures, giving me a biographical tidbit in the mosaic of an intriguing life.

My biography of Mrs. Frank Leslie, entitled *Purple Passage,* appeared over the University of Oklahoma Press imprint in 1953 and aroused the attention her fascinating career deserved. Although the book was finished and published, my pursuit of Mrs. Frank Leslie had not ended. It soon appeared that the art of detection was still needed in connection with one particular copy, which I learned about in another biography, a work about Max Beerbohm, the caricaturist and wit, by the playwright S. N. Behrman. To my astonishment I read that, knowing of Beerbohm's association with Oscar and Willie Wilde, Behrman had lent him "a book about Mrs. Frank Leslie" who had married Willie Wilde. According to *Portrait of Max,* Beerbohm "picked up the book and a pencil and, on the inside of the back cover, rapidly sketched Oscar and Willie for me. These are probably the last drawings Max ever did . . . they are quite remarkable." Max then proceeded to give "the now illustrated book" to Behrman.

Just as I had had to identify the congressman from Tennessee, so I had to possess this book. I opened a correspondence with Mr. Behrman, who informed me that he intended to leave the copy to Harvard's Houghton Library. Behrman's return address was 40 East Eighty-eighth Street—a detail that would take on some significance years later, when Leona and I moved to that very address. Meanwhile, I let some time pass before I returned to the pursuit and once again plied Mr. Behrman for permission, if not to purchase the copy, at least to view it. This time I was informed that the "deal" with Houghton Library had not materialized and the book had disappeared. Now the detective in me had to start sleuthing. I reminded Mr. Behrman that his *Portrait of Max* had been published by Random House, which had reprinted the "two marvelous caricatures" of the Wildes in the book. They must have had the copy at one time. Perhaps they still did.

Behrman's response was swift: "Your letter . . . threatens to bring Purple Passage back to me." A search disclosed it in the Random House safe. Behrman concluded his note: "When this book arrives I will at once telephone you."

A lengthy silence followed, broken by my doggerel reminder:

Dear Mr. Behrman, S. N.
Let me hear from you once again.

Alas, as Max Beerbohm had followed the Wildes to the grave, so S. N. Behrman followed Max. The widow Behrman called upon a colleague of ours to appraise her late husband's library, and I made a generous offer for the Beerbohm-illustrated copy of *Purple Passage*. That was a long time ago. I have not only been unable to purchase the copy; I have never seen it.

No—not all detection is fruitful, and not all sleuthing is successful. Despite our many exciting finds, we have suffered keen disappointments. In Cambridge, England, one year we visited the shop of R. C. Pearson, M.A., located on Hobson Street. His stock on the whole was indifferent, but just before our departure Leona suddenly entered an advanced state of agitation. She was looking at a quarto volume by one Elias Herckmans, printed in Dutch in 1634 and profusely illustrated. Its title, *Der Zeevaertlof*, or *Praise of a Sea Voyage*, rang a bell. Either from her years with Reichner or from one of the thousands of catalogues she had studied, she knew there was something unique about that book. One of its seventeen illustrations, she was certain, was by Rembrandt. How much higher could a book-seller aspire? Afraid to draw the attention of R. C. Pearson, M.A., to her find, she did not dare to hunt for the prestigious plate by the great artist, but simply added the volume to the small pile we had selected and told Mr. Pearson to send them on.

We returned to London in a state of unsubdued excitement. On a visit to E. P. Goldschmidt we discussed our find, and the great E.P. was duly impressed. He destroyed any doubt we may have had. That single plate by Rembrandt made the book one of the most desirable illustrated works of the seventeenth century. The *Zeevaert-lof* would more than pay for our *Zeevaert*.

Back home, with irrepressible anticipation, we opened the package from Hobson Street, Cambridge, England. Tremulously we began leafing through the illustrated quarto. It must have seventeen plates. We began to count them. Something was wrong. We counted again. We saw a telltale stub from which a print had been cut away. Our copy of the *Zeevaertlof* had only sixteen plates. Rembrandt van Rijn was in absentia. Sometime after 1634 an ardent print collector or ruthless printseller had extracted the engraving from the book and destroyed its stature. Sadder and wiser, we sent it back to England on what was probably its final *Zeevaert*.

The disappointments were always hard to take, especially when they concerned the truly great figures in art—like Rembrandt—or in literature—like John Milton. By the early 1950s we felt a close affinity with the author of *Paradise Lost*. Had not Leona unearthed his association with a Parliamentary *Scriptum* of 1652, and had not Madeleine spent much of her English Honors course at Barnard reading his soaring iambics? And so, we were ever on the prowl for John Milton.

Once again I believed I had found him at a bookshop in London's St. John's Wood during our annual buying trip. I quickly descended a ladder, a small calfbound volume in my hand, my eyes round with wonder, the book open to the title page. "Look at this!'' I whispered dramatically to Leona. The sight that had stopped my breath was an ownership inscription inked on the margin of the title page: "Jn Milton." Could this, by the remotest possibility, have been a book touched, and read, and owned by John Milton? To us at the moment there was every likelihood that he had indeed written his name on the title page of Giovanni Marliani's *Vrbis Romae Topographia (Topography of the City of Rome)*. The book we held in our hands had been published in Venice in 1588 and was a guidebook, a kind of Baedeker, to the marvels of the Eternal City. It had been designed for the Roman tourist, and in the late 1630s Milton had been a tourist in Rome. What more likely than that he had purchased a guidebook during his visit and placed his name on its title page? We could not hesitate. It was true that the name John Milton was not uncommon, but if it was *the* John Milton, then we would have ascended so high into the empyrean that someday we might even find a volume that had belonged to another bard—from Avon.

Holmes and Watson donned their deerstalkers as soon as they returned home. The multivolume Columbia Edition of Milton on the New York Public Library's open shelves contained a chapter on John Milton's library. The books traceable to the poet's collection were listed. The list included, as a possibility, the Marliani—*our* Marliani—and the ownership inscription reproduced was identical with ours. According to the Columbia Milton, the volume so signed had been sold at a London auction in the 1920s and after that seemed to have vanished.

"We own a book that Milton owned!" To that refrain we awoke each day; to that refrain we retired each night. It had been, my dear Watson/my dear Holmes, elementary. Too elementary. We reminded ourselves once again that nothing is elementary. Although the book bore the signature "Jn Milton," and although it had been mentioned in the Columbia Milton, we still had no firm proof that the signature was that of the poet and that the book had actually been his property. Milton's signature changed almost yearly. Our attempt to compare our example with the various facsimiles of those known to have been his was fruitless. We must seek out a Milton expert to verify our hope.

We found the expert, the late Professor Harris Fletcher, of the University of Illinois, who was skeptical: "Just send me a copy of the title page." We waited while our daily and nightly refrain underwent a slight change: "Do we own a book that Milton owned?" A telephone call from Illinois soon answered the query. "This is Robert Downs, Director of the University of Illinois Libraries." Holmes and Watson exchanged triumphant glances. "It's about that Milton signature." Holmes and Watson began respective calculations in mental arithmetic. "Professor Fletcher wants me to tell you it's an eighteenth-century forgery."

Leona and Madeleine   📖   AFTER CONSID-
erable correspondence with the Curator of Cornell's Department of Rare Books, we followed his suggestion and took our first selling trip to Ithaca, New York. Felix Reichmann was a charmer; now middle-aged, he had been a refugee from Vienna and still exuded continental bonhomie. We took to each other immediately. He selected many books from our satchel and we heard much gossip about European prewar booksellers, including of course Leona's irascible Herbert Reichner. We also heard the fascinating story of another, earlier political refugee from Europe and of a sensational book he had written.

"In 1822," Reichmann began, "a young Moravian monk named Karl Anton Postl disappeared from a monastery in Prague. He was fleeing," Reichmann continued, "from the dictatorial rule of Metternich, and after one year had passed Postl turned up in the city of New Orleans with a new identity and a new name—Charles Sealsfield." As Sealsfield he would write many books before his death in

1864, but the one that Felix Reichmann lusted after was entitled *Austria As It Is*. Published anonymously in 1828, it was a vitriolic denunciation of the kind of Austrian misrule that had made refugees of both the author and the Cornell curator. *Austria As It Is* had been banned as libelous by the Teutonic authorities. Today it was scarce indeed. Felix Reichmann craved a copy. And we determined we would find one for him.

A few years later, during a book hunt abroad, we visited a dealer new to us, a nondescript gentleman named Burke, whose shop in the outskirts of London seemed at the end of the Underground. Our letters home recorded the event:

> L made a splendid find yesterday. Here's the story: At a small dealer's, Burke's . . . in an area smelling of bubble and squeak, she spied—on his Travel shelves—Austria As It Is. It's really not a travel book at all, but an anonymous satire that was banned, & it has a fascinating history. Ever since we were alerted to it we've been hoping to find it. L grabbed it & only her unusual loquaciousness & pleasantries would have warned a dealer who knew her that something out of the ordinary had happened. It's a splendid copy but Burke knew nothing about it and priced it at 10 bob—$1.40.

Like its author, *Austria As It Is* took up a new life in America; Felix Reichmann was overjoyed; and we two thanked our serendipitous stars that we had heard its story and taken a long ride in the Underground.

The Prince of Serendip was more attentive to us in Paris than in London. As Felix Reichmann had alerted us to an intriguing political excoriation, a French colleague alerted us to a Utopian political manifesto. Michel Bernstein was a survivor of the war; he and his wife had been members of the Resistance, printing counterfeit stamps to foil the Germans. As a rare bookdealer he appropriately specialized in political ideology, of which he was a master. We were introduced to him—one had to be formally introduced before he would take one on as a new customer—and we became among his elect.

In the Paris district Issy-Les-Moulineaux he presided over a small and dilapidated château, which housed his wife, Monique, his boxer, Zouboulou, and his magnificent collection of books and pamphlets on political theory and French history. His extreme erudition was surpassed only by his Gallic patriotism: Monsieur Bernstein actually believed that the French Revolution had influenced the American! We visited him annually for many years, studying his *fiches,* or descriptive slips, and handing him our selections. Short, pale, precise, he would look at them, nod approvingly, walk to his ceiling-high bookcases, his gummed shoes creaking, immediately find the work he sought, and proudly carry it to us. He spoke nothing but French, although we were sure he understood many languages. A day with Monsieur Bernstein was guaranteed to exhaust—but it was also an education. It was he who educated us about the desirability of a certain discourse by a celebrated French publicist.

By then Monsieur Bernstein had moved to the heart of the Left Bank in the Sixth Arrondissement, the center of the antiquarian trade. His procedure, however, was unchanged. As we were going through his *fiches,* Leona picked out a slip describing a *Discours sur la Polysynodie,* by the Abbé Saint-Pierre, published in 1719. As Monsieur Bernstein brought the little octavo to us, he looked down his nose at it and remarked, "This second edition is nothing much. But, my friends, if ever you find this book in its first edition of 1718 in a larger, quarto format—buy it. Buy it, whatever it costs, and then sell it to me. I have been looking for it all my life, and I would pay anything to own it." When we inquired about his reasons, Monsieur Bernstein explained that the Abbé Saint-Pierre had described in his *Polysynodie* a new plan of government and had produced a great landmark in the history of political theory. However, like most innovations, his discourse had been regarded as anti-establishment and had been censored. Its printer was arrested and nearly all copies of this first edition had been suppressed. If any was still around, it was "rarissime."

A few days after Monsieur Bernstein's lecture on the Abbé Saint-Pierre's revolutionary treatise, we strolled the cobbled walks of the Left Bank to the rue des Écoles and entered the bookshop of Monsieur Thiebaud. Despite his blue eyes and white hair, Monsieur Thiebaud closely resembled a wily fox. He was guarded by three female assistants while he guarded his establishment, especially the upstairs portion, from any undesirables. Although we were always welcome to the main floor, we were not permitted to the upper floor, which contained not only Monsieur Thiebaud's uncatalogued recent acquisitions but his W.C.—a situation that often made for some uncomfortable moments. On this particular occasion, however, we were well content with the main floor. Almost as soon as we entered the establishment and glanced at the bookshelves, we saw in front of us a large quarto volume bound in calf with the arms of a nobleman impressed in gilt on the spine. We drew it from the shelf. This time we really could not believe our eyes. Monsieur Bernstein had given us a lengthy lesson on the first edition of the *Discours sur la Polysynodie,* published in 1718 in quarto size, censored, and suppressed. Now it was in our hands. We looked at each other with a wild surmise, not from a peak in Darien, but from a *librairie* on Paris's Left Bank; we had found Monsieur Bernstein's long-sought discourse in "rarissime" first edition, and we had found it for him in his own backyard.

Serendipity accompanied us not only in the Sixth Arrondissement of Paris but, one year, as far off as the Fourteenth. There, in the Alésia section, we concluded our Paris stay with a purchase that could not have been more appropriate. Although we had originally met when teaching Sabbath School and should have been aware of the day, we had completely forgotten—far away from home—that the Jewish New Year was about to begin. We were a trifle surprised when the proprietor, Monsieur Lévy, looked somewhat disconcerted as we entered his bookshop.

"I am just about to close for the Holy Day," he told us. Then it dawned on us. "We'll just be a minute," we apologetically replied.

"I'll phone my wife and tell her I'll be a little late."

It did not take us much more than a minute to find the most fitting accompaniment for the Holy Day that was about to begin. The purchase we made from Monsieur Lévy at that propitious moment was *Der Iudenstaat,* by Theodor Herzl. The great Zionist plea for a national homeland for the Jews had been published in Warsaw in 1896, the first Hebrew edition of a book that would lead to action. In 1948 the author's dream was realized and the State of Israel took its place among the nations of the world. Now, on the eve of the Jewish New Year, we had found *Der Iudenstaat.* Monsieur Lévy shook our hands as we made the purchase. "You could not have selected anything more fitting to commemorate the day," he said, "Happy New Year. *Gut Yontif.*"

We showed off some of our serendipitous finds in our catalogues. Mostly, however, we tried to shape our catalogues around a specific theme—a country, as in *La Belle France*—an era, as in *The Century of Conflict* (the seventeenth century). One of our most successful catalogues around this time viewed its subject from a new perspective. Instead of rehashing the *age* of the Renaissance we emphasized the *personalities* of the Renaissance, and we called our catalogue *The Man of the Renaissance.* There were 425 items in it, broken down into 27 sections. Each section was devoted to the followers of a particular profession, from "The Advocate" and "The Artist" to "The Statesman" and "The Tax-Collector." In between were "Courtier" and "Dramatist," "Historian" and "Philosopher," "Physician" and "Poet," "Ruler" and "Scientist." In that way we humanized not only the Renaissance but our presentation of that age—our catalogue. Among our highlights were Vasari's *Lives of the Artists,* Machiavelli's *Prince,* Petrarch's *Sonnets,* Rabelais's *Letters.* But all the 425 items, whether highlights or lesser lights, reflected the age through the individual and brought it intimately into the ken of the collector. Our catalogue's cover breathed the spirit of the Renaissance. It was adorned with a portrait of the *condottiere,* the Marquis of Pescara, in his plumed helmet and full armor.

Cover, contents, entire catalogue evoked the praise of our peers as well as of our customers. Clifford Maggs, of 50 Berkeley Square, hit the nail on the head when he wrote that he was "much impressed with your idea of stressing the man and not the impersonal subject. 'The Advocate' is more stimulating a heading than 'Law,' and so on. My warm congratulations." Another dealer, of the London firm of Stevens and Brown, assured us that "this is the kind of catalogue that starts people off collecting—just what is wanted as an offset to the depressing displaced commas of the bibliographical fanatics." And librarians too expressed their enthusiasm even when they did not buy—Moses Marx, the distinguished Curator of Hebrew Theological Seminary, commenting upon the "excellent organization of material" and the "very fine description of the books," and Lawrence Wroth of the John Carter Brown Library, letting us know "how much the catalogue was admired by the staff."

Very soon a professor at Rutgers was soliciting copies of our catalogues to use "for instructional purposes in connection with a course called 'Building Library Collections.' " Our reputation was growing, a development that stimulated us to reach still higher. By the time the four hundredth anniversary of Shakespeare's birth was celebrated, we had the temerity to issue a catalogue for that great occasion. We had not one Shakespeare folio; we had no quartos. Nonetheless, we applied what we had to our purpose and designed a catalogue containing one or two books published each year of Shakespeare's life. Each book was captioned with a quotation from a Shakespeare play, a challenge that gave us much delight and pleased our customers no end. *Books Published During Shakespeare's Lifetime* covered the years 1564 to 1616. Under the date 1566, and under the caption "O brave new world," we offered Sir Thomas More's Latin works, including the *Utopia;* under the date 1587, we described an oration on the death of Francesco de Medici, headed with the quotation "Good-night, sweet prince." Our labor of love evoked fine responses, the most gratifying of all coming from Lola Szladits, the unforgettable head of the Berg Collection at the New York Public Library. Lola wrote: "Yr. catalogue is worthy of the Globe and the Bard . . . I read it (twice) from 0 to End and enjoyed myself hugely. I bet you did too. Concept, timing, presentation are all brilliant and I salute you."

Despite our reluctance to take a downtown office, there was no doubt that the firm was expanding. A variety of customers found their way to our house on the hill in the Bronx. A day or two after our return from our trip abroad in 1949 we found David Wagstaff of Tuxedo Park at our doorstep. A noted collector of books on hunting and dogs, he had somehow heard on the bibliophilic grapevine that Rostenberg and Stern had purchased a book in Latin entitled *De Canibus Britannicis (On British Dogs).* Excitedly, he fondled the volume, all but ignoring our own American dog, Leona's beautiful Irish terrier Bonaventure Elzevier Rostenberg.

Unlike Mr. Wagstaff, who was after a single book, Mabel Erler ventured to the Bronx to select in bulk. Mabel prided herself on her position as Acquisitions Chief of Chicago's Newberry Library, but there was nothing at all stiff or formal about her: "I'm pretty good for a small-town gal from Kansas." Mabel loved books, bridge, and gin—not necessarily in that order. She appeared at East 179th Street at 11 A.M. during a heavy snowstorm, seated herself at a desk, and plowed through our book descriptions, a martini at her side. By evening she had selected some fifty books, fortified herself with additional martinis, and was ready to relax over a game of bridge. Eventually marrying the Director of the Newberry Library, Mabel came a long way. But she never really changed. Outspoken, natural, in love with fun, she was always the small-town gal from Kansas and the bookseller's friend.

From the sedate and beautiful "Molly" Pitcher, of the Folger Shakespeare Library, to Lord John Kerr, who pinched snuff while he scanned the shelves, we welcomed a variety of browsers and prospective customers. When George White, head of the Geology Department of the University of Illinois, came for lunch and books, Leona's charming mother took special pains to put him at ease by animatedly discussing the geology of the Grand Canyon.

By 1957 the New York Public Library had chosen us to act as its representatives at New York auctions, and later we served as agents for the Library of Congress, representing it at the extensive and highly publicized Streeter Sales of Americana at the Parke-Bernet Galleries. We were coming into our own.

Our correspondence testified to our expansion. Letters came to us postmarked from Buenos Aires, Australia, and Nigeria, and some of them were bibliophilic curiosities. A gentleman from Buenos Aires informed us that he had no interest in a book's subject or editor or date; all he wanted was books that measured less than eight centimeters for a "library of small volumes." An Australian collector hoped to obtain from us books, paintings, and manuscripts "preferably dating before 1000 A.D." A Nigerian hopeful wrote that it was his "sincere desire to order 2400 medical books to replace a collection that had been destroyed." And from nearby New Jersey we received the offer of a 1569 Luther Bible, fourteen inches wide, sixteen inches long, and ten inches thick (worth a few hundred dollars), for which the owners hoped "only to realize a reasonable price offer, which would enable my husband, myself & our 4 young children to purchase a small home."

Madeleine 📖 OUR MOTHERS TOOK AS MUCH pleasure in such letters as we did. They chuckled over them and recognized them as tokens of our expanding reputation. By early 1957 Leona's mother, who had welcomed Professor White with her winning charm, began to withdraw. In early March she suffered a fatal heart attack. Her great loss left the house on the hill almost empty and Leona heartsick for months to come. She stayed on with Babette and the books. Gradually she felt a sense of freedom and spent much time with my mother and me.

My mother had been far more than a mother to me. She had not only made a home that spread a warm and loving protective cloak around her daughter; she had been for me an intellectual companion, a sounding board for my writings, a creative source. She may have pushed me forward, but she never demanded anything else from me. "You must lead your own life," she had always insisted. Then, in 1958, after a brief illness, she died. Her shocking loss, the end of such a relationship, left me feeling like an amputee. Even during our brief book hunt abroad in the fall of 1958, that feeling persisted. The return home was especially difficult, since there was no mother at the dock to greet us.

There was never any real question as to our future. I simply moved into the Bronx house on the hill. The partners and friends now became companions for the life to be. Now we were on our own—but too we were truly together.

ABAA

Madeleine 📖 THE ABAA is really an anomaly in terminology. The letters stand for Antiquarian Booksellers Association of America. Antiquarian booksellers not only in America but all over the world are, almost without exception, individuals sufficient unto themselves, and the word "association" would seem to have no connection with them. Antiquarian booksellers may not live in an ivory tower, but they assuredly do live in a world of their own devising. And yet, in 1949—the same year the North Atlantic Treaty Organization was shaped by the Allies of World War II—a group of strongly individualistic antiquarian booksellers actually banded together to form an association.

We were among them. True, being so young in the trade, we were shy, if not fearful, sat together in the rear at meetings, and never enunciated an opinion. But we were there, and by the time five years had passed we moved up front to the first row. By then we were part of a closely knit group of antiquarians who discussed the technical points of books, explored second-hand shops together, relished country picnics in the summer and vociferous dinner parties in the winter. The role of women in the ABAA was never discussed. We were accepted without question in the ranks of antiquarian booksellers, but—as of today—of the twenty-four presidents of our association only three have been women. Leona was one of them, but that did not happen until 1972.

Meanwhile, like all the other members, we were learning the meaning of association and were developing a point of view about our trade to present to the public. When Radio Station WNYC, under the leadership of Ben Grauer, the well-known announcer, collector, and staunch friend of antiquarian booksellers, launched a program on aspects of book collecting, Leona participated. With all the panel she deplored newspaper headlines that featured millionaire princes as collectors and ignored the real backbone of the trade, the faithful, specialized collector of lesser means.

Antiquarian booksellers all over the world had found that, despite differences in nationality and individuality, they shared a common purpose: to make rare books understandable, desirable, a part of modern life. The ABAA was a member nation of the International League of Antiquarian Booksellers, which by 1954 was hosting biennial congresses in different cities. In 1954 the city selected for the congress was Vienna, and we were among the American delegates. After two days in occupied Vienna, I recorded my impressions in my journal:

> *Europe in limbo—Wien in transition—imperial, regal, monstrous architecture in decay—stone houses dilapidated & frequently riddled with bullet holes. Military police in evidence. East plus West. The Russian soldiers are everywhere but completely withdrawn & uncommunicative. It is a captive city, the prey of 4 nations . . . The city is one of the greatest contrasts: Renaissance, Hapsburg, Baroque, 19th-century dullness, Karl Marx Community houses & Russian occupation coupled with delightful café life, beggars, Tyrolean costumes and superb sacher torte & apfel strudel!*

In early September there were also antiquarian booksellers from all over the world in Vienna. They convened for a general assembly and we sat with the American delegation, our flag waving, all chauvinistically greeting one another. Despite the party politicking and the cliqueing, we came to know each other and enjoy each other over dinner at the Café Mozart or tea at Sacher's, at the Heuriger in celebration of the new wine or at a performance of *Fledermaus*. We bought books from the Viennese dealers and strengthened friendships with the American delegates and learned more about the nature of association.

We learned a little something about internationalism, too. Leona caused a minor crisis by informing the Directress of Seating Arrangements for the Farewell Banquet that she would not sit where she had been placed—with the German delegation. After her experiences in Strasbourg, after the revelations of the Holocaust, she simply could not bring herself even to an appearance of civility with the German booksellers. As a result, we were advised that, if we were not sufficiently international-minded, we should not have attended an international conference. All of which was of course true, but at the time neither of us was sufficiently objective to realize it.

As the ABAA was part of a larger international organization, the Middle Atlantic Chapter was part of the ABAA. By 1956 Leona was elected chair of MAC. Lively, well-attended, her meetings featured talks by librarians and collectors, discussions about cooperative catalogues issued by a group of members, and bookish chitchat. A few years later I followed as chair of MAC, achieving record attendance at meetings in the Club 1407 Restaurant and eventually launching a landmark event in the history of the American antiquarian book trade: the first rare book fair in the United States.

This seminal undertaking, which would spark a book fair contagion spreading to every hamlet in the country, began with my query at an MAC meeting: "Why don't we have a book fair?" News of the first British antiquarian fair and its success had reached all of us, and the members of MAC were convinced that we could work together in practical and productive cooperation. They were right. The first book fair committee was no advisory committee; it was a working committee. We selected Steinway Concert Hall on New York's West Fifty-seventh Street as our location and met regularly and frequently to arrange for all the minutiae essential to book fairs: book shelving, display cases and linings for display cases, signs and posters, publicity, announcements and keepsakes, a budget, hours and days for fair number one. I wasn't going to make the same mistake I had made back at Barnard when I did everything but advertise the Ben Shahn event.

The fair opened at 5 P.M. on April 4, 1960, with a preview, and lasted for five more long days, running from 10 A.M. to 10 P.M. Twenty-two dealers occupying twenty booths displayed a variety of rare books from incunables to twentieth-century first editions and enjoyed the long week of togetherness so much that they sorely missed their colleagues after the week was over. Before the fair opened, a few minutes before 5 P.M., Leona wondered out loud what we had all wondered silently: would our fair attract any visitors at all? Then, before I realized it, she had ducked outside to see whether anyone had come. When she returned, her face reflected radiance and disbelief. "They're standing on line to get in! There are crowds outside!" Despite rain and storm, the jams of people on opening night filled us with incredulity and exuberance.

Our visitors were enthusiastic. They did not seem to notice that we had tossed all our empty cartons behind a curtain on the dais of the concert hall. They noticed only our wares, from a fifteenth-century confessional to a first of *Ulysses,* from a book printed on vellum to a Poe illustrated by Manet. Besides noticing, they bought. Although one genuine prima donna swooped into the concert hall and in dismay demanded, "What have they done to Steinway Hall?," Arthur Rubinstein not only made his entry but bought two music manuscripts. And during the lulls of the long days, we all bought from one another. It is true that I also developed a case of giant hives while the fair was in progress, but success crowned our efforts, and dealers' reactions were more than gratifying. Polled when the fair was at long last over, we all agreed we would "definitely participate next year," and Elisabeth Woodburn, who dealt in gardening books, voiced the opinion of all when she exclaimed: "A real wahoo occasion! Haven't had such fun in years! Sold plenty, will sell more. When is next fair?"

There was the next, and the next, and the next—every year—and though the setting would change to New York hotels, the Plaza among them, and to the Seventh Regiment Armory, and the duration would be shortened, most of the modus operandi initiated at our debut would continue.

In 1969, our fair became an international one, and Rostenberg and Stern issued a catalogue and announced that they would be at Booth 33 of

NEW YORK'S RAZZLE DAZZLE BOOK FAIR
Both Ladies Will Dispense Humanities,
Literature, Art, Judaica, Philosophy,
Science, Turcica and
PLEASING CONVERSATION.

In 1971 we dispensed, inter many alia, a single book that was purchased for the University of Rochester by its chief of rare books, Robert L. Volz. After he had acquired our copy of poems by Pope Urban VIII, issued in 1634, with an engraved title page and a portrait by Peter Paul Rubens, in a binding made for a famous French collector, François Auguste de Thou, he wrote to us: "My thanks to you and to Madeleine Stern for the time and interest you gave to me in New York last Friday. I enclose our purchase order . . . for the finest book, or at least the most exciting book, at the fair."

Book fairs proliferated all across the country, and in 1964 we set up our booths with our colleagues in San Francisco and in 1967 in Los Angeles. The twenty-two dealers who had launched America's first Antiquarian Book Fair would increase as the decades passed to over two hundred twenty. But it is questionable whether the later, more professional versions engendered as much excitement as that first fair of 1960.

It was only a few years after the Steinway Hall fair that another milestone in bookseller association was reached. The antiquarian book fairs served as a kind of cooperative bookstore for three or four days. Visitors could sample the stocks of participating dealers and become acquainted with books on a variety of subjects published over five centuries. But the booths were vacated when the fair was over; the book fair was by nature a transitory event. Why not, it was asked, extend it? Why not attempt a lasting cooperative bookstore? Such a store, if centrally located, could be a meeting place for book collectors where they could not only buy books but talk books; for dealers it would offer a cornucopia of opportunities, for in such a bookstore participants would not only sell but buy books and do additional selling and buying by means of referrals. Such a bookstore could become a microcosm of the American rare book trade.

Through the concerted efforts of an MAC committee, the Antiquarian Booksellers Center, located at 630 Fifth Avenue, in the Concourse of the International Building of Rockefeller Center, was opened on October 14, 1963. Outside the entrance stood the huge statue of Atlas holding the world on his shoulders. Just so, the center held, in the thousand square feet it occupied, the infinite riches of the world of antiquarian books. The committee had not only found the shop, but had enlisted some fifty participants; in addition, it had arranged the shelving, scheduled exhibits, hired a secretary, and even sewn the backdrop for the enormous show windows.

On opening day the plaster, paint, and stain were still wet, and shelves had not yet been placed in the bookcases. But soon after, all was in readiness. Notices of this unique bookstore appeared in the media, from the *Saturday Review* to *Cue,* from the German *Börsenblatt* to *Publishers Weekly,* from the *Christian Science Monitor* to the *New York Times.* I served as first chair of the center and watched with joy as it became a revolving exhibition hall. It would last for a quarter century, most of the time under the devoted and enthusiastic guidance of its secretary, the late Edith M. Wells. It would attract visitors from all over the world, this truly cooperative bookstore in the heart of Manhattan.

Our first exhibition at the center took place early—the week of November 18, 1963. We prepared for it by displaying in the center's four enormous windows books that would, we hoped, appeal to the masses of people who passed by. Situated as they were in the Concourse, or basement, of the International Building, the center's windows faced corridors teeming with people—people on their way to a café or a subway, business people, pleasure seekers, tourists. In the gigantic windows of the shop we placed our early printed books, highlighting several by and about women. Our pioneer feminist display included an eighteenth-century French comedy, intriguingly entitled *La Femme Fille et Veuve (Wife, Daughter, and Widow);* a sixteenth-century Italian translation of Boccaccio's fascinating work on famous women; Madame Pompadour's *Letters;* and an illustrated Utopian romance of 1739, set in America, by Rustaing de Saint-Jory, *Les Femmes Militaires,* which proclaimed the absolute parity of men and women in work, government service, war, and life. Opened to a plate depicting women in military costume, this could not fail to attract the attention of the passersby. And attract it did; even while we were placing our books in the windows, people stopped in their tracks to gape.

Occasionally they also came in, and when they did, they also occasionally bought. As the *New York Daily News* would report: "Book collecting . . . mirrors the occupations, moods and concerns of bygone eras. The Antiquarian Booksellers Center is a fascinating place.'' That week in November, the center became our bookstore, exhibiting the results of what the *News* called our ''global treasure-troving.''

Our dear friend, the book collector Miriam Holden, sent a large basket of flowers to congratulate us. Petite, chubby, berouged, her hair always encased in a Venida hairnet, Mrs. Holden looked far more feminine than feminist. But she was a staunch feminist, not only in her political affiliations but in her book collecting, and it was to her that many of our feminist treasures passed in the 1960s. But the week of November 18, which had begun so gloriously, ended, alas, with tragedy. On the twenty-second, when we returned from lunch, our secretary had received the appalling news by telephone. The news was confirmed on a small portable radio. John Fitzgerald Kennedy had been shot in Dallas. The thirty-fifth President of the United States was dead. We placed Miriam's basket of flowers in the center of a gleaming window, closed the doors, and left. The bells of St. Patrick's Cathedral had begun their unforgettable tolling. We walked blindly toward the subway, meeting the hordes of bewildered, outraged, and mourning people who had all lost the grace of one brief period of our nation's history.

Our life in books, punctuated occasionally by great events, flowed for the most part peacefully on. Much of the excitement we experienced continued to stem from our bookish detection. And the results of our detection found their way to the windows of the Antiquarian Booksellers Center and to our catalogues, to our booths at fairs and to our shelves in the Bronx.

In a way, the area on the Paris quais where bookstalls clustered had something in common with our fairs and our center. What more appropriate for us to discover one day as we leafed through a thirty-two-page French political pamphlet of 1622 than a reference to a *''bouticque mobile . . . d'vn marchand Libraire en liures du temps passé''*—a ''movable boutique of a bookseller merchant dealing in

books of a time gone by." Surely we were such bookseller mer-
chants, and here—doubtless unknown to most of the world—was
probably the earliest mention of the Paris bookstalls. We had found
the pamphlet in a collection of four hundred tracts in the Paris
emporium of Monsieur Michel Bernstein and paid, prorated, three
dollars for it. The *Povrmenade Dv Pré Avx Clercs,* unbound, stitched,
just as it had come from the press in 1622, described the promenade
of a seventeenth-century collector on the recently constructed Pont
Neuf of Paris, where he finds the *"bouticque mobile,"* browses
through the titles on display, and selects a book to read if not to
purchase. On the sunlit quais of the City of Light, our collective
lives had been foreshadowed.

Another French pamphlet bought from a Paris dealer brought us
not only to our bookselling roots but to our home port. *Diverses
Pieces Servans de Reponse Avx Discovrs Pvbliez Par Les Hollandois* made no
reference in its title to either America or New Amsterdam, but they
were assuredly in residence. The date of the pamphlet started the
Finger-Spitzengefühl vibrating: 1665. Had not the Dutch been ousted
from New Netherlands in August 1664 and New Amsterdam metamorphosed into New York? By any chance was there any mention of
that earthshaking event in these *Diverse Pieces Serving as Reply to Public
Discourses by the Dutch?* Indeed there was—no need to read between
the lines. The lines were clear: New Netherlands was discussed,
along with the relations of Dutch residents with the English and the
role of the West India Company. "Rare and remarkable," we called
this tract, as well as "apparently little known" and "yet another
source for New Netherlands." The pamphlet went precisely where
it should have gone—to the library of the New-York Historical
Society.

Yet one of our most memorable discoveries took place in a small
London bookshop on Grape Street, off Shaftesbury Avenue. We
arrived at that most halcyon of moments, just when the dealer had
finished preparing his new catalogue but before he had sent it off to

the printer. "I have a catalogue in preparation. Perhaps you would like to glance at the advance slips," is probably the most titillating invitation a bookseller on the hunt can hear. We two sat hunched at the dealer's desk, examining his precious slips. We went through the As quickly. It happened when we came to the Bs—more specifically to BEAUMONT, WILLIAM, whose *Experiments and Observations on the Gastric Juice, and the Physiology of Digestion* had been printed in Plattsburgh, New York, in 1833. The book had pioneered medical history, for in it the author-surgeon Dr. Beaumont had for the first time described the physiology of digestion in a living man. We had heard the extraordinary story about a Canadian halfbreed who had been wounded by a musketshot in 1822 and left with a small hole in his side. Through that hole Dr. Beaumont had studied the workings of the stomach, later writing his observations in his *Experiments and Observations on the Gastric Juice*. We seized the slip, looked at each other in a state of glory, and asked our dealer for the Beaumont. In a few minutes it was in our hands—an unimposing octavo, poorly printed in upstate New York, but an incomparable treasure, worth today about $2500, priced at the equivalent of $19.

We have told the story of our Beaumont find whenever we had the chance. The last time we told it was when we gave the keynote speech at a Colorado seminar on rare books. After the speech was printed we had a charming letter from a woman bookseller in Plattsburgh, who wrote:

> It was thrilling to read about Dr. Beaumont's book . . . My store is 1 block from the location of Dr. Beaumont's office. We once acquired a copy of the 1st Ed. back in our early bookselling days. We bought it for $400.00 & sold it for $800.00 to a local history professor who then spent $1200.00 to have it restored at a Vt. Monastery. He then donated it to Plattsburgh State Univ. where it is in the library on display in a glass case.

Another book suitable for display in a glass case was one we found on the grimy, dusty shelf of Francis Norman's bookshop.

When he moved from his Gower Street cellar to Hampstead Heath, he had moved not only his books but all the dust and grime and debris, among which we made an astounding discovery. Robert Boyle the great English chemist died in 1691, and the following year his library was sold by what was called "private agreement." In the centuries that have passed since then not a single volume surfaced that could be identified as having belonged to Robert Boyle. Now, in the shambles of Norman's shop on Hampstead Heath, we found the first. The book, a French attack on the Jesuits published in 1688, bore a Latin inscription on the flyleaf stating that the work had come from the library of "the most illustrious and renowned Robert Boyle." The distinguished author of *The Sceptical Chemist* had also had a deep interest in theological matters, and this attack on the Jesuits would have been precisely his cup of tea. Once our little book had had a place in Boyle's library in Pall Mall. After Boyle's death it had passed to the writer of the Latin inscription. And a couple of centuries later it had somehow been picked up by the war-ravaged bookseller Francis Norman. Now it was ours, and we would pass it on to Dr. John F. Fulton, of Yale University Medical Library, where it would doubtless repose in a glass showcase—perhaps next to a copy of the *Experiments* of Dr. William Beaumont.

We showcased our finds, along with bread-and-butter books, in our catalogues. Most of our catalogues—*Century of Conflict, Persons & Places, Fare for the Fair*—consisted of a few hundred items on specialized subjects and were aimed at the nation's libraries. Still hungry for books, such institutions as Folger and Newberry, Yale and Princeton, Michigan, Texas, and Stanford were acquiring early printed materials with gusto, and we were happy to supply them.

Now, in the 1960s, it occurred to us that we should aim, not at selling three or four, or six or eight items to a library, but an entire catalogue—a whole glorious collection of related material that we could assemble and then pass on at a lot price, as a unit, or, in booksellers' parlance, *en bloc*. And what could be more appropriate for such a purpose than our sixteenth- and seventeenth-century

French pamphlets that unrolled a panorama of France's dramatic history?

There was plenty of space in the Bronx house to store books and pamphlets and keep them on ice until we were ready to research them. The enormous room on the third floor had once been Adolph Jr.'s, and in his day it had held a Ping Pong table, along with all the other paraphernalia assembled by a young man who enjoyed six or seven hobbies. Now we would store our collections there, catalogue them, and sell them *en bloc*.

Our Catalogue XXXIV was entitled *One Hundred Years of France 1547–1652: A Documentary History*. It comprised 755 pamphlets that reported events in France during the century that began with the accession of Henry II and his notorious spouse, Catherine de Medici, and ended with the malevolent deeds of Mazarin. In between our tracts portrayed the Valois-Guise-Bourbon rivalry, the Huguenot struggle, the triumph of the great Bourbon monarch Henry IV and his assassination, the emergence of Richelieu—a whole century reflected by reformer and critic, soldier and merchant, with a cast of characters that included Coligny and Condé, Sully and Richelieu. In these 755 ephemera the opinions of churchman and dissenter, courtier and peasant, scholar and diplomat were enunciated, and the pattern of a hundred turbulent years was traced. The preface to our catalogue stressed the immediacy of the ephemeral pamphlet: "An accumulation of pamphlets reflects the multi-faceted history of a particular age." The *en bloc* purchase of the collection was recommended as "a precious nucleus for the study of the political, religious, social and economic history of the period." Some of the royal coats of arms and woodcut portraits that appeared in the pamphlets were reproduced. And our preface ended with the words *"Vive la France!"*

Our joy in the preparation of Catalogue XXXIV was climaxed only by our joy in its *en bloc* sale. We had three orders for the collection, the first from the University of Buffalo, where an ardent history professor was avid to acquire it, the second from Yale, and the third from Michigan. The contents of Catalogue XXXIV were sold to the University of Buffalo, and our remaining copies of the catalogue were rubber-stamped with the proud statement: "Catalogue XXXIV—One Hundred Years of France/Has Been Sold En Bloc/It Is Being Circulated as a Courtesy."

It did not take long for us to consider that if the pamphlet could so graphically mirror the sixteenth and seventeenth centuries in France, it could even more graphically present that turmoil of the late eighteenth century known as the French Revolution. Thousands upon thousands of pamphlets had been printed during those eventful years, and it seemed to us that revolutionaries were spouting tracts even as they stood in the tumbrels en route to the guillotine.

Catalogue XXXVII—*The French Revolution*—was bound in bloody scarlet covers. It contained over 1650 pamphlets that documented revolutionary France and its major periods: the precursors of revolution; the 1789 meeting of the States-General; the abolition of feudalism; the new leaders; the destruction of the monarchy; the spread of terror; the Thermidorian Reaction; and the dictatorship of Bonaparte. In these on-the-spot reports were traced the rights of man and the new social platforms, and here were heard the comments of Danton and Robespierre, Mirabeau and Marat, of Girondist and Jacobin. Our foreword to our French Revolution catalogue invited "inquiries" regarding an *en bloc* purchase and ended with the words *"Vive la Liberté, l'Egalité, la Fraternité."*

The first "inquiry" came by telephone from the Eleutherian Mills Historical Library, near Wilmington, Delaware. That library, recently founded by the Du Ponts—had we not represented Pierre Samuel at auction?—concentrated upon the period 1750 to 1820 in France, when the family was rising to prominence there. The French Revolution was important for Eleutherian Mills. An agreement was reached, and in early November 1966 we drove to Greenville, near Wilmington, to deliver the 1659 pamphlets we had catalogued. Our trade journal, the *Antiquarian Bookman,* reported: "This is [the] second time in 2 years that Rostenberg has sold a complete catalog en

bloc! She and her associate, Madeleine B. Stern, specialize in form-
ing collections on single subjects." And Miss Grace Ottey, librarian
of Eleutherian, wrote to us, "To me, the collection is the outstanding imprint acquisition in our 10 years of existence."

Our third *en bloc* catalogue, *The Aldine Press,* was actually a far
more outstanding "imprint acquisition." For some years now we
had been placing on the shelves of the big third-floor room the
vellum- and morocco- and calfbound volumes that had been published by the great Aldine Press of Venice between 1495 and 1595.
In 1967, when the 258 items in our Catalogue XXXIX had been
described, we believed that Aldus Manutius, founder of the press,
and his family were the greatest publishers of all time. We still
believe so.

It was with increasing admiration and delight that we examined
each of the Aldines we had collected and, seated at two bridge tables
in the big room, catalogued them: the great 1496 *Thesaurus
Cornucopiae,* edited by Aldus himself; the 1501 Horace, first of the
pocket classics, to be stowed in the saddlebag of a wandering
scholar; Artemidorus on dreams and Castiglione on the courtier in
first edition; the first edition of Plato's complete works; the 1502
Dante *Divine Comedy,* the *Terze Rime,* the first in portable format,
executed from a manuscript sent to the publisher by his friend the
humanist Pietro Bembo; and Bembo's own *History of Venice,* in which
the author inserted an unexpected account of America and of Co-
lumbus, whom he described as "a man of sharp intellect, who
traversed many immense regions and much of the ocean." The
House of Aldus also traversed "many immense regions," from the
realms of ancient scholarship to those of the sixteenth-century avant-
garde.

In the preface of his *Thesaurus Cornucopiae* Aldus Manutius expressed his joy at rescuing such writings from the "buriers of
books" and his desire to give them "freely to the world." Our
Catalogue XXXIX was a tribute to Aldus and his heirs. Its white

covers bore in black the Aldine colophon of Anchor and Dolphin—
Anchor for firmness and deliberation, Dolphin for speed of production. And it was with considerable speed after considerable deliberation that our Aldine collection was transported to the steadily expanding Humanities Research Center of the University of Texas. In
1982 the assistant to the director of that center was preparing a
book, *Great Catalogues by Master Booksellers,* including our most accomplished catalogue, XXXIX.

It was item 113 in that catalogue, the first edition of Lorenzo de
Medici's *Poesie uolgari,* that soon led us from the House of Aldus to
the House of Medici. By the end of the 1960s we had assembled our
fourth grand collection. Its setting was a city we had grown to
love—Florence, Firenze—a cornucopia out of which flowed the
Middle Ages and the Renaissance. We had stood before the Medici
tombs designed by Michelangelo; we had wandered through the
Ricardi Palace and seen Gozzoli's fresco of Lorenzo on a white
charger; we had often walked past the Baptistery with Ghiberti's
golden doors; near one of our Florentine booksellers we had gazed
again and again at Michelangelo's *David.* In the Palazzo Vecchio on
the Piazza della Signoria we had seen the *studiola* of Francesco de
Medici. The fortress of the Strozzi Palace had brought the Medicis
home to us. Wandering through the narrow streets of Florence, with
its dull yellow houses, its ancient faded frescoes, its glimpses of the
Arno, we had felt the presence of the Medicis. Their shadow was all
over—in the Santa Croce and the Duomo, in Giotto's Campanile, in
all the shrines and niches, the courtyards and cells, the chapels and
palaces of this unbelievable Tuscan city. In Florence, on the Via
Vente Settembre, dear delightful Signor Cesare Olschki plied his
trade in rare books. From his establishment, so freely thrown open
to us, we had selected many of the books that restored the Medicis
to life.

Now, in the late 1960s, we brought them all together—more
than three hundred in total. The younger Aldus Manutius had writ-

ten a life of the first Grand Duke of Tuscany, Cosimo I de Medici, and we thought it appropriate to highlight our presentation with that work, the first book printed by the Aldine Press at its Bologna branch. There were orations by friends and sycophants on Medici births and Medici deaths, from Vasari's account of the festivities honoring the baptism of Francesco de Medici's daughter, in 1567, to funeral orations on the death of Cosimo I de Medici, in 1574. There were sixteenth-century histories of the Medici family and of their city-state; there was a great eighteenth-century portrait book presenting full-page engravings of 104 Medici *illustrissimi*. The Bulls issued by Pope Leo X found a place in our collection, for Leo X was a Medici, the son of Lorenzo the Magnificent. The account of a carnival pageant held in the Medici court in Florence on Shrove Tuesday of 1565 was part of our collection, and, though we seldom dealt in autographed materials, we included a letter signed by Catherine de Medici in her role as Queen Mother of France. We even added an illustrated two-volume set of George Eliot's *Romola,* bound in white vellum cloth with red and gold stamping. The historical novel had been written after the author's stay in Florence in 1860; it had been reprinted in Boston in 1890 as a de luxe gift book; and in 1902 it had been presented to my mother as a wedding present. We thought it would end up appropriately as part of our Medici holdings.

The collection was illuminated by many great names—writers who had enshrined the Medicis or their domain in their books: Boccaccio, whose *Decameron* consisted of tales supposedly narrated at the time of the Florentine plague of 1348, a work edited at the order of the Grand Duke of Tuscany; Aretino, whose *History of Florence* traced the rise and influence of the Medicis; Michelangelo the Younger, nephew of the great artist, who had delivered a eulogy of Cosimo II de Medici at Santa Croce in 1621. We included Cellini's autobiography with our Medici books, for the Medicis had been his patrons. Along with Cellini's *Vita* we included his two treatises on art theory and the masterpieces he had created for the Medicis. Vasari, who had been Cosimo's "right-hand man in all matters relating to art," was represented with the first illustrated edition of his *Lives of the Artists,* fittingly dedicated to the great art patron Cosimo. The Florentine poets were there with the Medicis in all their grandeur: Dante in a 1515 Aldine edition, cased in a gilt-stamped Grolieresque calf binding; Petrarch, trailing clouds of glory all over Tuscany, in a charming 1539 edition with his laureled portrait on the title page. Machiavelli was present with his *Prince,* justifying the wily Medici rule, and Savonarola was present too, the friar-preacher who had foretold ruin in the midst of the prosperity of Lorenzo de Medici, with an edition of his commentaries on the Psalms.

Toward the end of 1969 our Medicis followed our Aldines to Texas. We had now sold four *en bloc* collections. We had many copies of our catalogues left, so we distributed them to our collectors and libraries accompanied by a card imprinted as follows: "These catalogues have been sold *en bloc.* They are being distributed as a courtesy only. Please do not order from them." From the four sales we had grossed approximately $125,000. Although a goodly portion went to the tax collector, a goodly portion remained with us. It was time for the two book ladies of the Bronx to change their address and their domicile.

A move had been impending for some time. The lovely house was vulnerable to the neighborhood's increasing violence. A commodious front porch tempted access from the street, and the french windows of the dining room made entry all too inviting. The garden in the back and the hedges in the front regularly suffered the onslaught of boys bent on destruction. The house was especially vulnerable to the aging process: it was hard to keep up with broken leaders, peeling paint, cracked window frames, a leaking roof. Although, with our car ever ready in the alleyway next to the house, *we* felt extremely mobile, the comments of friends and customers added to our problems. We were so far "up," they complained—so hard to reach.

On and off over a period of three years we made half-hearted attempts to become more reachable. But every time an agent showed us an apartment or a townhouse in Manhattan, we returned to the rambling Bronx house with relief. Where else could we revel in so much space—space for our books and for ourselves? Where else could we find such comfort? Where else would we find another beloved housekeeper? Babette, we knew, would return to Germany as soon as we moved. Her heart, like ours, was in the house. Now, it would be sold, and most likely torn down, the appurtenances of the past, except those in the heart, obliterated.

Finally, in 1969, we moved to Manhattan. A caring and persistent agent had found a handsome co-op for us in the Carnegie Hill section, between Madison and Park Avenues. At the same time we took a small office on East Eighty-sixth Street. After the move was accomplished a friend asked if Leona missed the Bronx house, now that she had such a beautiful downtown apartment. "Of course I do." "But what can you miss?" "I miss the beautiful staircase," she said. "I miss my home."

Actually, beyond the roots of childhood, there was nothing left to miss. The Bronx had changed, and no longer were we a true part of the community. Once we were settled, on December 4, 1969, we circulated an announcement to inform our customers that the book ladies of the Bronx had relocated. But, fearful that the tenant-owners would object to our business operation, we couched the terminology on our change of residence cards cagily, not even mentioning the word *books,* and we concluded with the following: "By Appointment Only." It was that little appendage at the bottom of the card that raised a few eyebrows. Our innocent card somehow found its way to the nonbookish population, and late one evening one such recipient telephoned to us. His accent was foreign, his voice determined. "I get your card in the Boston airport," he stated. "I want to make appointment." Delighted to learn that our reputation extended to out-of-town airports, we were still a bit puzzled and asked, "What is your particular specialty?" "My specialty?" "Yes," we persisted. "What do you collect?" Now *he* was puzzled, and before he hung up, he asked with some exasperation, "Tell me, ladies—vat you do?"

Vat we did after the move to Manhattan was what we had been doing right along in the Bronx: detecting and buying abroad, sleuthing and researching, writing and cataloguing, building collections and selling. The thrills that had come with our discoveries brought us both inner gratification. In a very few short years those thrills would intensify and we would assume a more public image.

In April 1972 the Antiquarian Booksellers Association of America elected a new president, named Leona Rostenberg.

OUR DOUBLE LIVES

Leona I WAS WELL aware that this was only the second time in twenty-three years that a woman had been given the high post of president. I wanted to make sure that the membership was also aware of it, and in my inaugural address I gave a cursory sketch of the role played by women in the five hundred years of the antiquarian book trade. Had not, I gently reminded my constituents, a woman been responsible for the invention of printing by movable type? Had not old Johann Gutenberg borrowed the gulden from his mother to launch his great experiment? And, as the centuries rolled by, had not women been active in the printing, publishing, and bookselling fields, frequently as helpmates or heirs to their husbands and sometimes in their own right? My own compendium on publishing, printing, and bookselling in seventeenth-century England had found space for the productive career of the late seventeenth-century English woman publisher Anne Baldwin, and my partner had devoted an entire book to the fascinations of the nineteenth-century American publisher Mrs. Frank Leslie. Now, in the twentieth century, we were presumably on equal terms—the men and women of the book trade. Were we not? Of course there were exceptions. Most irksome was that the prestigious association of book collectors, the Grolier Club, did not yet admit women. Nonetheless, where there were liberty and fraternity, there must eventually be equality. This would be one of my goals for a trade devoted to the acquisition and dispersal of books for the joy and betterment of man—and woman.

The feminist intentions expressed in my inaugural were carried out subtly and more or less by implication. The fact that I was a woman was not underlined, for I was seeking not mere acceptance but complete parity. And the technique seems to have worked. My domestic reign was for the most part a smooth one.

The climax of my tenure was reached in a remote city halfway across the globe—Tokyo. It was there that the biennial congress of the International League of Antiquarian Booksellers, hosted by the Japanese Association, was held in the autumn of 1973. When I was informed of this, my reaction was a mixture of excitement, anxiety, and eagerness. Knowing that each national president was expected to deliver a thank-you address at the farewell banquet, I casually remarked to Madeleine, "I wish I could deliver mine in Japanese."

I should have known better. The gal who had had Rostenberg's firm stationery imprinted in 1943 presented me with another surprise gift in 1973: four long-playing high-fidelity records offering forty lessons complete in *living Japanese*. I couldn't waste the stationery. Now, I couldn't waste the records. During our summer in East Hampton I sat on the terrace listening to the *dóozos* and *arigatoos* and *konnichi was*, and although I never did attain the promised fluency within six weeks, I was able to write a brief speech in Japanese, or in what I believed was Japanese. Mady was not so sure. At her suggestion I tried out my presentation before the two amiable proprietors of an Oriental notions shop on Fifty-seventh Street. They were politely enthusiastic, although they did remark that the speech seemed to have been written in nineteenth-century Japanese.

Mady was worried. After we embarked on our long journey, she decided to have my composition auditioned again. In Tokyo, a San Francisco dealer in Orientalia listened to my rendition, deleted the remaining "thees" and "thous," improved the phrasing, and gave me an encouraging imprimatur.

The gala farewell banquet had been preceded not only by congressional meetings but by excursions to the shrines of Nikko and Nara, the palaces of Kyoto, the great library of Tenri. We had dined and drunk hot *sake* at the beautiful Hannya Yen Restaurant, enjoyed tea and kimono ceremonies, and browsed along Tokyo's book row, the Kanda. Now came the crowning point of the congress, the farewell banquet at the elegant Imperial Hotel. The banquet room was ablaze with the Japanese women's gorgeous kimonos and obis. For the first time the Oriental dealers' wives had been permitted to join in such a mixed assemblage, and their shyness was as notable as their sartorial magnificence. At the tables visitors from all over the world were seated with the Japanese. I was on the dais, along with all the foreign presidents, while Mady, I saw, had been placed at a table graced mainly by Japanese. The custom in Japan was to present the speeches before the banquet was served, rather than after. Perhaps they believed that empty stomachs encouraged better listening than surfeited ones. One after another, in alphabetical order of country, the presidents—all male—arose and, each in his own tongue, delivered a boring speech. Belgium followed Austria; Germany and Great Britain followed France and were followed by Italy, the Netherlands and Norway, Sweden and Switzerland. In French and German, English and Italian, Swedish and Schweizer-Deutsch, the clichés of gratitude succeeded one another. The Japanese at Mady's table and across the huge room were obviously wilting with boredom, unable to comprehend a single word. Stomachs rumbled. Finally, I heard the summons: *The United States of America.* I was last to speak. But not least.

As soon as I opened my mouth, the entire banquet room awoke.

Mady's table—the Japanese all practically asleep—started to ap-
plaud, and then their attention was riveted. I addressed the audience
as gracefully as I could—charmingly, succinctly, and in Japanese.
When I concluded my remarks on the hospitality of East to West,
the gala farewell came to life. The applause was thunderous. The
Emperor's brother, the Prince, rose and bowed low before me.
Here, I had delivered a speech in Japanese, the American president
and specialist in European books, epitomizing the meaning of internationalism. It was an added fillip that the speaker just happened to
be a woman.

For this particular American president 1973 was an *annus
mirabilis*. In that same year, I finally received the degree of doctor of
philosophy that had so long been denied me. As the *AB Bookman's
Weekly* put it, "Dr. Leona Rostenberg: Columbia U Reverses Itself."
And as one letter of congratulation put it, "In point of fact, I really
think the congratulations should go to Columbia University for dem-
onstrating a rare good sense."

The reversal began with the June 1972 issue of *Columbia Reports*.
Under the heading "Forthcoming Intermediate Degree to Be Retro-
active," there was an article by Dean Richard C. Robey that began:
"A new degree soon will be offered at Columbia to students who
have completed all work for the Ph.D. except the dissertation." The
article also indicated that "in lieu of a dissertation, a body of original, scholarly published work" might be presented. Mady got more
and more excited. I myself was unimpressed. So many years had
passed since the rejection of my dissertation that I had lost interest
in pursuing the whole business. Besides, what if I did get the degree?
The only people in the world who would have cared—my parents—
were not here to rejoice. And who wanted an "intermediate degree"? I was entitled to a full-fledged one. "Yes!" Mady shouted.
"And you still are entitled to that degree. It's a simple matter of
justice and you MUST pursue it. Let right be done."

Reluctantly, I dispatched a letter to Dean Robey, presenting the facts of my case: my passing the oral examinations "with honor"; my dissertation on "The Influence of the Strasbourg Printers upon Humanism and the Reformation" and its rejection as invalid by Lynn Thorndike. I listed my published writings during the intervening years, offered to submit them in lieu of a dissertation, and expressed readiness to discuss my request for "this long delayed degree."

Almost immediately the wheels started turning. An interview with the chair of the History Department, Dr. Eugene Rice, Jr., was encouraging. Columbia already had two copies of each of my publications, but would need five copies of the works selected. In addition, I would need to defend my publications much as I would have defended my dissertation—before a committee of five university pundits. The dissertation defense took place on March 12, 1973, in Fayerweather Hall, where I had taken so many courses and heard so many lectures. My emotions were mixed: I was stirred by the return to a *temps perdu;* I was eager now for right to be done; I wanted the degree. At the end of the in-depth questioning, I was invited to retire to the student lounge to await the committee's decision. The young occupants eyed me with considerable surprise and amusement, but soon I was escorted back to the defense room. As I entered, the committee rose and greeted me in unison: "Congratulations, Dr. Rostenberg."

In the April 9 issue, an *AB Bookman's Weekly* article on "Dr. Leona Rostenberg" began: "Yes, Virginia, there is justice. On Monday, March 19, Leona Rostenberg, President of the ABAA, was awarded the Degree of Doctor of Philosophy from Columbia University." I was happy with the satisfaction of a task accomplished, a wrong righted. The elation I would have felt over thirty years earlier was missing. It was really Mady who experienced that elation. Her joy was unbounded. She immediately arranged a grandiose celebration—a graduation party—attended by nearly a hundred well-wishers. One of them gave me an album filled with all the appropriate rhymed aphorisms for a girl graduate, from "Roses are red, violets are blue" to "Long may you live, happy may you be, blessed with 40 children, 20 on each knee." Those who could not come wrote—some exulting in the thought that "it is good to give an institution its comeuppance"; others seeing it not only as a personal honor but as one "for our whole profession"; but most simply wondering, "Where do you go from up?"

The first place we went was commencement. I rented a cap and gown and on May 16 marched in the academic procession to the terraced plaza of Low Memorial Library. The sun shone on a crisply cool day. No war protests cast a shadow upon academe that day. Only the Watergate break-in marred the national horizon. Nothing marred mine, except perhaps the thought that it was all a little late. But a doctor of philosophy, I reminded myself, had better be a philosopher.

By 1973 we were both beginning to think that the story of our thirty years in the rare book business might make a good book. We dedicated our chronicle of those thirty years in the book business "To our friends in the trade: *On Approval*." They approved. We traced the stages of our business, from apprenticeship days to book hunts abroad, from Holmesian detections to the final chapter that presented a kind of philosophy of the antiquarian trade. There, we wrote that "it is one of the excitements of life to understand fully that there is nothing new under the sun, that in one way or another, by suggestion or indirection, hints of the present have been given in the past, and that over all seeming chasms there are bridges. This is one of the excitements imparted by the antiquarian book." In antiquarian books, we mused, could be found all the *causes célèbres* of our own day, from liberty of the press to perpetual peace, from space travel to Utopia, from modern medical break-throughs to the Xerox machine. In our book *Old & Rare* we tried to see connections, especially connections between past and present, and in tracing connections we both experienced the joy of discovery.

"To be writers *and* rare book sellers—how much nearer Heaven can you get than *that?!*" wrote our charming and outgoing colleague Ardis Glenn, proprietor of Glenn Books in Kansas City, after reading about our thirty-year partnership. We had been heading toward Heaven in the books we had written individually over the years. Now, in our first collaboration, we set out for the empyrean together.

Madeleine 📖 For many years I had been leading not only a double life, but an *entwined* one. My life in rare books was closely connected to my life as a writer; in some instances the former actually shaped the latter. I spent a good part of the late 1950s researching and writing a book whose subject had been suggested by our feminist collector Miriam Holden.

Miriam had entered our lives with a phone call requesting a few books from our Renaissance catalogue—the 1539 poems of Vittoria Colonna and the letters and orations of Cassandra Fedele—books that reanimated the place of women in a sixteenth-century Rialto. Then she had asked, "By the way, is the Madeleine Stern associated with the firm the same Madeleine Stern who wrote biographies of Margaret Fuller and Louisa Alcott?" That question and its answer paved the way for what would become an enduring association. I borrowed books from her shelves almost as often as she purchased books from ours. Now, one day in the late 1950s, Miriam remarked to me, "We need a good book on women who pioneered the professions in this country." "Of course," I immediately concurred. "They are the women who reached for economic independence—the backbone of the women's movement."

And that was the beginning of a book that would be called *We the Women: Career Firsts of Nineteenth-Century America,* which I naturally dedicated to Miriam, "who suggested that this book be written

. . . and [whose] splendid library of books by and about women helped bring it to completion." I included twelve biographies of women who lived equal rights by storming the professions and trades, arts and sciences previously closed to them: the first American women in architecture and law, dentistry and chemistry, interior decoration and stockbrokerage. Margaret Fuller had written, "Let them be sea-captains, if you will," and my women had taken her at her word.

Unlike Margaret Fuller and Louisa May Alcott, the protagonists of *We the Women* had for the most part been completely overlooked. Tracing their lives and careers, therefore, often required the expertise of Sherlock Holmes. He came to my assistance frequently, notably in the case of the first American woman ophthalmologist, who also happened to be the first woman stenographic reporter for congressional committees. I knew her name—Isabel C. Barrows—but little else; the nineteenth-century press had apparently paid her scant attention. Yet records must exist about a woman who had achieved two such important firsts, and Holmes and I decided to go after them.

One fact that I did unearth was that she had hailed from Vermont; another was the name of her husband: Samuel June Barrows. The name "June" for a man seemed unusual, and at that point I suddenly recalled another man with the same name. In connection with research on an earlier book I had at one time been in touch with one June Barrows Mussey, also of Vermont. There could be—there must be!—a connection. As Sherlock lured me on, I traced Mr. June Barrows Mussey, no longer in Vermont, but now settled in Düsseldorf, Germany. Had he, I asked, ever heard of Isabel, wife of Samuel June Barrows?

The answer came with stunning swiftness. Mr. Mussey had indeed heard of Isabel Barrows. She was his grandmother. What was more, she had written an autobiography—never published—and he had a typescript copy of it. Would I like it? Ten days later, the lengthy document, entitled "Chopped Straw, or the Memories of Threescore Years," was on my desk. Its dateline was Washington, D.C., February 23, 1908. It became a major source for my reanimation of a woman whose background shifted from Vermont to Washington, from New York and Boston to Vienna, from India to Russia, a woman who lived many lives and pioneered two professions, who had begun life on a Vermont farm and ended it attempting to rescue a prisoner in czarist Russia. The fortuitously detected "Chopped Straw" (Bits and Pieces) became my link with the past, my source for the reconstruction of a life.

Other lives in *We the Women* were reconstructed, often with Sherlockian assistance. My first American woman dentist, Lucy Hobbs Taylor, received her degree from Cincinnati's Ohio College of Dental Surgery in 1866, the only woman in a class of nineteen. The valedictory, addressed to the "Gentlemen Graduates," disregarded her completely. But she was awarded a parchment that became a historical document, recording a professional first for women. In the Kansas State Historical Society I found it—a document almost as telling to the woman dentist's biographer as to the woman dentist herself. The diploma of this "young girl [who] had so far forgotten her womanhood as to want to study dentistry" ended her long struggle for admission to dental school. It adorned the office of "the woman that pulls teeth."

Taylor's struggle for a dental education was duplicated by Ellen Richards's struggle to enter the Massachusetts Institute of Technology, a struggle dramatized by the discovery of the minutes of the institute's meetings. Richards, a pioneer environmentalist who would devote her life to that triangle upon which all life is built—air, water, and food—was early determined to study chemistry, and after her graduation from Vassar applied to MIT for admission as a special student. The story of her progress is disclosed in the minutes of that institution. On December 3, 1870, "the question of the admission of female students was postponed till the next meeting."

The following week, although the faculty were of opinion that "the admission of women as special students is as yet in the nature of an experiment," they admitted the applicant as a special student in chemistry, with the understanding that her admission would set no precedent for the future. My chemist did not care. She had "the chance of doing what no woman ever did . . . To be the first woman to enter the Massachusetts Institute of Technology, and so far as I know, *any scientific* school." The minutes of faculty meetings for December 3 and 10, 1870, still preserved at the institute, became telltale testimonials for *We the Women.*

First published toward the end of 1962, shortly before the appearance of Betty Friedan's influential *Feminine Mystique, We the Women* was a precursor to the feminism that was one of many isms attracting followers in the 1960s. My own literary contributions to that offbeat decade were two wildly divergent books. In *The Pantarch: A Biography of Stephen Pearl Andrews* I traced the deviational career of an eccentric nineteenth-century reformer who attacked any infringement of individual freedom. Abolitionist, champion of free love, he tried to free the Texas slaves almost single-handedly; he organized a community of individual sovereigns on Long Island; he campaigned for the presidency of the seductive Victoria Woodhull; he invented a universal language; and he talked interminably before the Manhattan Liberal Club. A man out of his own time, he would have been extremely comfortable in the sixties.

My second response to that deviational decade was a book on a firm of phrenologists who were also publishers: *Heads & Headlines: The Phrenological Fowlers.* My Fowlers were also sovereign individuals who taught a Delphic gospel: Know thyself. To any who would attend, they imparted self-knowledge through phrenology, examination of the skull to determine the faculties of the brain. Walt Whitman, who worked at one time for the Fowlers, was extraordinarily receptive to their phrenological beliefs and teachings. As a system, phrenology attracted some and repulsed some. It surely would have attracted the offbeat generation of the 1960s. Indeed, if it had only been true, it would have attracted us all.

It was in connection with the Fowlers that I made another exciting discovery: nothing less than the first book appearance of daguerreotypes by the photographer who would become Mr. Lincoln's camera man, the renowned Mathew Brady. The book, published in 1846, was entitled *Rationale of Crime,* and was the illustrated, annotated American edition of an English publication on the phrenological interpretation of criminal jurisprudence. Phrenologists had a profound interest in crime, believing that the discovery of criminal tendencies in a subject could dissuade the potential criminal from a baleful course of action. Criminal leanings, like every other evil trait, could be overcome. The view blended well with nineteenth-century American optimism, and doubtless increased the clientele who flocked to Fowler headquarters on New York's Nassau Street to have their heads examined.

It was natural for Lorenzo Fowler to play a role in the American edition of the *Rationale of Crime.* It was he who selected some of the criminals on Blackwell's Island as case studies. It was natural too for Eliza Farnham to edit the book, since she was matron of the women's prison at Sing Sing and a strong believer in phrenology. When I examined the *Rationale* at the New York Public Library, I turned first to Farnham's "Introductory Preface," in which she acknowledged the help of Mr. Fowler and of the artist Edward Serrell. When I read on, the *Finger-Spitzengefühl* came to life. "Nor must I omit to name . . . Mr. Brady, to whose indefatigable patience with a class of the most difficult of all sitters, is due the advantage of a very accurate set of daguerreotypes." Mr. Brady! Could this possibly have been the earliest, previously unidentified work of the Mr. Brady whose first name was Mathew? There was no doubt that the nineteen engraved daguerreotypes were marvelous: the Irish vagrant, the Indian half-breed, the grand or petit larcenist—all seemed alive and desperate.

Now research had to bolster *Finger-Spitzengefühl*. It was not difficult to ascertain that the twenty-one-year-old Mr. Brady—Mr.
Mathew B. Brady—was listed in the New York City Directory for
1844–45 with a "Daguerrian miniature gallery" at 207 Broadway,
corner Fulton. The corner of Fulton and Broadway was not far from
Nassau Street, where the brothers Fowler were examining heads.
The young daguerreotypist must have been attracted to the Phrenological Cabinet and must also have shared in the newness of reform
that saw crime as avoidable. There was no doubt that, with his
cumbersome camera and his copper plates coated with silver, young
Mathew Brady had crossed to Blackwell's Island and there exercised
"indefatigable patience with a class of the most difficult of all sitters." There too he had produced extraordinary likenesses of the
convicts. Included in the American edition of the *Rationale of Crime*
they formed the first public appearance of America's first great
photographer. My article in the *Quarterly Journal of the Library of
Congress* shook the dust from the *Rationale of Crime* and opened a
window on Mathew Brady's earliest work. It had resulted from a
brief acknowledgment in a forgotten book, along with a touch of
Finger-Spitzengefühl.

Shortly before Mathew Brady set up a "Daguerrian" gallery on
Broadway, corner Fulton, an eighty-year-old Franco-American died
in Paris. My interest in Joseph Nancrede stemmed from the fact that
between 1795 and 1804 he had published and sold books in Boston
that introduced to American readers French Revolutionary philosophy. He had been a citizen of two worlds, serving as a young soldier
in the American Revolution, teaching French at Harvard, increasing
Franco-American understanding. I wanted to reconstruct his career
for a book on the Franco-American book trade, but unfortunately
original sources seemed wanting. It occurred to me then that often
the end explains the beginning. Perhaps a last will and testament
would bring to life the motivations and actions and accomplishments
of Monsieur Joseph Nancrede. Sure enough. It had been preserved

in the Archives de Paris—the "Déclarations des Mutations par Décès," or dispositions of property of the deceased. It was dated June 15, 1842, and there indeed were sketched the trappings of a long rich life: his furnishings, his silver money, his investments. And there too were described the objects of my hunt. Nancrede had bequeathed to his friend, a French-Canadian exile in Paris, Louis-Joseph Papineau, all his books and all his papers. Fortunately for me, Louis-Joseph Papineau proved a faithful legatee. When his exile ended, Papineau, I discovered, had returned to Canada and taken with him the bulk of Nancrede's correspondence. Where had he deposited all this? My correspondence with Canadian manuscript depositories was extensive, but eventually I hit the target. In the Public Archives of Canada, among Papineau's own papers, were all the Nancrede documents I sought: his family letters and the correspondence of printers and booksellers with whom he had dealt; communications from William Cobbett and Joel Barlow; the letters of statesmen and rulers—Timothy Pickering and John Jay, Lafayette, Bonaparte, Louis Philippe. Here, in short, were the source materials for a life, the bricks to build or rebuild the past.

Leona 📖 AS FAR AS I WAS CONCERNED, my original thesis was still in my blood, and I was determined to prove that thesis as an independent scholar. After all, the imprints of many of the books we bought led me to the study of the printer-publisher. Had he issued them because they reflected his own point of view or for financial gain, or both?

In 1949 we had purchased from the prestigious London firm of Quaritch a run of the monthly *Philosophical Transactions* of the Royal Society from 1665 to 1702—thirty-six wonderful years when Newton and Boyle, Leeuwenhoek and Hooke were introducing the new science to England. Their articles on light and vision, chemistry and biology, blood transfusion and microscopy were ground-breakers. Their discoveries were published by John Martyn, Printer to the Royal Society, and my attention was focused upon him. Had he, as publisher, advanced the scientific innovations of his time?

John Martyn had assuredly been identified with the new scientists. Hooke browsed at his shop, The Bell, where the proprietor coddled that avid purchaser but slow payer. Martyn published Hooke's masterpiece, the *Micrographia*. It was doubtless through his connection with Hooke that he became Printer to the Royal Society and as publisher to its members was responsible for most of the highlights of the scientific resurgence. I determined to investigate the printing and advertising, the distribution and sale of those works. In our run of the *Philosophical Transactions* I found John Martyn's catalogue and lists, substantiating his specialization in the sciences. I followed him through the plague and the fire of London; I researched his career in the Stationers' Company; I studied his advertisements and his wants in the *Philosophical Transactions;* I saw him as his contemporaries had seen him in their diaries. In a lengthy article published in the *Papers of the Bibliographical Society of America* I reanimated that "thriving man in his trade," John Martyn, and indicated beyond doubt that he, too, though no scientist, had with his imprints "stimulated the intellectual and scientific development of the English Restoration . . . and . . . helped preserve for posterity an indelible record of an age of diverse experimentation, abounding curiosity, and enviable genius."

The new science had helped crush Puritanism in England. Before reform took over, however, crusades for faith alone enjoyed a mighty sway. The archpriest of Puritanism during the first part of the seventeenth century was William Prynne, almost pathologic in his pursuit of godliness. His contempt for the pleasures of life was expressed in a famous book, *Histrio-mastix,* a violent excoriation of stage players published in 1633 by another staunch Puritan, Michael Sparke, himself the author of a work appropriately entitled *Crums of*

Comfort. As Martyn had advanced the pursuit of science, Sparke aided and abetted Puritanism. At the time, the Queen of England, Henrietta Maria, French wife of Charles I, resented this intrusion upon the lighter side of life. The queen had brought performers from France to her adopted country, and it was not long before both Puritans, author Prynne and publisher Sparke, were tried in the Court of Star Chamber and a life sentence imposed upon Prynne. All copies of the *Histrio-mastix* were burned as the publisher stood in the pillory assailed by the stench of the conflagration. Subsequently, Sparke paid tribute to the Puritan author of *Histrio-mastix* by compiling and publishing the *Catalogue of Printed Books Written by VVilliam Prynne . . . Before, During, Since His Imprisonment.* This curiosity in the history of Puritanism we acquired at a Boston book fair, inspiring me to include in my gallery of influential publishers the life of Michael Sparke, uncompromising moralist, who with his "bleak and unadorned quartos" preached a bleak and unadorned doctrine.

Yet another publisher who aroused my keen interest was Nathaniel Thompson. He, too, like Michael Sparke, was tried and sentenced to stand in the pillory, but for precisely the opposite reason. Nathaniel Thompson of Fetter Lane was as staunch a Catholic as Sparke was a Puritan, regarding himself as Protector of the Faith. From our old English bookseller friends, the brothers McLeish of Little Russell Street, we purchased a copy of *The Tryal of Nathaniel Thompson . . . for Writing, Printing and Publishing Libels,* published in London in 1682. We would sell that transcript to the University of Sydney, Australia, but before we did so I would use it as a principal source for my article on Thompson and the Catholic reaction in England. As I had pursued the printer to the Royal Society and the Puritan crusader, I pursued the Papist publisher—all members of minority groups, all persistent riders of hobbyhorses, defiant tilters at windmills, whose tool was the printed word.

It was Anne Baldwin who, as a woman, represented for me the most interesting of the minority groups, even though her imprint usually read "A. Baldwin," much in the ambivalent style of A. M.

Barnard. She flourished at the end of the century and was the first woman publisher whose publications crusaded for the "Rights & Liberties" of the people. It was true that she inherited her business from her husband, but she had been and would be far more than his "help meet." At the Oxford Arms near Warwick Lane after Richard Baldwin's death she became, through the writings she issued, a proletarian force. Anti-Bourbon, anti-Papist, she published writings that championed the common people of England. From her office flowed tracts and books that advanced the rights of seamen and the wages of coachmen, opposed a standing army and exposed the state of the prisons.

Between 1709 and 1710 Anne Baldwin's imprint appeared on a periodical, *The Female Tatler,* edited by one Mrs. Crackenthorpe, *"a Lady that knows every thing."* Mrs. Crackenthorpe would be identified as Mary de la Rivière Manley, whom Swift described as "about forty, very homely and very fat," with an amazing capacity for intrigue and slander. But Anne Baldwin would use anything, including *The Female Tatler,* to espouse social justice in England until the paper, its editor, and its publisher were indicted. The career of Anne Baldwin and her crusade for English political freedom took shape from my researches at the Stationers' Company in London and the McAlpin Collection at New York's Union Theological Seminary. My study joined its predecessors in the pages of the Bibliographical Society *Papers.*

In time I added to my portraits of seventeenth-century English printer-publisher-stationers whose careers were reflected in *Literary, Political, Scientific, Religious & Legal Publishing . . . in England, 1551–1700.* And when I had completed twelve such studies, in 1965, they were assembled and published in a two-volume edition.

As the Yale librarian Donald Wing commented in his preface to the work:

A good many of us have watched the steady flow of articles from Miss Rostenberg's pen with increasing respect and I am sure many others have also urged her to collect them into a volume. Here they are . . . These twelve essays cover the seventeenth century philosophically as well as chronologically—with a nice degree of emphasis on each facet of the publishing trade. Here is meat for the historian of science, of journalism, of theology, of Americana, of literature, and of politics . . . here is a feast. Bon appetit!

In my ardor for tracing the lives and productivity of publishers, I had also covered the careers of English printsellers, portrait book publishers, and purveyors of art texts, decorative arts, and map publishers, the architecture publisher of a London swept by catastrophic fire—all who had introduced the graphic arts into "my" area of seventeenth-century England. My publisher, Burt Franklin of New York, issued my richly illustrated *English Publishers in the Graphic Arts* in 1963. Burt was a large man in every way. He was an insatiable collector of books on economics, an antiquarian dealer in that specialty, and a compulsive publisher of books for book people. Everything he did was on a grand scale. He ate hugely; he talked with indefatigable gusto; he had grandiloquent ideas. He loved to add books to the numerous series he launched. My graphic arts venture was issued as Burt Franklin Bibliography and Reference Series Number 42. Dedicated to my parents, "who would have been pleased," it carried a preface by A. Hyatt Mayor of the Metropolitan Museum of Art, and was hailed as "a lasting contribution."

The publisher of my third book was a study in contrast to the exuberant Burt Franklin. Bob De Graaf was a sober Dutch citizen with a passion for books—the antiquarian variety, which he sold, the modern variety, which he published. Annually we spent a day at his house near the canal in Nieuwkoop, selecting books from his shelves and enjoying his wife Emmy's company and cuisine. During one of our visits I discussed my project for a book on the minority press in England, a book that would encompass the English attitude toward religious subversion during the reigns of Elizabeth I and James I. In those days religion was not only synonymous with politics—it *was* politics. Deviation from the established church, whether Catholic or Puritan, was heresy. Once again I was determined to trace the role of printer-publisher in the more or less unexplored field of minority belief and thought. The result was *The Minority Press & The English Crown: A Study in Repression,* which appeared in 1971 over the imprint of B. De Graaf.

I had long before been introduced to an exciting example of deviational printing. Had not my first major find been the Calderwood, published at the Pilgrim Press in Leyden by the English expatriate William Brewster before he boarded the *Mayflower?* Had we not sold another example of Brewster's clandestine printing to the Leyden University Library, located "about two hundred yards" from the press's birthplace? In between, unexpectedly, serendipitously, and incredibly, we acquired still another even more noteworthy Pilgrim Press book. By then we were aware that Brewster's very first publication from his underground press in Leyden had been a Latin work by a Puritan divine named William Ames, expressing his Separatist views. Ames's book was not only Brewster's first; it was one of only three in which he actually included his name in the imprint. It was a prize to be sought after. And we found it on the floor of the basement in a bookshop in London's Cecil Court.

When we first entered the shop and asked the proprietor for old and rare, he suggested we descend to the lower depths, where he had stored "bits and pieces" from a theological library he had bought about fourteen years earlier. We descended without much hope. Theology per se was not to our liking. Once in the basement we were paralyzed by the quantity of calfbound books surrounding us—on shelves, on chairs, on tables, and especially on the floor. Languidly, we picked up a little calfbound duodecimo that had presumably reposed for fourteen years on that floor. We opened to the title page. It was a Latin work by the Puritan divine William Ames. We looked at the imprint and needed no detection to read, also in Latin, "Leyden: William Brewster, 1617." Here was the first issue from the underground press established in Leyden by our Pilgrim Fathers. The book bore the ownership inscription of one of the Lords of the Treasury, George Baillie, and the price he had paid for it in 1704: 2 pounds 9. We did better in Cecil Court centuries later. We paid one guinea—$2.90. Our book would go for $900 to our friend Donald Wing at Yale.

I had long ago been fascinated by the friendship between the Printer to the Royal Society, the bookseller John Martyn, and his illustrious but difficult customer Robert Hooke. For me, Hooke epitomized the seventeenth-century English book collector: he did not hesitate to spend hours browsing, haggling over prices, taking books on approval, returning them, and buying the same books at another dealer's. He bought books not for decorative purposes but for use. In my study of Hooke and his library, *The Library of Robert Hooke: The Scientific Book Trade of Restoration England,* published in 1989 by Modoc Press of Santa Monica, California, I discussed at length the scientific book trade of Restoration England. I profited, as my subject had, from the importation of scientific texts from abroad. With him I journeyed to the second-hand bookstalls of Duck Lane and Moorfields; I visited purveyors of mathematical texts and alchemical specialists, and attended auctions of his day. When, researching Hooke at the British Museum, I read the catalogue of his library auctioned after his death at Exeter-Exchange in the Strand, I decided to reprint it in my study of Hooke, analyze it, and draw bibliographical and ideological conclusions from it.

Long before I saturated myself in the life and reading of Robert Hooke, I had applied my love of books to another mania, stamp collecting. For years I had been collecting stamps that depicted every phase of bookish history, from the invention of printing to early printers and publishers, from the printing press to libraries, from first editions to woodcuts and illustrations, from bookplates to book fairs. Stamps from Malta and Iran, the Cook Islands and Ceylon, Israel and Barbados, the Congo Republic and the Maldive Islands lent color to my collection, and I pursued a book on a stamp with almost the same fervor as I pursued a book in an English basement. I invented a name for my mad passion—Bibliately—and decided to make a book out of my books on stamps. *Bibliately* was published serially in 1977 and later in book form by *The American Philatelist,* introducing a new "philatelic topical" to the hordes of stamp collectors and a new book about books to bibliomaniacs.

The books and articles—*We the Women* and *Heads & Headlines, Publishing in Seventeenth-Century England* and *Robert Hooke*—were produced against the continuing background of business as usual. Business as usual meant attendance at auctions. At the great Thomas W. Streeter sale of Americana at the Parke-Bernet Galleries in 1968 we sat on tenterhooks with a Library of Congress bid of $25,000 for Pigafetta's *Narrative of the Voyages of Magellan* and, becoming glummer and glummer, watched in agony as the bids climbed beyond us to the hammer price of $56,000.

Business as usual meant catalogues that punctuated the years and offered to our clientele works on *The Court of Louis XIV* and *Sources of History, The French Revolution* and *The British Connection.* Many of our catalogues were of course designed for the book fairs in which we continued to participate. *Plums at the Plaza* offered a fruity assortment for an elegant fair at the Hotel Plaza. We gave, tongue-in-cheek, a self-promotional title—*New York's Finest*—to our catalogue for the 1980 book fair, and were duly thrilled to read in a letter from an Ann Arbor dealer to our trade journal: "Our unanimous choice for the most delightful bookseller duo at the Fair was that redoubtable team, Leona Rostenberg and Madeleine Stern." In his *Times* survey of the 1983 book fair, Herbert Mitgang singled out for comment our feminist books from Pope Joan to Mary Wollstonecraft, our first edition of *The Wealth of Nations,* and a Brewster Pilgrim Press imprint. The next year, when our fair catalogue was entitled *Showcase,* we celebrated the fortieth anniversary of the firm and had a poster printed to mark the event. Our booths at book fairs were graced not only by our own "Fare for the Fair," but by our browsers and visitors. At one fair Irving Wallace chewed the literary rag with us, discussing his books and ours. At another, Jacqueline Kennedy, who of course needed no introduction, was introduced to us and left us with an enchanting memory. By the time of the 1989 book fair we were described as a "venerable firm." The "venerable firm" commented, "We never think about retirement, because we're continually invigorated by new discoveries."

THE BLOOD-
AND-THUNDER

Madeleine 📖 IN 1983
the American Printing History Association conferred upon us jointly
its annual award "for distinguished
contributions to the study and dissemination of printing history." In
doing so, the association broke with
precedent, for it was the first time
the award was given to rare book
dealers and the first time it was given jointly. We were asked to give
acceptance speeches at the presentation in Columbia University's
Butler Library, and we chose to give them in tandem. It was indeed
appropriate that the award of the American Printing History Association was bestowed upon us jointly. In many ways the two recipients
had led and were leading joint lives. We were partners in business;
we lectured in tandem; and although we had written many books
separately, we had also written in collaboration. We continued to do
so.

All our joint publications were written in the Barnes Landing
section of East Hampton at the eastern end of Long Island during the
long summer months when we recessed our book business. We
began renting a cottage in 1962 and—foolish as it may seem to

investors in property—we have been renting ever since. At first we rented for a month, later for three months, and always we have loved our island summers. We spend our mornings writing, our afternoons beaching, swimming in the bay, and enjoying the lazy summer talk of our good beach friends. As one of our guests sagely commented, "It's a way of life you could easily get used to."

Our first collaboration was written in a house on Winding Way. It is a toss-up whether we had more pleasure in the writing than in the reading aloud to each other, or vice versa. We wrote about the "Public Relations" of antiquarian dealers; of "Books That Swing the Pendulum"—political writings that led to action; of books that escaped our net; of catalogues and collections. Books and their life cycles formed the basic theme of our works. Then, in 1993, our third collaboration was produced. Unlike its predecessors, this was a novel centering on our search for a "fabulously rare copy of the 1511 Erasmus *Praise of Folly.*" We traced its history from its publication in Strasbourg, its experience of fire and flood, war and epidemic. We told the tale of the colorful personalities through whose hands it passed: a Nuremberg patrician, a great artist, a celebrated Czech engraver, a woman hawker, a seventeenth-century auctioneer, a London butcher, a chandler of Southwark, an adventurer in the New World. We related it, too, to our country house guests, and in the end we described its discovery at a Ladies' Village Improvement Society Fair in East Hampton. We called our concoction *Quest Book—Guest Book: A Biblio-Folly.*

But it was our greatest find ever, the one that most mirrored our own double lives, that continues to enthrall today's reader; that is, of course, the unmasking of Louisa May Alcott. Had she lived today, Louisa May Alcott—or, rather, her alter ego, A. M. Barnard—would have written this chapter as a sensation story. Her cast of characters would have included an ambitious, self-promoting male villain and a woman ignored. Her plot, based upon an attempt to mislead the public, may well have involved a pact with the devil.

After riding on the heroine's coattails, the Mephistophelian hero would abandon her utterly and, indifferent to her fate, bask on his own in literary glory. The plot would of course demand a subplot, hinging on a rejected sensational manuscript and its eventual resurfacing. But the Alcott version of this thriller would end in triumph for the woman scorned and doubtless find a place in such a collection as *The Feminist Alcott: Stories of a Woman's Power*.

It was toward the end of 1973 when it dawned on me that nobody had ever thought of digging up those wonderful stories that Leona discovered Alcott had written anonymously or under the pseudonym A. M. Barnard. Leona's discovery, announced to the public thirty years earlier, had been briefly applauded before being completely disregarded. No one, including myself, had thought of tracing the Alcott blood-and-thunders and making them available to the public. Until now.

The other projects of my double life over the past thirty years had deflected me from the fascinating spinster of Concord. But now I was drawn to her again. If the world could learn that the author of *Little Women* had penned stories of violence and revenge when she was not writing wholesome domestic sagas, surely the world would take note. For my anthology of blood-and-thunders I selected a quartet of shockers, including the earliest I had uncovered, the anonymous prize winner of *Frank Leslie's Illustrated Newspaper,* "Pauline's Passion and Punishment." Against the background of an exotic paradise, Pauline Valary, a "handsome woman, with bent head, locked hands, and restless steps," paces "to and fro, like a wild creature in its cage," planning revenge upon the man who has abandoned her. "Leave Gilbert to remorse—and me," she declares, and proceeds to weave her vengeful web and the author's suspenseful plot.

The feminist gallery was joined—climaxed—by the enigmatic figure of Jean Muir in A. M. Barnard's masterpiece, "Behind a Mask: or, A Woman's Power." Originally issued in *The Flag of Our*

Union, which Leona had discovered, this four-part serial of 1866 came to me in photocopy from the American Antiquarian Society. I devoured it voraciously as the pages followed one another. Pauline Valary was more femme fatale than feminist; Jean Muir reversed the proportion. One of A. M. Barnard's most fascinating heroines, she is actress and witch, enchantress and feminist. Motivated, like Pauline, by thwarted love, she sets out to ruin the Coventry family and succeeds in captivating every one of its male members, including the head of the House of Coventry.

Why had the future author of *Little Women* created such characters and woven such stories? There were many reasons. Economic need was one. Bronson Alcott had no gift for moneymaking, and the cost of coal, the price of shoes, increased along with the family debts. "Pauline's Passion" had yielded its author—"a lady of Massachusetts"—$100, and "Behind a Mask" brought $80 (more than the publisher's original offer) to the Alcott sinking fund.

But A. M. Barnard had another, perhaps even stronger motivation to spin thrillers in which feminism was so often an ingredient. In a way, "Behind a Mask" is a *roman à clef* in which the past not only of Jean Muir but of Louisa May Alcott sits for its portrait. Like Jean Muir, Alcott had gone out to service, experiencing at age nineteen what can only be called her Humiliation at Dedham. She had consented to work for the Dedham lawyer the Honorable James Richardson and his sister, but when she retreated from his maudlin advances she had been assigned all the household work, from digging paths through the snow to fetching water from the well, from splitting the kindling and sifting the ashes to blacking the master's muddy boots. After seven weeks of drudgery she left, receiving for her labors the sum of four dollars. It required little detection to perceive that the Humiliation in Dedham had been converted into feminist anger in a sensation story.

A few years later, frustrated in all her attempts to find work, Louisa looked at the waters of the Mill Dam and was momentarily tempted to find the solution of her problems in their depths. Surely such a temptation, like her service in Dedham, was part of the psychological equipment of a writer who needed to let her hair down.

Many details that would appear in the large corpus of sensation narratives eventually traced to her pen found their source in the author's life. From a passion for acting to hashish experimentation and opium addiction, from mind control to madness, the themes are traceable not only to Alcott's readings and imaginings but often to her observations and experiences.

To "Pauline's Passion" and "Behind a Mask," I added A. M. Barnard's Gothic romance "The Abbot's Ghost: or, Maurice Treherne's Temptation," a four-part serial from *The Flag of Our Union* of 1867, and *The Mysterious Key, and What It Opened,* which had been published as a "Ten Cent Novelette" by Elliott, Thomes & Talbot. Once I gathered my gaudy foursome together, I offered the collection to the firm of William Morrow. Joni Evans, the charming, vibrant senior editor, was, at the end of January 1974, "tremendously excited"; a "contract letter" was "in the works"; by the end of May a marketing meeting promised further excitement over a volume now definitely entitled *Behind a Mask.*

Behind a Mask: The Unknown Thrillers of Louisa May Alcott was published on my birthday, July 1, 1975. And the hoopla began. The next morning I was interviewed on the "Today" show by Barbara Walters, who, I must confess, was really more interested in why Louisa Alcott had never married than in the complexities of her double literary life. The excitement continued, now that the titillating disclosure had been made: the author who touted the wholesome delights of apples and ginger cookies in her family sagas also expressed remarkable familiarity with murder and mayhem, drug addiction and the sexual power struggle in the thrillers of *Behind a Mask.* Reviewers were astonished with the array of "wild melodrama and mad passion" in *the* Miss Alcott, the most astute remarking, "A most fascinating find. Never again will you have quite the same image of this particular 'little woman.' "

As eyes were opened, eyebrows were raised. *Behind a Mask* was reprinted: by September a fourth printing had been scheduled; foreign rights were sold to W. H. Allen of London; a Bantam paperback vastly increased the readership. A second volume of anonymous and pseudonymous shockers by the "Children's Friend" was contemplated.

The last paragraph of my introduction to *Behind a Mask* had stated:

The four narratives selected for Behind a Mask: The Unknown Thrillers of Louisa May Alcott *are, it is hoped, an earnest, a foretaste of others that will follow. For Louisa Alcott was indeed a natural—an almost limitless—"source of stories." Here her "gorgeous fancies" and her flamboyant characters do "cavort at their own sweet will." And here, in an extraordinary union, the excitements of escape are coupled with the excitements of self-discovery. She writes in a vortex behind her mask and she proves, if proof is needed, that "the writers of sensation novels are wiser in their generation than the children of sweetness and light."*

Behind a Mask was a foretaste of *Plots and Counterplots: More Unknown Thrillers of Louisa May Alcott,* published exactly one year later. The title narrative—"V.V.: or, Plots and Counterplots," "By A Well Known Author"—had originally appeared in *The Flag of Our Union* in 1865 and reappeared as a Ten Cent Novelette. V.V.—Virginie Varens—is a far cry from Jo March. A malevolent, devious Spanish dancer, she is probably Alcott's most evil heroine, perpetrating sins that range from peccadillo to crime. An exciting femme fatale, V.V. had "the nerves of a man" and "the quick wit of a woman," not to mention the malignancy of Satan and the conniving skills of Machiavelli. Even in the act of appalling, she enchants.

To "V.V." I added another A. M. Barnard serial plucked from

the pages of *The Flag of Our Union*, "A Marble Woman: or, The Mysterious Model," a narrative presenting Alcott's variation on the Pygmalion-Galatea theme. Here the heroine is molded into marble by a sculptor whose clay is flesh and blood. Here too the author deftly interweaves other delectable themes: the child-bride; a hint of incest; a brief bout with opium addiction. Louisa Alcott had surely been ministered laudanum during the illness that followed her service as Civil War nurse, and as a result A. M. Barnard found in tincture of opium a useful narrative device. The final story of *Plots and Counterplots*, "Perilous Play," originally published in *Leslie's Illustrated Newspaper*, is concerned entirely with drug experimentation. A short, dramatic shocker, "Perilous Play" is devoted exclusively to an experiment with hashish, "that Indian stuff which brings one fantastic visions." It ends with the exclamation "Heaven bless hashish, if its dreams end like this!"

With two other sensation stories, "The Skeleton in the Closet" and "A Whisper in the Dark," *Plots and Counterplots* made a popular sequel to *Behind a Mask*. The page turners that appealed to the general public were at the same time spurring scholars on their revisionist course. Reinterpreting the "Children's Friend" in the light of her shockers, they highlighted the darker aspects of Alcott's life and character, applying the new criticism not only to her oeuvre but to her persona. The sexual politics in her newly uncovered sensation fiction was traced, her "midnight fantasies" examined, her "gender relations" explored. Louisa May Alcott was recognized as a far more adventurous writer than had been believed, a many-faceted professional as adept at the sensational as at the sentimental. From behind her mask, a new Alcott image was emerging.

The critics were soon joined by the dramatists. Katharine Houghton, actress-playwright, created and performed a delightful monologue entitled *To Heaven in a Swing*, a one-woman show about the life of Louisa May Alcott. *Necessities*, Rita Kohn's one-woman script on Alcott, was an award-winner. Two dramatists in California collaborated on a play based upon "V.V.: or, Plots and Counter-plots," and off Broadway in New York the story "Behind a Mask" was charmingly transposed for the theater by Karen L. Lewis. A musical adaptation of that story is being prepared by Polly Pen for the McCarter Theatre in Princeton, New Jersey.

The unmasked Alcott seemed to attract attention from a wide range of readers and viewers, and many curious reactions found their way to my desk. One correspondent who worked in a sawmill informed me that he was writing a book containing postcards to Louisa May Alcott and was looking for a "woman editor" whose "instincts" were compatible with his. Another correspondent sent me a lengthy opus written after she had revealed in a series of hypnotic sessions that *she* was Louisa May Alcott.

The producers of "Bookshelf" on BBC Radio interviewed me for a program entitled "A Double Life," which they characterized as "a splendid sidelong way of viewing Alcott." Leona and I were invited to lecture on "Louisa May Alcott: What Was Behind Her Mask?" The library of Brigham Young University in Provo, Utah, enlisted us to build a collection of writings by and about Louisa May Alcott that has continued amassing for many years. A. Dean Larsen, Associate University Librarian and a dear friend, wrote to me in appreciation: "When you meet Louisa May Alcott in the next life she is going to embrace you and say, 'Madeleine, you, more than any other person ever to live, have furthered my literary reputation.' "

It was only natural that, by the 1980s, scholars should have begun the task of collecting Louisa May Alcott's *Letters* and revising and completing the nineteenth-century edition of her *Journals*. For those two indispensable undertakings, Professor Joel Myerson of the University of South Carolina and his then research assistant, Daniel Shealy, were largely responsible. I was delighted to join with them in both major projects. The new edition of Alcott's *Journals* included "Notes and Memoranda," kept by the writer in a ledger bound in half-leather. In it she entered a brief summary of her year's activities and—most important—a list of stories she had written, the titles usually abbreviated, and the sums they had earned. In those lists some surprising titles appeared, titles of stories I had never heard of, much less read. For example, in the early 1860s "A Pair of Eyes" earned the author $40; in 1864 she received $50 for "The Fate of the Forrests"; in 1865, when she earned $50 for "V.V." and $75 for "A Marble Woman," she also earned $50 each for "A Double Tragedy" and for "Ariel."

The titles of those unread narratives seemed appropriate for the blood-and-thunder genre, and I had a very good idea of where they had appeared. In re-editing Alcott's *Journals,* the twentieth-century editors had included all the telltale names and statements that the nineteenth-century editor, Ednah Dow Cheney, had seen fit to delete. Louisa Alcott, it appeared, had been far more prolific than her biographers had dreamed. The Concord Scheherezade had hidden an Arabian Nights Entertainment behind her mask. Many of her tales had been written, as she noted in her *Journals* during the 1860s, "for Leslie"—the L. I had long ago identified. Here he was again, with his fleet of magazines and newspapers. I had only to plow through them for titles I now knew were by Louisa May Alcott. The hunt was on once more.

No one who has not experienced the urgencies of search-and-find can share the palpitations and bated breath that accompany the turning of crumbling nineteenth-century folio newspaper sheets for hidden nuggets. Frank Leslie's major publication, his *Illustrated News-paper,* lay before me in bound volumes of the 1860s. I knew they must contain some of the unsigned stories I was seeking. In these pages my tireless author awaited her huntress. I found her first in a two-part narrative published in October 1863, anonymously, of course. I quickly scanned my find. "A Pair of Eyes; or, Modern Magic" was modern magic indeed—a remarkable narrative focused upon mind control through mesmerism, extraordinary preoccupa-

tions for the author of *Flower Fables*. In November 1863 Alcott recorded in her journal: "Recieved [sic] $39 from Leslie for 'A Pair of
Eyes,' not enough, but I'm glad to get even that . . . Paid debts
with it as usual." How right she was. Not enough for such an
intriguing narrative, even in 1863.

I tracked down "The Fate of the Forrests" in three issues of
Frank Leslie's Illustrated Newspaper for February 1865. Here, my anonymous, multifaceted writer had left the lure of mesmeric influences
for the shocking theme of Hindu Thuggism. Even in this foray into
the exotic, the power struggle between the sexes runs like a scarlet
thread. The author of *Little Women* found the sexual conflict an
enormously productive literary theme.

In March 1865 Alcott wrote in her *Journal:* "Leslie asked me to
be a regular contributor to his new paper 'The Chimney Corner,' &
I agreed if he'd pay before hand, he said he would & bespoke two
tales at once $50 each. Longer ones as often as I could & whatever
else I liked to send. So here's another source of income & Alcott
brains seem in demand."

Frank Leslie's Chimney Corner was planned, started, and edited by
that genuine femme fatale Miriam Squier, who would shortly become Mrs. Frank Leslie. On the first page of its first issue was
emblazoned an anonymous narrative entitled "A Double Tragedy:
An Actor's Story." Leafing the pages, I found in the weekly for July
8 and 15 the two-part tale "Ariel: A Legend of the Lighthouse."
Both stories owe much to the theatrical passion of their stagestruck
author. "A Double Tragedy" is not only a story of guilt and murder, but quintessentially a story of the stage. "Ariel," set on an
enchanted island, borrows heavily from Shakespeare's *Tempest*, almost translating it for a nineteenth-century readership. The surname
Alcott gives her heroine Ariel is, incidentally, March.

Those four stories discovered or rediscovered in Leslie news
sheets would have been sufficient for another collection of Alcott
thrillers. But I had a delectable plum to add to them. In December
1866 the writer noted in her *Journal:* "Wrote . . . a wild Russian

story 'Taming a Tartar.' " Listing the year's earnings, she cited "Taming a Tartar" at $100. An Alcott narrative with such a title had to be both melodramatic and feminist. And indeed it was. It was spread—again anonymously—over four installments of *Frank Leslie's Illustrated Newspaper* in 1867, and it was the most explicit version of the power struggle between the sexes that Alcott had ever produced. The contest between the slender, pale-faced English teacher Sybil Varna and the "swarthy, black-eyed, scarlet-lipped" Tartar Prince Alexis is an exciting and intense battle of wills. Its final dialogue dramatically designates the victor:

> *ALEXIS : I might boast that I also had tamed a fiery spirit, but I am humble, and content myself with the knowledge that the proudest woman ever born has promised to love, honor, and—*
> *SYBIL : Not obey you.*

The quintet of "Newly Discovered Thrillers of Louisa May Alcott" was gathered together under the title *A Double Life,* and the collection was published by Little, Brown in 1988.

Three years later another collection of Alcott shockers, traced and assembled by colleagues Daniel Shealy and Joel Myerson, was published by Greenwood Press as *Freaks of Genius.* And in 1993 still another anthology of Alcott's "Stories of Intrigue and Suspense" appeared under the title *From Jo March's Attic,* over the imprint of Northeastern University Press. That collection was dedicated to Victor A. Berch, "Literary Detective." I had sent to that persistent researcher a list of some of the still untraced titles from Alcott's account book and, doubtless after the usual palpitations, he uncovered them in yet another Leslie publication, *Frank Leslie's Lady's Magazine* edited by none other than Miriam Leslie. Where Alcott listed "Dr Donn" [sic] $22, Mr. Berch found "Doctor Dorn's Revenge"; where Alcott cited "Countess Irma," Mr. Berch pounced upon "Countess Varazoff," whose first name was Irma; Alcott's "Made-

moiselle" showed up as "My Mysterious Mademoiselle," and "Betrayed" materialized as "Betrayed by a Buckle."

Between 1975 and 1993, five collections of Alcott thrillers were
resuscitated from the fragile weeklies of the mid-nineteenth century.
The page turners disclosed the author's strange familiarity with sexual power struggles, narcotics addiction, murder, revenge, and feminist triumph over the male lords of creation. The prolific double
literary life that had been a well-kept secret in the nineteenth century was revealed to the public. Or was it? In two decades much can
be forgotten.

There was still one long sensational story that Louisa May Alcott
had written but had never published. She had called it "A Modern
Mephistopheles, or The Long Fatal Love Chase" and had written it
in 1866, shortly after her return from abroad, where she had served
as companion to a young invalid. It had been suggested by A. M.
Barnard's publisher, James R. Elliott, of Elliott, Thomes and Talbot,
who had written:

> I would like to have you write me a story of from 200 to 250 pages your Ms.,
> in 24 chapters, & the close of each 2nd chapter so absorbingly interesting that
> the reader will be impatient for the next. The twelve parts (24 chapters) may
> vary 5 or 6 pages as to length, but not more than that. I want it to run
> through 12 numbers of our Magazine, and I think you can write a story that
> you, myself and our readers will like. For such a story I shall be willing to give
> you an extra $25, over the half dollar per Ms. page. Will you write it, so that
> I can have it (or one half of it) by October 1st?

Since family debts had mounted during the breadwinner's stay
in Europe, she was quick to comply with Elliott's request. But James
R. Elliott, for reasons Alcott cites in her diary, rejected the manuscript. As Alcott put it, "Mother sick . . . Got a girl & devoted
myself to mother, writing after she was abed. In this way finished
the long tale 'A Modern Mephistopheles.' But Elliott would not

have it, saying it was too long & too sensational! So I put it away & fell to work on other things.''

''A Modern Mephistopheles'' had been rejected, but Alcott was a thrifty Yankee who seldom threw away anything useful. I knew she had re-used the title, *A Modern Mephistopheles,* for a book requested by the publisher of her later work, when, as America's beloved author of juveniles, she commanded dazzling prices and an enormous readership. In 1877, long after *Little Women* had brought her fame and fortune, Thomas Niles of Roberts Brothers asked his illustrious author to contribute a novel to his No Name Series, a series of books published anonymously but written by famous authors. Why not, Niles had suggested, use that old unpublished story and rework it for the No Names?

Alcott had followed his suggestion, and her *Modern Mephistopheles*—the story of a Faustian young man who sells his soul for literary fame—appeared in the series in 1877, intriguing readers and setting them to guessing at its authorship. In 1987 I had the pleasure of editing that novel for Praeger, and it was then that Joel Myerson alerted me to the fact that the manuscript of the original ''Modern Mephistopheles,'' rejected by Elliott, was still extant, in Harvard's Houghton Library.

In short order a Xerox copy was on my desk. The story, entitled ''A Modern Mephistopheles, or, The Long Fatal Love Chase,'' consisted of some 284 pages—indeed ''too long'' for Elliott's purpose. In the title, however, I noticed that the words ''A Modern Mephistopheles'' had been penned out, leaving only ''The Long Fatal Love Chase,'' whose first paragraph contained the enticing words ''I often feel as if I'd gladly sell my soul to Satan for a year of freedom.''

It was an accurate title for the rejected manuscript, which had no relationship at all to the plot of Alcott's No Name narrative. Had ''The Long Fatal Love Chase,'' besides being too long, been too sensational? The plot line of each novel is clearly the power struggle between good and evil, but beyond that basic theme they had very little in common. The heroine of the "Chase," Rosamond, is artlessly frank, unconscious of her power, in love with a sinner but hating the sin. The sinner hero is Phillip Tempest, a man who has tasted every pleasure, obeyed no law but his own will, roamed all over the world, and at thirty-five become "unutterably tired of everything under the sun." The interaction of hero and heroine triggers an elaborate plot with a number of sensational subplots. Rosamond, to begin with, is won over a card game; a pretended wedding deludes her into thinking she is married to Phillip Tempest; in a chapter entitled "Cholera" Phillip leads a friend to his death; Rosamond's escape from her sinner husband and his untiring pursuit entail disguises, assumed names, the discovery of a corpse, a stay in a convent, and a stay in a madhouse. Tempest's chase after his fugitive inamorata is indeed long and fatal, involving sudden reappearances, false reports, and the frequently inaccurate firing of pistols. Midway through the manuscript Father Ignatius is introduced, a priest who falls in love with the heroine. The long chase does end fatally, with Rosamond's death and Phillip's suicide. But before he destroys himself, the hero gathers the dead woman in his arms and claims a final macabre victory: "Mine first—mine last—mine even in the grave!"

In my introduction to the second and much revised *Modern Mephistopheles* of the No Name Series, I discussed the early rejected version in some detail. And as far as I was concerned, that was the end of "The Long Fatal Love Chase." I had seen little in it to argue with James R. Elliott's rejection of the manuscript. In my wildest imaginings—never, to be sure, as wild as Alcott's—I could not have foreseen that it would, 130 years after it had been conceived, generate a *cause célèbre* and a reputed fortune.

Then, some time later, I was sent a copy of Occasional List Number 93, issued by a New York dealer in rare books, Ximenes, Inc. Item 299 in that list offered—under the heading "Six Hundred Pages of Manuscript"—two autograph manuscripts by Louisa May

Alcott: *Jo's Boys* and *A Long Love Chase*. The *Long Love Chase* was described as "the original manuscript of an unpublished novel, a gothic tale about a restless and strong-willed young woman . . . who is rescued from her dull existence by the demonic Phillip Tempest; the subsequent tale involves bigamy, murder, and suicide." The two manuscripts were offered as a pair, the price (reputedly over $400,000) available "on request."

Alcott manuscripts on deposit at the Houghton Library were for the most part still owned by the Alcott family. In the case of the "Love Chase," which had never appeared in print, the right to publish was also vested in the family. When I read the Ximenes offer, I of course informed Dean Larsen of Brigham Young, who would have been delighted to add the manuscript of *Jo's Boys* to the library had the price been less astronomical. *Jo's Boys,* the final volume of the *Little Women* trilogy, had been written during Alcott's last years and had rung the curtain down upon the March—and Alcott—family. By contrast, "The Long Love Chase" seemed a minor acquisition. I took the liberty of suggesting to my colleague of the Ximenes firm that, since the two works had nothing in common beyond their authorship, it might be wise to offer the two manuscripts separately.

At this point yet another character walked on stage to participate in the ensuing drama. Kent Bicknell, in his mid-forties, was principal of a private school in New Hampshire and, not unlike the Transcendentalists, had long been under the influence of East Indian philosophy and mysticism. A former collector of Nathaniel Hawthorne, he had recently switched his collecting interests to Louisa May Alcott, and in this connection he paid occasional visits to the firm of Rostenberg and Stern. We talked Alcott; he made a few purchases; and, in exchange for a number of my articles on various phases of Alcott's career and Leona's groundbreaking article on the Alcott pseudonym, he presented us with a large quantity of local maple syrup.

During this seminal period, another cast of characters walked on stage with a revised film version of *Little Women*. I found the new rendition too free with its reading of the original text, and the whole far too saccharine. Remembering only Katharine Hepburn as Jo March, I thought Winona Ryder too beautiful and too unruffled. But the majority of viewers loved the new *Little Women,* and the movie would do much to heighten interest in the Concord spinner of tales.

While the film was in preparation, Kent Bicknell purchased the manuscript of "A Long Fatal Love Chase" and paid the family for the right to publish it. It was not long before he engaged the services of an agent, who had no trouble stirring up interest in a previously unpublished sensational Alcott novel, and Random House acquired the prize for a reputed seven figures. History, once again, repeated itself, and the publishing world savored the idea of a new discovery. Of course, Louisa May Alcott had been "hot" for a long time.

By January of 1995, earlier publishers of Alcott's sensation stories were hoisting themselves on the bandwagon. The blood-and-thunder style apparently filled a twentieth-century need, too. *A Long Fatal Love Chase* was published, without introduction but with considerable hype, by Random House in 1995. Along with it came the reissues of my earlier collections and the proposals for new ones. Vindication loomed for the women ignored—for Leona, known to many as "the Little Grandmother of the Alcott Revolution," for me, and most of all for Alcott herself.

As it turned out, the new generation of readers was captivated by the reprinted *Behind a Mask*. In October 1995, in an article entitled "Dead White Females," Michele Slung wrote for the *Washington Post:*

> Collector Kent Bicknell, the man who'd bought and [peddled] the manuscript of Love Chase, was really only riding on the distinguished coattails of book dealer/scholar Madeleine Stern, who'd begun staking out the territory of Alcott rediscovery as long ago as the early 1940s.
>
> Thirty years after she'd gotten on the case, in an era when the cobwebby

shelves of out-of-print fiction by women writers were finally starting to be scrutinized . . . William Morrow . . . took a chance and . . . brought out her edition of Alcott's mesmerizing and lurid Behind a Mask, *to the delight of anyone who happened to come across it.*

Stephen King, reviewing the *Chase* in the *Times,* concluded that it was "not the best of Alcott's sensation stories; that is probably 'Behind a Mask.' " General critical opinion concurred. Maureen Corrigan, in her joint review of *Mask* and *Chase* for the *Washington Post,* wrote that "*Behind a Mask* is by far the better way to become acquainted with Alcott's racier side." Corrigan ended her critique with a delicious suggestion: "If they ever make a movie of 'Behind a Mask,' forget Winona Ryder; this Alcott heroine calls for the likes of Leona Helmsley."

Meanwhile, I had received a phone call from Random House. Would I supply them with an Alcott volume for their Modern Library division? The request was irresistible to me. I selected for the volume five shockers whose themes would appeal to twentieth-century readers: "A Pair of Eyes," based on mind control; "The Fate of the Forrests," with its ethnic barbarism and violence; "Behind a Mask: or, A Woman's Power"; "Perilous Play," on hashish experimentation; and "My Mysterious Mademoiselle," with its suggested transvestitism. In my introduction I wrote that "Louisa May Alcott would have found herself at home in the twentieth century . . . In her stories of . . . mind control, Eastern violence and woman's power, drug experimentation and transvestitism, she transcends her own time . . . The enchantments she has conjured up are as modern as they are magical."

The new compilation, *Modern Magic,* was joined some time later by yet another, requested by Northeastern University Press, a house that had already issued my omnibus volume, *Louisa May Alcott Unmasked: Collected Thrillers.* Now I provided them with *The Feminist Alcott: Stories of a Woman's Power,* including "Pauline's Passion and Punishment," "V.V.: or, Plots and Counterplots," "Behind a

Mask: or, A Woman's Power,'' and "Taming a Tartar"—four stories selected "because in them the sexual power struggle is . . . the fiber that knits the narrative together" and "in each of the four . . . the canny author has offered fascinating variations on the theme.''

The climax of *my* Alcott renaissance was reached when Random House elected to reprint my biography of Louisa May Alcott, first published in 1950, as a paperback. Needless to say, its bibliography of Alcott writings was expanded to 314 numbered items, including of course all the traced sensation stories.

In the 1950s, after that biography was issued, I sold the majority of the Alcott books I had collected to make room for books related to my next biography. In the 1970s, when I began tracking down the Alcott thrillers, I assembled another Alcott library. Now, in the 1990s, I am doing the same thing. If there has been a persistent ghost in my literary life, it is certainly that of Louisa May Alcott. Early on, identifying, as so many adolescents have done, with Jo March, I gloried in that heroine's forthright independence and daring. Surely she was, as I was, a feminist in the making. Later I would realize that she was a role model for all women who said what they thought and did what they believed in, regardless of world opinion.

Thanks to Leona's discovery, we had learned that, like Jo March, Louisa May Alcott had written sensation stories that were published anonymously and pseudonymously. The forthright Louisa Alcott had led in secret a tumultuous double literary life. Later on, tracing those stories to their original printed sources, we became aware of Alcott's familiarity with—and delight in—"forbidden" subjects: violence and revenge, hashish and opium, the lust for power, the struggle of the sexes, and, long before the twentieth century, feminism articulated. Alcott had written not only of hearth and home, but of the strange and exotic. She inspired discovery and—as with *A Long Fatal Love Chase* and the recently published juvenile novel *The Inheritance*—rediscovery. Alcott was a woman for

all seasons, a writer for all ages, complex and fascinating, capable of
shocking, still capable of surprising.

To disclose the fascinations we had uncovered in Alcott, I spent
much of my own creativity pursuing her, revealing her secrets to the
world. Leona started all this with her discovery of A. M. Barnard.
Together, we rejoiced as unacknowledged Alcott narratives were
traced and read and assembled. The ghost of Louisa Alcott further
cemented our relationship with each other.

By the 1990s it almost appeared as if my own productivity was
attempting to rival Alcott's. In an article, "The Sensational Miss
Alcott," in *The New Criterion*, James W. Tuttleton commented that
"Madeleine Stern, Miss Alcott's first scholarly biographer, has long
made a cottage industry out of editing and anthologizing" Alcott's
potboilers. That "cottage industry" soon generated several interesting interviews with Leona and me. Our opinions were elicited by
the BBC for a production on women's literature and women's lives,
captioned "Behind a Mask." Then, early in 1995, Michael Warner
consulted us on the "recent" Louisa May Alcott revival and produced a provocative article for the *Village Voice Literary Supplement,*
entitled "The Secret Behind the Secret Writings of Louisa May
Alcott." He ended his lengthy exploration of the roles of Rostenberg, Stern, and Alcott with a tantalizing query:

> Will the thrillers and the feminist writing ever have the same foothold in
> the popular imagination that Little Women has? Will we learn to see Jo
> March and Jean Muir as sharing more than their initials? Or will Jo remain
> the figure portrayed by Winona Ryder, drained of all internal conflict and
> comfortingly normal? At 750 pages, [Louisa May Alcott] Unmasked may be
> just enough ballast to outweigh that image. And who knows; it may not even be
> the end of Alcott's secret ventings. After all, there's always Madeleine Stern.
> "Mady will find more," says Leona Rostenberg. "She's a sleuth."

EPILOGUE

THE SENSATIONS—THE BLOOD-AND-THUNDER—IN our own lives have all been derivatives of our detection and scholarly sleuthing. These have been our lifelong passion. They still are.

Even now, as octogenarians, we rise to the excitement of the hunt, the thrill of the find. And yet all too frequently we are made aware of our age. At book fairs, where we have a booth every year, we hear from browsing visitors, "We can't believe you two are doing the fair again. We never thought to see you here." The implication is obvious.

Glancing around us at those book fairs, we find ourselves looking for what is absent. There are but few booths operated by our contemporaries, so many of whom have died. The ghosts of retired librarians visit our stand, along with collectors who have given up collecting. Thanks to all this, as well as to health scares over the years, we recognize the intimations of mortality. We no longer fly overseas semiannually or annually to buy from our European colleagues, whose ranks are diminished. Yet we still hanker for the musty whiff of a Left Bank *librairie* or the calf and vellum vistas of a bookshop in Cecil Court. When we visit dealers closer to home, we no longer climb ladders to explore the topmost shelves. Serendipity has not disappeared, however, and so we find treasures on the lower shelves of bookcases. There is no doubt that we still search for them.

When we open a book and make a discovery, our hearts palpitate wildly—not from angina, but from excitement.

Young people—people, say, under sixty or seventy—see us as old and frail. We recall Walter Savage Landor, who, having "warmed both hands before the fire of life," wrote that he was "ready to depart." The point is that he wrote those lines at age seventy-five, but he lived to be almost ninety. One of us has diminished sight and the other diminished hearing. We have become each other's eyes and ears and so survive. We do more than survive—we experience the passion that has dominated our lives; we continue our hunt for books, practice our Sherlockian exploits, and, living our double lives, write and co-write our books. It is true we may be stepping back. We are not stepping out.

We have become keen observers of the generations who have succeeded us. Every age is critical of the next, and we are no exceptions. Although we admire and befriend many young dealers who do not confuse value with price, we deplore the all too popular conception entertained by many dealers that books are to be regarded primarily as investments. Such booksellers go in for dollarship, not scholarship. We deplore too the concentration upon books that require next to no research, the modern first editions in English whose interest lies less in their content than in their mint dust jackets. Then we retreat happily to our Renaissance octavos and quartos published by Aldus Manutius and Johann Froben, by the Estiennes and Colines, bound in vellum that has become stained or calf that has become scuffed, and as we turn their pages we still find unexpected, unknown riches. We still reach avidly for the small pile of seventeenth-century French pamphlets that may refer in passing to a brave new world. Our reference library is filled with books that after half a century of use have become—like us?—worn and tattered. But they yield us clues and insights that we would never be able to glean from intimidating computers.

Our untraditional lives have given us few regrets. We would

certainly have delighted in children. At the same time we realize that growing offspring would have given us, for all the joy, a continuing awareness of our own aging process. Not having had children, we have often been blissfully unaware of the passage of time. Somehow our beloved dachshunds have been able to give us joy without reminding us of the Grim Reaper.

One deep disappointment of the 1930s—Mr. Thorndike's rejection of the doctoral dissertation on the printer's role in humanism—has turned into a blessing. Had that dissertation been accepted then, one of us would have been stranded in some small Midwestern college teaching names of kings and dates of battles; the other would have continued unhappily explaining *Ivanhoe* and *Silas Marner* to uninterested high school students. There is no doubt that we both owe a debt of gratitude to that saturnine, green-suited necromancer who sidled into the lecture room, mumbled on about magic, and unwittingly—magically—changed our lives forever.

Instead of abiding in academe, we have sought and discovered, independently and together. We have introduced the past to the present. One of our greatest thrills was our discovery of the double literary life of America's best-loved writer of juvenile fiction. The revelation that the author of *Little Women* was also the author of clandestine sensational shockers was our blood-and-thunder story.

We have had good reason to revel in the joys of scholarship, the gratifications of sleuthing. We still have. One of us still sits comfortably at the typewriter while the other makes suggestions or offers plans and ideas. When the younger generation tells us we are legendary figures, we sometimes think they really mean has-beens. It is true that they study our catalogues, buy our rare books, consult us from time to time, read and collect our co-authored publications. They search our eyes for a legacy.

Our lives are our legacy, and it is a legacy dominated by the first person plural. The delights we have discovered in detection were possible only because we have detected and discovered together. We have been companions in the search; we have rejoiced in unison. We share our achievements as we share our hopes. We still end each other's sentences. Together we look to the future—to our next find, to our next book, to our next adventure.

ACKNOWLEDGMENTS

Those who helped construct and shape our lives are no longer here to enjoy our acknowledgments of gratitude. But to those who helped us reconstruct our lives we give our heartfelt thanks:

To Betsy Lerner, our editor, who suggested that this book be written and then expertly guided it to its completion;

To Frances Apt, our extraordinary copy editor;

To Helen Keppler Miller, our dear friend since childhood. She saved our early letters to her; recently she enthusiastically read *Old Books, Rare Friends* in manuscript—and so she had a double role in the creation of this book;

To Jane Lowenthal, Barnard College Archivist, who provided copies of articles from Barnard periodicals of the 1930s;

To E. Dennis Rowley, of Brigham Young University, for photocopies of materials in the Louisa May Alcott Collection;

To Dorothy Warms, classmate at Hunter College High School, for her recollections and a copy of the 1928 *Argus;*

To Liane Wood-Thomas, Executive Director of the Antiquarian Booksellers Association of America, for some photographs of LR and MBS.

INDEX

ABOUT THE AUTHORS

Eighty-seven and eighty-four years old, respectively, Leona Rostenberg and Madeleine Stern have been rare book dealers for over
half a century. Madeleine has written fourteen books, including
biographies of Margaret Fuller and Louisa May Alcott, and Leona, a
former president of the Antiquarian Booksellers Association of
America, has published five books on seventeenth-century printing
and publishing in England. In addition, they have co-authored six
books about books, including *Old Books, Rare Friends.* They reside in
New York City with their dachshund Bettina and summer in the
Hamptons.